Frances Eales
Steve Oakes

speakout

Upper Intermediate
Students' Book

with ActiveBook

PEARSON

Longman

BBC

CONTENTS

CONTENTS

CONTENTS

CONTENTS

LISTENING/DVD	SPEAKING	WRITING
	talk about different ages; discuss similarities and differences between generations	
listen to a radio programme about writing letters to your future self	talk about your future hopes and plans	write a letter to your future self; learn to use linkers of purpose
listen to a radio phone-in programme about life's milestones	role play a radio phone-in; learn to ask for clarification	
BBC **How to Live to 101:** watch an extract from a documentary about people who live to a very old age	plan and take part in a debate	write a forum comment giving your opinion
	talk about TV watching habits	
listen to an expert talking about hoax photographs	discuss answers to a quiz; discuss celebrities and the media	write a discursive essay; learn to use linkers of contrast
listen to people talking about recent news stories	talk about the press; discuss 'top five' lists; learn to make guesses	
BBC **The Funny Side of the News:** watch and understand a programme about live news	retell a recent news story	write a news article
	discuss difficult decisions	
listen to people talking about their attitudes to time; listen to a radio programme about people's daily rhythms	talk about your attitude to time	write an informal article; learn to use an informal style in an article
listen to someone talking through an awkward situation.	talk about how to handle awkward situations; role play an awkward situation; learn to soften a message	
BBC **The Human Animal:** watch an extract from a programme about body language	describe a family or cultural ritual	write about a family ritual
	discuss how good a witness you are; talk about what you would do in difficult situations	
listen to people talking about getting tricked	speculate about how scams work	write an advice leaflet to help visitors to your city; learn to avoid repetition
listen to someone reporting an incident	role play reporting an incident; learn to rephrase	
BBC **999:** watch an extract from a documentary about a sea rescue	discuss items to take on a life raft	write a story about a lucky escape
listen to a film review on a radio programme	talk about films	write a film review; learn to write more descriptively
	talk about popular culture and arts experiences	
listen to tours of two different places	learn to express estimates; role play showing a visitor around part of your town	
BBC **The One Show:** watch an extract from a programme about a famous graffiti artist	choose a new artistic project for your town	write a description of a favourite work of art or building

COMMUNICATION BANK PAGE 158   AUDIO SCRIPTS PAGE 164

PARTS OF SPEECH

1A Work in pairs and complete the questionnaire.

HOW I LEARN

1 It's useful to know grammatical terminology...
a) because it's [1]**much** easier to talk about grammar rules.
b) to read and understand grammar books [2]**better**.
c) ... actually, I don't think it's [3]**useful**.

2 When I meet a new word, I...
a) [4]**look it up**, then write it in my notebook with a translation.
b) write [5]**a** phrase or sentence with [6]**the** word in it.
c) think about it, but don't write anything down.

3 I enjoy using English outside the class...
a) to communicate on social networking sites.
b) when I'm [7]**watching** films and listening [8]**to** music in English.
c) ... I [9]**don't** use English outside class.

4 In addition to [10]**doing** homework, I study English...
a) [11]**every day**.
b) two or three times a week.
c) not at all – I don't have time!

5 I think it's important [12]**to speak** English in the lesson...
a) 100% of the time.
b) whenever we [13]**can**.
c) only when we're [14]**told** to.

B Match the grammatical terms a)–n) with words 1–14 in bold above.
a) dependent preposition
b) past participle
c) present participle
d) gerund
e) infinitive with *to*
f) adjective in comparative form
g) gradable adjective
h) adverbial phrase
i) quantifier   *1*
j) auxiliary verb
k) definite article
l) indefinite article
m) modal verb
n) multi-word verb

VERB PATTERNS

2A Correct the sentences.
                           working
1 I can't stand ~~to work~~ with music on.
2 I learned driving last year.
3 I want that the teacher corrects everything I say.
4 I'd rather to eat out than at home.
5 I'd like travelling abroad this year.
6 I enjoy be alone.
7 I like it when the teacher tells to repeat words.
8 I'd better to spend more time studying or I'll never make progress in English.

B Find two examples above for each pattern:
1 verb + gerund   *1*
2 verb + infinitive
3 verb + infinitive with *to*
4 verb + object + infinitive with *to*

C Work in pairs. Which sentences are true for you? How would you change the other sentences to make them true?

PRONUNCIATION

3A Work in pairs. Complete the table with words from the box.

completely   extremely
guarantee   future   minutes
push   public   system   reach
thorough   took   absolutely

1	/ɪ/	th<u>i</u>s	w<u>o</u>men
2	/iː/	th<u>e</u>se	l<u>ea</u>ve
3	/ə/	<u>a</u>gain	pr<u>o</u>nunciati<u>o</u>n
4	/æ/	<u>a</u>ctually	<u>a</u>ngry
5	/ʌ/	f<u>u</u>n	m<u>o</u>ney
6	/ʊ/	b<u>oo</u>k	p<u>u</u>ll

B ▶ 0.1 Listen and check. Then listen and repeat.

C Work in pairs. How can phonemic symbols help you learn new words?

COLLOCATIONS

4A Cross out the noun or noun phrase that does not collocate with the verb in the word web.

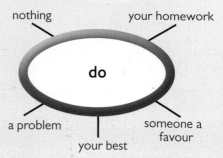

nothing — your homework — **do** — a problem — someone a favour — your best

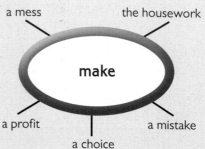

a mess — the housework — **make** — a profit — a mistake — a choice

a break — an exam — **take** — a chance — a noise — your time

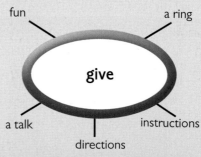

fun — a ring — **give** — a talk — instructions — directions

a dream — a good time — **have** — a break — trouble — care

B Work in pairs and take turns. Student A: say a noun or noun phrase. Student B: say the verb that collocates with it.

UNIT 1

UNIT

1

beginnings

SPEAKING

1 Work in pairs and discuss the questions.

1 Who do you live with?

2 Do you think it's easier to live with family, friends or on your own?

LISTENING

2 Read the programme listing and look at the photo. What do you think happens at a 'speed flatmating' event?

3A ▶ 1.1 Listen to the first part of the programme and answer the questions.

1 What happens during the evening?

2 What two things are given to you when you arrive?

Speed flatmating

You might have heard of speed dating – those events for the young, free and single who are just too busy to find the love of their lives – but what about applying the same principle to finding a lodger for your spare room? In today's *You and Yours* on BBC Radio 4, reporter Natalie Steed experiences 'speed flatmating'.

B ▶ 1.2 Listen to the rest of the programme. Match each person with the way they feel about speed flatmating.

1 First man

2 Second man

3 First woman

4 Second woman

a) It's important to be honest.

b) It's easy.

c) Confused

d) He/she doesn't say.

C Listen again. Are the sentences true (T) or false (F)? Correct the false sentences.

1 A white badge means you ~~are looking for a room~~.
F have got a room to rent.

2 The first man wants someone who will be there most of the time.

3 A pink badge means you are prepared to 'buddy up' (share a bedroom).

4 The second man started looking for a room a fortnight ago.

5 The first woman thinks you can tell a lot at first sight.

6 However, she thinks speed flatmating is embarrassing.

7 The second woman asks quite personal questions.

8 She hasn't found anyone at the speed flatmating event.

4 Work in pairs and discuss the questions.

1 Would you use speed flatmating to find or rent out a room?

2 If you were looking for a flatmate, which of the topics in the box below would you ask about? What sort of questions would you ask?

relationships	work	daily habits	finances	politics
future plans	music	references	weekends	diet

GRAMMAR   direct and indirect questions

5A Look at the conversation from a speed flatmating event and complete the questions.

A: So where ¹ _____ you staying at the moment?

B: Quite near here.

A: Oh, who are you living ² _____?

B: Some friends from college. I'm just staying there on a temporary basis until I find a flat.

A: Right. And what ³ _____ you decide to come to the city in the first place?

B: I work for a big sportswear company and they've just relocated here.

A: And have you any idea how ⁴ _____ you want to stay here?

B: At least a year, I hope. I suppose it depends how it works out.

A: Do you mind me asking ⁵ _____ you're in a relationship?

B: No, that's OK. No, I'm single at the moment.

A: One more question. Er, what are you ⁶ _____ in the mornings? It's just that I'm not at my best early in the day.

B: Me neither. I don't usually talk to anyone till after my first coffee at work!

B ▶ 1.3 Listen and check your answers.

6A Check what you know. Look at the questions in Exercise 5A and find:

a) two indirect questions.

b) a subject question (one where the question word is the subject).

c) a question with a preposition at the end.

d) an alternative to *how*.

B Underline the correct alternative to complete the rules.

Rules:

1 *Direct / Indirect* questions are used to make a question more polite or when the question is personal.

2 The word order in indirect questions is *the same as / different from* direct questions.

3 In indirect questions, *use / don't use* the auxiliaries *do* or *did*.

4 In indirect questions add *if* or *whether* for a *yes/no / Wh* question.

C ▶ 1.4 Put the underlined words in the correct order to make indirect questions. Then listen and check.

1 <u>wondering was I</u> if I could see the flat.

2 <u>you tell me could</u> how much the deposit is?

3 <u>mind do me you asking</u> how old you are?

4 <u>interested be I'd know to</u> how you organise the cooking.

5 <u>I can ask</u> you how noisy it is?

6 <u>know you do</u> how soon the room will be available?

7A Listen again. What are the main stressed words in each sentence?

B Does the intonation start high or low?

➠ page 128 **LANGUAGEBANK**

PRACTICE

8 Make sentences with the prompts.

1 Could / tell / how much / earn / each month?

Could you tell me how much you earn each month?

2 mind / asking / how much time / spend / on the phone and Internet each day?

3 think / will / usually spend weekends here / or / will / often / go away?

4 What / be / last flatmates / like?

5 What / annoy / you / most / about / sharing a flat?

6 What kind / music / like / listen to?

VOCABULARY personality

9A Read the descriptions from a flatmate finder site. Which person would be the best flatmate for you? Why?

▶ **Mikhail, age 24**

I'm a post-graduate student studying geology. I'd be a good flatmate because I tend to **keep myself to myself**. I'm not unfriendly but my idea of a perfect evening is to spend the night in, order a takeaway and watch a DVD or maybe play computer games. I'm not a computer **geek**, though. Like any student, I'm often short of cash, but I'm not **tight-fisted**, I don't mind paying my share. I can be quite messy – I often bring rocks home to work on. I'm usually up and out before 7.30 in the morning.

▶ **Claudia, age 34**

I'm a professional cook in an Italian restaurant. I work late so I don't like being disturbed in the morning. I'm a **people person** and love inviting friends round and cooking for them. I **am** very **particular about** order, especially in the kitchen – if there's one thing I hate, it's a messy kitchen. I also get annoyed if I'm the only one cleaning up or people don't **pull their weight** around the house. My friends say I'm very sensible and practical, really **down-to-earth**.

▶ **Pat, age 28**

I'm a lawyer and sing with a band in my spare time. I've got a good job and a decent salary, but at the moment I'm being careful with my money as I'm saving up for a new sound system for the group. I'm often **out until the early hours** because of late night gigs with the band. People say I'm **a good laugh** but I can be pretty serious too – I sometimes bring the band back after a gig and I can really **get into** talking about politics – I love a good discussion.

B Work in pairs. Match meanings 1–10 with the phrases in bold from the descriptions in Exercise 8A.

1 feel this is important   *am particular about*

2 away from home very late

3 be introverted

4 someone who is sociable

5 someone who is obsessive and boring (about a topic)

6 enjoy (a topic or activity)

7 someone who is fun to be with

8 realistic about things

9 mean with money

10 do one's share of work

➠ page 148 **VOCABULARYBANK**

SPEAKING

10A Work in pairs and discuss the questions.

1 Which of the people in Exercise 8A would you enjoy meeting socially?

2 Who do you think you would get on with least well?

3 Which phrases would you use to describe yourself?

B Write six questions to find someone you would get on with socially. Use indirect questions where appropriate. Look at Exercises 5A and 8 to help.

C Ask other students your questions. In what way would each person be a good match for you?

WRITING an informal email

10A Work in pairs and answer the questions.

1 How often do you write informal emails in your own language? Who do you write them to?

2 Do you ever write emails in English?

3 What kind of things do you write about?

B Read the email and answer the questions.

1 What do you think the relationship is between the writer and the recipient?

2 Where is Jorge living and who with?

3 How did he find the flat?

> **To:** kiri.b@mailbank.com
>
> Hi Kiri,
>
> Thanks for the email. Great to hear the news about your job – and that you're feeling much better now. Hope you're enjoying your summer.
>
> I got to London a couple of weeks ago and I'm staying in a place called Swiss Cottage. Do you know it? It's very handy for the underground – only takes twenty minutes or so to get to school every day.
>
> My flatmate, Winston, is great. He's originally from Jamaica and is divorced with two kids, who are often around. He's a good laugh and he's happy to chat with me any time so I can practise my English, which is great!
>
> You'll never guess how I found the flat. I found this thing called 'speed flatmating' on the internet. You go to a kind of party and you chat to a lot of people who've got rooms to rent. I met Winston there and we just clicked! I moved in the next day.
>
> Must go now as it's time for class. Be in touch soon.
>
> All the best,
>
> Jorge

C Work in pairs and complete the guidelines for writing informal emails. Use the email in Exercise 10B to give you ideas.

1 For the salutation, use Dear / _____ + name.

2 For the ending, use *All* _____ *best*, _____ *wishes*, or *Love* + name.

3 Paragraphing: try to stick to _____ topic(s) per paragraph, though writers don't always follow this guideline.

4 To convey an informal style:

a) use informal punctuation such as _____ and _____.

b) use informal language, such as _____ meaning *convenient*, _____ meaning *liked each other straightaway*, and _____ meaning *in contact*.

c) use contracted forms, for instance _____, _____ or _____.

d) leave out some words, for example in these phrases in the first and last paragraphs: _____, _____, _____, _____.

LEARN TO check for accuracy

11 Read the email and correct the mistakes . Use the teacher's correction code at the beginning of each sentence.

Correction code:	sp = spelling
v = verb form	p = punctuation
gr = grammar	wo = word order
ww = wrong word	st = style

> **To:** jorge.67@mailbank.com
>
> Hi Jorge,
>
> Thanks for the email. [gr] Sounds like you're having good time. [v] I never hear of speed flatmating before but it seems like a great idea. [wo] The job is still fantastic and I like very much the people there.
>
> [sp] One of my colleagues, Paolo, comes from Italy and so we often practice English together at lunchtime.
>
> [ww] He's a very sympathetic person and great fun.
>
> [p] Last weekend I took him to a party at a friends' apartment – we didn't get home till five o'clock the next morning! The photo is of us dancing.
>
> [st] Have to go now as it's getting late and tomorrow's a work day. I look forward to hearing from you again soon.
>
> Best wishes,
>
> Kiri

12A Write an email (120–180 words) to another student in the class describing your current living situation. Include information about:

- the place
- who you live with
- how you found it
- how you feel about it

speakout TIP

After you have finished any piece of writing, go through and check for accuracy. Remember to check grammar, verb forms, vocabulary, word order, spelling and punctuation. Also check that the style is suitable for the person you are writing to. Check your email now.

B Work in pairs. Exchange your emails and write a reply.

▶ **GRAMMAR** | present perfect & past simple   ▶ **VOCABULARY** | feelings (1)   ▶ **HOW TO** | discuss experiences

VOCABULARY feelings

1 Work in pairs and look at the photos. Which of the activities have you done?

2A ▶ 1.5 Listen. Which speakers can you see in the photos. What do the other two speakers talk about?

B Work in pairs and complete sentences 1–10 with an adjective from the box. Then listen again and check.

> embarrassed   exhausted   satisfied   thrilled
> awkward   relieved   anxious   fascinated
> frustrated   impressed

1 For a start, I was very _____ and I think animals can sense it when you're nervous and worried.

2 Actually, I was extremely _____ when the lesson finished.

3 I came second so I was really _____.

4 I was absolutely _____ to see how different people behaved when they got in front of the microphone.

5 It took me ages to do and I got really annoyed and _____ at one point because I couldn't make it straight.

6 I felt really _____ when I'd finished because it was the first one I'd ever put up on my own.

7 Most people were there for the first time and I was really _____ by how quickly they learnt the steps.

8 I was very _____ because I kept treading on her toes.

9 I suggested calling the repair company. I felt very _____ about it but I thought we'd never get home.

10 I didn't get to bed till two in the morning and I was completely _____.

C ▶ 1.6 Underline the stress in each adjective in the box in Exercise 2B. Listen and check. Then listen and repeat.

3A Work in pairs and answer the questions.

1 In the sentences below, which adjective in bold is used for feelings and which for something that causes the feelings?

 a) Putting up a shelf was a really **satisfying** thing to do.

 b) I was really **satisfied** when I'd finished.

2 Which adjective in each pair below is gradable (G) and which is extreme/ungradable (U)?

 a) tired/exhausted

 b) excited/thrilled

 c) interested/fascinated

3 Which modifiers in the box can be used with gradable adjectives (G), with ungradable (U) adjectives and with both (B)?

> fairly G   very   really   absolutely   completely

B Work in pairs and cross out the incorrect alternative in each sentence. Explain the reason for your choices.

1 A: I'm *very/absolutely* interested in languages.

 B: Yeah, I'm *very/completely* fascinated by them too.

2 A: I'm *really/very* exhausted.

 B: Yes, I'm *fairly/absolutely* tired too.

3 A: I felt really *embarrassed/embarrassing* because I kept forgetting people's names.

 B: How *embarrassed/embarrassing*!

4 A: What was the most *frustrated/frustrating* thing about it?

 B: I got very *frustrated/frustrating* when I forgot the steps.

4A Choose five adjectives from Exercise 2B and think of times you felt these emotions. Write notes to help you.

B Work in pairs and take turns. Tell your partner about the experiences.

I've Never Seen *Star Wars*

1 *I've Never Seen Star Wars* is a BBC programme based on a simple idea: Take a celebrity and persuade them to try five experiences they've never done before; not extraordinary things but **mundane** and fairly **trivial**
5 activities that they've either always avoided or have never had the opportunity to do. The programme's producer thought of the name a few years ago because, amazingly enough, he'd never seen the film *Star Wars*.

Every week, the host, comedian Marcus Brigstocke,
10 encourages his guests to undertake challenges such as constructing flat-pack furniture, changing the oil in a car, having a tap-dancing lesson, wearing extremely high heels, or listening to a punk album. The show has recently moved from radio to TV and, so far, one guest has had a piano
15 lesson, another has tried online social networking and a third has built a wall (in the studio!). No one has refused a challenge yet. After each experience, Brigstocke interviews his guest to find out how they rated the experience from one to ten and whether they would like to try it again.

20 The programme's appeal lies in Brigstocke's charm and humour and his interaction with the guests, but also in the normality of the experiences. We, the viewers, can relate to the guests' reactions because we know the frustration of trying to put together flat-pack furniture or the pain of **tottering** around in high heels.

25 Guests' reactions vary from genuine enthusiasm, as when Barry Cryer, a grandfather of seven tried changing a baby's nappy and awarded the experience a maximum ten out of ten, to absolute **loathing**: 'I couldn't bear it. Everybody is jolly or cooking or laughing or making music with not a genuine emotion
30 in the whole thing!' said Joan Bakewell, after watching the film *Mamma Mia*. Another guest, when asked to change the oil in a car admitted, 'I've never tried to fix anything in a car, I've maybe opened the **bonnet** a couple of times.' Three weeks ago, comedian

Arthur Smith gave his piano lesson nine out of ten, 'I was quite
35 excited, actually, genuinely. Very quickly, it sounded like a tune.'

Brigstocke, who hosted the programme on radio for two seasons before it moved to television, says, 'I've just discovered the quickest way to get to know a person is to have a list of things that most people have done, and then ask them if they have or haven't
40 done the things on the list. It's really simple, but for example, Paul Daniels the magician has owned an original Beatles *Revolver* album since the sixties and not only has he never played it but he has never listened to any album of any kind, ever! I also think the show **taps into** something that has been a **recurring** theme in my
45 life – the need to explore new things, have new experiences, turn over every stone.'

At its best, the show lets us see the very familiar through fresh eyes. It's entertaining, amusing and can even, on occasions, be inspiring. Who knows, it might give us all the motivation to try
50 something new!

READING

5A Read the review. Overall, is it positive or negative?

B Read the review again and answer the questions.

1 Which activities are connected to making something?

2 How do the guests give feedback on their experiences?

3 Why do people like the programme? Give two reasons.

4 What was the most negative reaction from a guest?

5 Why does the presenter like the idea of the show?

6 How might viewers benefit from watching the show?

C Work in pairs. Match meanings 1–7 with the words in bold from the review.

1 not serious or important *trivial*

2 hating

3 repeating

4 ordinary and boring

5 the front part of a car over the engine

6 makes use of

7 walking but almost falling over

D Work in pairs and discuss the questions.

1 How many of the activities in the review above <u>haven't</u> you done? Are there any you would like to try?

2 What other 'ordinary' activities have you never done but would like to try? Ask your partner if they have tried them.

GRAMMAR present perfect and past simple

6 Check what you know. Match examples 1–5 with rules a)–e).

1 Brigstocke hosted the programme on radio before it moved to television.

2 I've just discovered the quickest way to get to know a person is to have a list of things …

3 Paul Daniels has owned an original Beatles *Revolver* album since the sixties.

4 I've never seen *Star Wars*.

5 The programme's producer thought of the name a few years ago.

Rules:

a) Use the past simple for a single completed action in the past where the time is specified or understood.

b) Use the past simple for a longer state or series of actions which began and finished in the past.

c) Use the present perfect for a completed action or experience in a period of time up to now, often in one's lifetime. The time is not specified.

d) Use the present perfect for a recent completed action in the past that is relevant to or has a result in the present. The time is not specified.

e) Use the present perfect for a state or series of actions which began in the past and continue to now.

7A Underline the time phrases in the sentences.

1 ... and, so far, one guest has had a piano lesson ...

2 No one has refused a challenge yet.

3 I've already seen *Mamma Mia*, so let's get another DVD.

4 Three weeks ago, comedian Arthur Smith gave his piano lesson nine out of ten.

5 I've put up five shelves this morning and it's only 10 a.m.

6 I put up five shelves this morning before lunch.

7 We've watched the programme for five weeks now.

8 We watched the programme for six weeks.

B Which verb form is used with each time phrase above? Why?

C Look at the time phrases in the box. Which are usually used with the present perfect? Which with the past simple? Which can be used with both?

so far\ ago2 up to now\ this time last week 2
last month2 yet\ since\ for3 already\
last night2 lately\ earlier today 2 in the summer 3
over the last fortnight \

8 ▶1.7 Listen to the examples of fast connected speech. Write past simple (PS) or present perfect (PP) for each sentence.

1 _____ 3 _____ 5 _____ 7 _____ 9 _____
2 _____ 4 _____ 6 _____ 8 _____ 10 _____

▶ page 128 **LANGUAGEBANK**

PRACTICE

9A Complete the sentences with the correct form of the verbs in the box.

do give be go live play try learn buy get

What would you like to try on *I've never seen Star Wars*?

• I ¹_____ (always) afraid of water, but I finally ²_____ to swim last year. Now I'd like to swim in the sea.

• I ³_____ (just) a video camera; my sister ⁴_____ it to me for my birthday. So I'd like to learn how to edit a film.

• I love music and I ⁵_____ the piano for many years now, but there's one instrument I ⁶_____ (not yet): the guitar.

• I ⁷_____ (never) anything online – I'm paranoid about giving my credit card details, but I know it's cheaper, so that would be my choice.

• Hiking in the Alps. I ⁸_____ in Austria since I was born, and everyone in my family ⁹_____ to the Alps hiking loads of times. But somehow I ¹⁰_____ (never) a proper hike.

B Work in pairs and discuss. Which activity in Exercise 9A would you most like to try?

VOCABULARY *PLUS* word formation

10A ▶1.8 Work in pairs and complete the table with the noun form of the adjectives in the box. Then listen and check.

~~frustrated~~ awkward satisfied nervous embarrassed
similar disappointed generous exhausted anxious

A -ion	B -ment	C -ity/-ety	D -ness
frustration			

B Underline the stressed syllable in each of the nouns in your table. Use a dictionary to help. Then listen again and check.

C Match the noun suffixes (endings) in the table with the rules below.

1 The stress is on the syllable before the suffix.

2 The stress is on the same syllable as in the adjective.

11A Complete the sentences in the personality quiz with the correct noun or adjective form.

B Read the quiz again. For each sentence decide if you strongly agree (✓✓), agree (✓), disagree (✗) or strongly disagree (✗✗).

C Work in pairs and compare your answers.

personality quiz

1 I often hesitate to speak in groups because I get emb*arrassed* easily.

2 People often comment on how gen_____ I am.

3 I notice sim_____ between myself and other people more than differences.

4 My greatest fru_____ are related to my relationships rather than money.

5 When I was younger, I was often awk_____ in social situations, but not any more.

6 I get a lot of sat_____ from helping people.

7 I often feel quite dis_____ in my friends, for example when they don't have time for me.

8 For me, the best cure for exh_____ is exercise.

9 I get ner_____ in large groups.

10 I often feel intense anx_____ in lifts.

▶ page 148 **VOCABULARYBANK**

VOCABULARY adverts

1A Look at the adverts A–E. Which two would interest you most?

A

Olympia Sports Centre

FREE INTRODUCTORY OFFER. Print the flyer on the right, **fill in** your details and present it at the gym to **sign up** for a FREE training session with a certified trainer, worth €30. Offer ends 30th January.

B

EXCEL SCHOOL OF ENGLISH

Advanced course in business English
Real business scenarios including telephoning, presentations, meetings and negotiations.
Limited enrolment – guarantee your place with a €50 **deposit** (**non-refundable**). Phone 0472 981634 to enrol.

C

The Bengal Tiger Restaurant
42 The High Street,
Tel: 0472 777421
Two-for-one deal.
Come any weekday and bring a friend. Offer extends till May 24th only.
Phone to reserve a table.

D

☆ **Keira Knightley** ☆
to star on stage in *Twilight 2*.

Pre-book on our hotline from November 16th.

Group discount for **matinée** performances.

Limited run March 16th to July 1st.

Phone 0100 900 200 for tickets.

E

✂ SnipSnip Hair Salon ✂
6 WEST GREEN ROAD
Free hairstyling by diploma students working under the supervision of a trainer. Come to SnipSnip this Saturday from 10 a.m. Styling will be offered on a **first come first served** basis.

B Work in pairs and match meanings 1–8 with the words/phrases in bold from the adverts.

1 If you go, your friend can come for free! *Two-for-one deal*
2 An afternoon show
3 You need to pay part of the cost now, but this money can't be returned.
4 You can't book a place, just get there early!
5 Put your name on a list for a course
6 It's only on for a short time
7 Write your name, etc. on a form
8 There's a maximum number for this course.

C Which of the words/phrases can be used to talk about a concert, a cookery course, a sale in a shop and a hotel booking?

FUNCTION polite enquiries

2A ▶ 1.9 Listen to the phone conversation and answer the questions.

1 Who is the woman phoning?
2 Why is she phoning?
3 What does she need to do?
4 What does the receptionist do?

B Complete the sentences. Then listen again and check.

1 I ___would___ like to _____ about a course.
2 I _____ wondering _____ it _____ be _____ for _____ to change to that group.
3 Can _____ tell _____ why I have to do it in person?
4 Would _____ be any _____ of doing the level test on the phone?
5 Do you _____ me _____ what it involves?
6 I'd be really _____ if you _____ hold a place for me till Saturday morning.
7 Would you mind _____ that in an email for me?
8 _____ you tell me _____ the school opens?

C ▶ 1.10 Listen and mark the intonation at the end of each enquiry. Does it go down and up ⤴ or just down ⤵? Then listen again and repeat.

I'd like to enquire about a course. ⤵

▸ page 128 **LANGUAGEBANK**

3A Make the enquiries more polite using the words in brackets.

1 Which one do I need to catch to get there by noon? (Could / tell)
2 Can I use your two-for-one deal on a Friday night? (wondering / possible)
3 Tell me about your policy for returned tickets. (like / enquire)
4 I want a window seat. (Would / chance)
5 Tell me about withdrawal charges. (Would / mind)
6 How much experience do your student hairdressers have? (mind / asking)
7 Explain that again, from the bit about downloading the software. (I / grateful)
8 Where exactly would the cheaper apartment be? (Can / tell)

B Work in pairs. In which situations could you make the enquiries above?

LEARN TO manage enquiries

4A Work in pairs. Read phrases 1–6 from the phone conversation. Who do you think is speaking, the receptionist (R) or the caller (C)?

1 Bear with me a minute.
2 Sorry to keep you.
3 Sorry to be difficult, it's just that …
4 I'd really appreciate your help.
5 Can you hold on a minute? I'll just see.
6 I've got one more question, if I'm not keeping you.

B Look at the audio script on page 164 and check your answers.

C Work in pairs and find:

1 two phrases showing the caller thinks she may be causing a problem.
2 one polite phrase from the receptionist meaning *please be patient*.

5 Work in pairs and role-play a phone conversation to a sports centre. Use the flow chart to help.

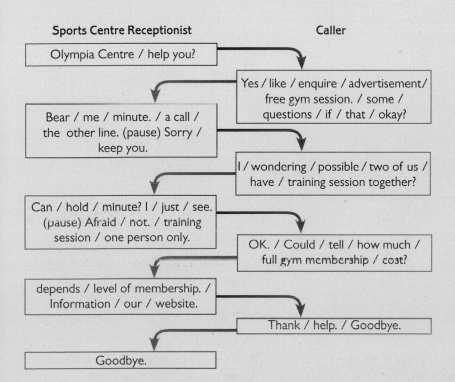

Sports Centre Receptionist — Caller

Olympia Centre / help you?

Yes / like / enquire / advertisement/ free gym session. / some / questions / if / that / okay?

Bear / me / minute. / a call / the other line. (pause) Sorry / keep you.

I / wondering / possible / two of us / have / training session together?

Can / hold / minute? I / just / see. (pause) Afraid / not. / training session / one person only.

OK. / Could / tell / how much / full gym membership / cost?

depends / level of membership. / Information / our / website.

Thank / help. / Goodbye.

Goodbye.

SPEAKING

6A Work in pairs. Student A: look at Situation 1. Student B: turn to page 158.

> Situation 1 – Student A (**Customer**)
>
> You booked a flight online, but you entered the wrong date for the return flight by mistake. Complete your information:
>
> From _____ to _____ on _____
>
> Returning on _____ (you put _____ by mistake).
>
> Phone customer service and try to change the booking. To prepare, make notes on two or three enquiries you will make and predict what the customer service person might say.

B Work in pairs. Student A: Look at Situation 2. Student B: turn to page 158.

> Situation 2 – Student A (**Service person**)
>
> You work at the front desk of a hotel and handle reservations. Complete the information:
>
> Name of hotel _____
>
> Cost of upgrading to a better room _____
>
> A customer calls to check a booking and possibly upgrade to a better room. When the customer calls make sure you:
>
> • ask what the customer's name is.
>
> • don't find the booking immediately … only after a delay.

speakout TIP

Before making a phone enquiry, note what you want to say and what the other person might ask you. This can help your confidence, especially in formal situations.

DVD PREVIEW

1 Work in pairs and discuss the statements. Which ones do you agree with?

1 If I go into a new situation, I prefer it if no one I know is there.

2 I sometimes try to reinvent myself when I move into a new situation.

3 I find it hard to be open with people I've just met.

4 I enjoy social situations where I don't know anyone.

2A Look at the photos. What do you think the programme is about?

B Read the programme information and check.

B|B|C Off The Hook

Off the Hook * is a comedy set on a British university campus. It focuses on the adventures of a group of new students having their first experience of life away from home. The story centres on Danny, a young man who wants to leave his past behind and start afresh, but whose plans are foiled from the start by the arrival of an old friend. Tonight's episode takes us from Danny's arrival at the campus with his mum, through his initial encounters with characters who will be a big part of his life for the next three years. These include the beautiful Becky and Danny's annoying friend, Shane.

*off the hook – no longer in trouble.

▶ DVD VIEW

4A Watch the DVD. Who does these things? Write D (Danny), M (Danny's mum), B (Becky) or S (Shane). Sometimes there is more than one answer. Who ...

1 asks for a kiss? *M*

2 says 'I love you'?

3 makes a joke?

4 embarrasses Danny?

5 introduces themselves?

6 introduces someone else?

B Watch the DVD again and complete the sentences.

Mum: Why don't you just let me come up and make I _____ _____ _____?

Danny: And maybe you should just stay for the first night and make 2 _____ _____ _____.

Becky: Inhaler boy.

Danny: Oh, you saw that. Good. I was 3 _____ that not everyone had seen it.

Becky: I thought you were 4 _____. I wouldn't let my 5 _____ within a mile of the place.

Shane: I made it, man. Can you 6 _____ it? There was one 7 _____ left on moral philosophy with comparative philology. I don't know what it is man, but it's only four hours of 8 _____ ... a week!

Keith: Sorry, if you're not in the 9 _____, could you just maybe go to the back?

Shane: Chill out, Granddad. What are you 10 _____ like that for, charity or something?

C Work in pairs and discuss the questions.

1 What do you think will make it difficult for Danny to make a new start?

2 What do you think will happen to the characters in the series?

speakout a first encounter

5A ▶ 1.11 Listen to someone talk about a first day at work. Why did he feel embarrassed?

B Listen again and tick the key phrases you hear.

Keyphrases

One of my [worst / funniest] memories is when I ...

I've had some very [embarrassing / awkward / strange] [experiences / dates / first encounters] in my life

I'll [always remember / never forget] the time I ...

It started as a [typical / classic] [first day / first date]

I was feeling [excited / embarrassed / nervous / shy / worried / out of my depth]

I spent the whole time [wondering / looking at] ...

By [now / this time] I was feeling ... so I ...

I (suppose) I was [surprised / relieved / amazed] when ...

6A Think about your first time in one of the following situations:

*   starting a new job
*   starting a school or university
*   meeting a host family
*   moving into a new flat
*   going for an interview
*   moving to a new country
*   starting a new course or class

B Make notes about what happened, your first impressions and how you felt.

C Work in pairs and take turns. Tell each other about your situation. Try to use some of the key phrases in your story.

writeback a summary

7A Read the summary of the story. What two facts are different from the recording?

Dave's story was about his first day at a new job. He was twenty-three and a trainee in a law firm. He described it as a typical first day, with everyone feeling very nervous and trying to make a good impression. Dave was at his desk reading a report and his new shoes were hurting, so he took them off.

He had been sitting there for over an hour when the head partner called him in to his office. Dave jumped up and rushed in, forgetting to put on his shoes. The partner looked at him, and Dave felt incredibly embarrassed. When the partner asked him why he didn't have shoes on, he couldn't think of anything to say, so he told the truth and said he had forgotten to put them on. The partner simply smiled, and that was the end of it.

B Write a summary of your partner's story.

C Exchange stories with your partner and check the facts.

DIRECT AND INDIRECT QUESTIONS

1A Choose a topic from the box and complete the questions.

> transport   family   travel
> shopping   study   fashion

1 Do you like ... ?
2 What's ... like?
3 How often do you ... ?
4 Have you ever ... ?
5 Would you like to ... ?
6 Why do you ... ?

B Make your questions indirect using the phrases below.

Can I ask ...
Could you tell me ...
Do you mind me asking ...
I was wondering ...
I'd be interested to know ...

C Work in pairs and take turns to ask and answer your questions.

PERSONALITY

2A Rewrite the sentences using the words in brackets so that the meaning is the same.

1 He's quite reserved. (keep) *He keeps himself to himself.*
2 He doesn't like working alone. (person)
3 She never lets herself become unfit. (particular)
4 She's so uncomplicated and easy to talk to. (earth)
5 He's fun to be with. (laugh)
6 She's quite short of cash, but she often buys everyone coffee. (fist)
7 He does his share of the work. (weight)
8 I do my best work after midnight. (hours)

B Work in pairs and discuss. What combination of personal qualities above would make a good colleague, a good friend and a good accountant?

FEELINGS

3A Complete the conversations with adjectives from the box.

> satisfied   thrilled   awkward
> embarrassed   exhausted
> anxious   frustrated   relieved

Conversation 1

A: I had a terrible night last night. I couldn't sleep.
B: You must be [1] _____.
A: Then this morning, I answered the door in my pyjamas. It was my boss.
B: I bet you were [2] _____?
A: I certainly was!

Conversation 2

A: I got the job!
B: Congratulations! You must be [3] _____.
A: Yes, I'm [4] _____ because I thought I'd done badly at the interview.
B: We were all sure you'd get it.

B Work in pairs and add *very, really, absolutely, fairly* or *completely* before adjectives 1–4 in Exercise 3A. Then practise the conversations.

PRESENT PERFECT AND PAST SIMPLE

4A Complete the sentences with the present perfect or past simple form of the verbs in brackets.

1 Since I started this course, I _____ my speaking. (improve)
2 I _____ to the United States yet, but I'd like to. (not go)
3 I _____ a real celebrity. (never meet)
4 When I was young, I _____ in a band, and lately I _____ again. (play / start)
5 I _____ two good films so far this month. (see)
6 I _____ breakfast this morning and it's two o'clock now. (not eat)

B Work in pairs and discuss. Are any of the sentences in Exercise 4A true for you?

POLITE ENQUIRIES

5A Rewrite the sentences to make them more polite. Use the phrases in brackets.

1 I need some information about train times to Vienna. (I'd like to enquire)
2 Which train do I need to take to get to Vienna by 3p.m.? (Can you tell me)
3 How far is it from the Western to the Southern train station? (Can I ask)
4 Where can I get information on local transport in Vienna? (Do you mind me asking)
5 Do I need to book a seat on the train? (I was wondering)
6 Can I book on the phone? (Could you tell me)
7 Could you book it for me? (I was wondering if)
8 Could you send me an email confirmation? (I'd be grateful if)

B Work in pairs and take turns. Role-play a phone conversation between a tourist information officer and a customer. Use the sentences in Exercise 5A to help you.

A: *I'd like to enquire about train times to Glasgow.*
B: *Certainly. What would you like to know?*
A: *Can you tell me what train I need to take to get to Glasgow by 6p.m. please?*
B: *Let me just check ...*

UNIT 2

SPEAKING

> Talk about big issues
> Discuss surveillance society
> Learn to give and respond to opinions
> Do a class survey

LISTENING

> Listen to opinions about surveillance
> Listen to people debate
> Watch a BBC programme about happiness

READING

> Read about a charity
> Read a letter of complaint

WRITING

> Write a letter of complaint
> Write your top tips for how to be happy

BBC CONTENT

▯ Video podcast: Does money make you happy?
◉ DVD: The Happiness Formula

UNIT

2

issues

▶ Comic Relief   p20   ▶ We're being watched   p23   ▶ Just what I was thinking! p26   ▶ The Happiness Formula p28

READING

1 Look at the photos and discuss. What are the people doing and why are they wearing red noses?

2A Read the articles and answer the questions.

1 What is Comic Relief?

2 Who participates in Comic Relief events?

3 What happens on Red Nose Day?

4 How often does it happen?

5 Which of the activities described in the second article involve:

a) looking silly?

b) not talking?

c) not sleeping?

B Work in pairs and discuss the questions.

1 Would you be willing to do any of the activities in the article?

2 Do you think Red Nose Day would be successful in your country?

C Guess the meaning of the words in bold in the second article. Use questions 1–3 below to help you. Then work in pairs and compare your answers.

1 Which part of speech is each word?

2 Is there anything in the surrounding context to help you work out the meaning?

3 Do you recognise any parts of the word, or is it similar to another word you know in English or in your language?

Eye-opening:

1) It's an adjective

2) She may be surprised or happy

3) It's made of eye and open so it probably means surprising

❝❞ speakout TIP

When you are reading, try to guess the meanings of new words so that you don't stop reading in order to look them up. Ask yourself about the part of speech, context and similarity to other words.

Comic Relief is a charity that was founded in 1985. It has been raising money for over twenty years to fund projects that help poor and vulnerable people both in the UK and across the world's poorest countries.

One of the ways Comic Relief raises money is through its Red Nose Day fundraising campaign, which is held in the spring every other year.

Red Nose Day involves fundraising events all around the UK including, as the name suggests, the wearing of Red Noses. Ordinary people all over the country participate, often doing unusual, silly things to attract attention to the cause and raise money. In the evening, the BBC hosts a seven-hour telethon which features celebrities in comedy sketches as well as powerful films about the projects Comic Relief supports in the UK and around the world.

To date, Comic Relief's Red Nose Day campaign has raised over a half a billion pounds, has sold nearly 60 million red noses, has produced fourteen singles (including eleven number ones) and has transmitted more than 190 hours of television. International versions of Red Nose Day have also been held in Canada, Finland, Iceland, Norway and Germany.

Would you be funny for money?

According to its website, Comic Relief's biggest tool 'is the ability to inspire people across the whole country – especially those who don't normally do charity – to do charity.' Red Nose Day seems to bring out the best and craziest in people, and this afternoon we were out and about asking people what they were doing.

'We came to work this morning in our pyjamas and took a bucket round to collect money from our colleagues,' said Maria D'Angelo outside the office where she works. 'It's been **eye-opening** actually. I've been working here for a year and it's the first time I've spoken to some of my colleagues.'

Down the street, outside a shoe shop, manager Chris Bayley was sitting in a bath full of something green. 'I've closed the shop and I'm spending the day in this **jelly**,' he explained, 'Do you want to try some? It tastes good!' How did he feel? 'I'm freezing! I've been sitting here for four hours now. But people walking by have been very generous.'

Traffic control officer, Sonia Gold, was taking a break from directing traffic. 'I've had this red nose on since eight o'clock this morning and I've had a great time. Everyone is in a good mood. A lot of the drivers have been waving at me or **hooting** and quite a lot of the cars are 'wearing' red noses too.'

And at Oakfield Junior School everyone had their red noses on but it was strangely silent in the **corridors**. One student, Wesley, wrote for us in his notebook: 'We're having a sponsored silence. I haven't opened my mouth all day, except to eat. Only one more hour now.' The teachers, I noted, seemed to be enjoying the **unaccustomed** quiet.

There was music, though, coming from the school hall where about forty people were taking part in a twenty-four-hour dance **marathon**. Paul Yelder looked **worn out**. 'I'm totally exhausted. We've been dancing for twelve hours, and I'm not sure I can survive till the end.' His partner, Yasmin McKay, was bursting with energy. 'Only twelve hours to go,' said Yasmin. 'My friends have said they'll double their **donations** if we finish!'

Everyone was getting involved: with cake sales, pub quizzes, sponsored swims; you name it and someone was doing it. If this town is anything to go by, it looks as if Red Nose Day is set to break all records this year.

GRAMMAR present perfect simple and continuous

3A Work in pairs and check what you know. Complete the sentences with the present perfect simple or continuous. Then check your answers in the articles.

1 I' _____ here for a year. (work)

2 It _____ money for over twenty years. (raise)

3 To date, Comic Relief's Red Nose Day campaign _____ over half a billion pounds. (raise)

4 I' _____ this nose on since eight o'clock this morning. (have)

5 I'm totally exhausted. We' _____ for twelve hours. (dance)

6 I' _____ the shop. (close)

B Match rules 1–3 with the sentences in Exercise 3A.

Rules:

1 Use either the present perfect simple or the present perfect continuous (both are correct) for an activity or state which started in the past and continues up to now. *1, 2*

2 Use the present perfect simple:

  a) with a state verb.

  b) for a completed action.

  c) for a completed result, in answer to *How much / many?*

3 Use the present perfect continuous:

  a) for a repeated or continuous activity.

  b) when there is present evidence of a recent activity.

4A ▶ 2.1 Listen and write the sentences.

B Underline the main stresses and mark any weak forms (/ə/ or /ɪ/) in the auxiliary verbs. Listen and check. Then listen again and repeat.

How long have you been working here?
       /ə/   /ɪ/

▶ page 130 **LANGUAGE**BANK

5 Complete the text with the present perfect simple or continuous form of the verbs in the box. If both are possible, use the continuous form.

| work   follow   become   visit |
| meet   live (recently)   recruit   know |
| double   grow |

1 I *'ve been working* with Fairtrade organisations to help developing markets get fair prices for goods since I finished university, and I 2_____ over thirty countries in connection with my work. This year 3_____ in one of my favourite countries, Ghana.

I 4_____ so many wonderful people here and been impressed by their strength and optimism. One of my closest friends is Kufuo, who I 5_____ since I started coming here.

He 6_____ cocoa all his life and 7_____ Fairtrade guidelines for producing cocoa for several years now. He 8_____ more than thirty other farmers into our group and they 9_____ the volume of cocoa exported. As a result, Fairtrade 10_____ one of the most important movements in this region.

6A Complete the questions with the present perfect simple or continuous form of the verbs in brackets. If both are possible, use the continuous form.

1 _____ hard recently? (you/work)

2 How long _____ your closest friend? (you/know)

3 You look well! What _____ ? (you/do)

4 How many times _____ your favourite film? (you/see)

5 _____ the same name? (your country/always/have)

6 How long _____ to this class? (you/come)

7 How many coffees _____ today? (you/drink)

8 How long _____ on this exercise? (you/work)

B Work in pairs and take turns. Ask and answer the questions in Exercise 6A.

VOCABULARY social issues

7A Complete the table with the social issues in the box below. Some issues can go with more than one category.

pollution ~~poverty~~ drought famine
drunkenness and drug abuse divorce
domestic violence debt obesity
lack of drinking water homelessness

SOCIAL ISSUES	
money	*poverty* debt homelessness
health	*poverty*
environment	
family	

B Put a cross next to the issues that are <u>not</u> a major problem in your country. Then work in pairs and compare your answers.

SPEAKING

8A Work in pairs and make notes on questions 1–3.

1 What do you think are the three main social problems in your country?

2 Do you think these problems are present all over the world or are they specific to your country?

3 For each problem, can you suggest one change or action that could make a positive difference?

B Work in groups and discuss questions 1–3 in Exercise 8A.

➔ page 149 **VOCABULARY BANK**

VOCABULARY *PLUS* verbs/nouns with the same form

9A ▶ 2.2 Complete the conversations with the correct form of one of the words in the box. Then listen and check.

~~decrease~~ record sponsor export
increase permit appeal project

1 **A:** Has malaria _decreased_ in recent years?
   B: Yes, there's been a huge _decrease_ because of the use of nets.

2 **A:** Does the BBC _____ Comic Relief?
   B: Yes, the BBC is one of their main _____.

3 **A:** Has there been an _____ in people's awareness of Fairtrade?
   B: Yes, and sales _____ by about thirty percent in Europe last year.

4 **A:** The UN has launched an _____ for the disaster.
   B: Yes, they're _____ for money and also tents and blankets.

5 **A:** When did Bonnie Tyler _____ her song *Total Eclipse of the Heart*?
   B: In 1983, and in 2008 it set a _____ for the most popular karaoke track ever.

6 **A:** What types of fruit do you _____ each year?
   B: Our main _____ are bananas and oranges, mainly to Canada.

7 **A:** Your latest _____ is research into rising sea levels.
   B: Yes, we _____ a rise of at least one metre in the next fifty years.

8 **A:** Do we need a _____ to enter the park?
   B: No, but we're not _____ to leave the main tracks.

B Which words in Exercise 9A are nouns (N) and which are verbs (V)?

C Listen again and mark the stress on the words. Which ones have the same stress in the noun and verb form and which are different?

🖝 speakout TIP

When the noun and verb form have the same spelling, the noun is usually stressed on the first syllable. Mark and practise the stress on these words: *an import/to import, a reject/to reject, a desert/to desert.*

10A Work in pairs. Student A: look at the quiz. Underline the stress in the words in bold. Student B: turn to page 158.

QUIZ

1 Which country **imports** more Japanese used cars than any other? Canada, Brazil, or Kenya?

2 In India, what colours is it unlucky to wrap a birthday **present** in? Black and white, red and green, or purple and yellow?

3 Which fruit do some plant experts **suspect** was the earth's first? The apple, the banana or the pear?

4 Which is the largest subtropical **desert**? The Arabian, the Kalahari or the Sahara?

5 **Research** has shown that what percent of homemade dinners served in the US include vegetables? 43%, 63% or 93%

B Work in pairs and take turns. Student A: read out your questions and possible answers. Student B: close your book and guess the correct answer.

C Check the answers on page 162.

➔ page 149 **VOCABULARY BANK**

▶ GRAMMAR | the passive   **▶ VOCABULARY** | technology and privacy   **▶ HOW TO** | talk about surveillance

VOCABULARY surveillance

1A Look at the photo. How does it make you feel? Why?

B Work in pairs. Match the types of surveillance technology in the box with quotes 1–6.

> phone cameras   speed cameras   CCTV cameras
> microchips   street level cameras   number plate recognition

1 I think they're **an invasion of privacy** because people can see the area where you live and how to get into your house or apartment.

2 There's not much evidence that they really prevent accidents and **law-abiding citizens** who drive safely have nothing to fear.

3 They act as **a deterrent to crime** because potential criminals know that their actions might be filmed.

4 These can make people more **accountable for** their actions because their photos can be taken and put up on the internet, so it's a good thing.

5 Because these are in all our credit cards and travel passes it means people can **monitor** and **log** information about our habits and movements as we move around a city but I don't like the fact that personal data on our shopping habits can be **handed over** to other companies.

6 I worry that the authorities can now **keep track of** you and where you are every minute of the day, that is if you drive, of course. It's all part of the growing **surveillance society**.

C Match meanings 1–8 with the phrases in bold in Exercise 1B.

1 record   *log*
2 a way to stop people from doing something illegal
3 given
4 responsible for
5 people who aren't criminals
6 getting information about someone's private life in a way they don't like
7 watch or follow (two phrases)
8 a situation where there is a lot of observation, filming or recording of people

D Work in pairs and discuss the statements in Exercise 1B. Do you agree with them? Why?/ Why not?

LISTENING

2A ▶ 2.3 Listen to people discussing surveillance. Which types of technology do they talk about?

B Listen again and complete the table.

Speaker	For (✓) or against (✗)	Reasons
1		
2		
3		
4		
5		

GRAMMAR the passive

3A Check what you know. Look at the sentences and underline the passive forms.

1 They're just used by the government to make money.

2 More crimes are being solved because of CCTV cameras.

3 A few months ago I was robbed by two men but thanks to CCTV, the people who did it were all arrested.

4 In my area, four cameras have been placed along one stretch of road.

5 The technology will be used to tell us what we can and can't eat.

6 Everyone has to be more careful because their photos might be sent to the newspapers.

7 I hate being watched like that.

8 I certainly don't want to be sent adverts from companies I don't know.

B Underline the correct alternative to complete the rules.

Rules:
1 Use the passive to put the focus on the person or thing *doing the action / affected by the action*.

2 Use the passive when the person who did the action:

a) *is / isn't* obvious

b) *is known / unknown*

c) *is / isn't* important

3 Use the passive to bring the object of the verb to *the beginning / the end* of the sentence.

C Work in pairs. Match each of the rules above with the sentences in Exercise 3A.

4 ▶ 2.4 Mark the stress in phrases 1–6. Listen and check. Then listen again and repeat.

1 They're just used by the government ...

2 I hate being watched like that.

3 I don't want to be sent adverts ...

4 I was robbed by two men.

5 Crimes are being solved ...

6 ... their photos might be sent to the newspapers.

▶ page 130 **LANGUAGEBANK**

PRACTICE

5A Complete the sentences with the correct form of the passive.

1 In some companies, emails _____ (always / filter) for particular words and in this way company secrets _____ (can / keep) safe.

2 Many people don't like _____ (tell) to carry their identity cards with them all the time.

3 At this moment, your actions _____ (probably / film) by a camera somewhere.

4 In the future, microchips _____ (place) in food packaging, so that you _____ (can / remind) when it's time to buy more.

5 In the future, genetic screening _____ (may / use) to predict whether someone might commit a crime.

6 Last year, thousands of people's personal data _____ (lose) by officials.

7 To date, many criminals _____ (catch) because their details are on the DNA database.

8 Social network websites _____ (often / infiltrate) by hackers in the last few years and people's personal data _____ (steal) .

B Work in pairs and discuss. Which ideas in Exercise 5A do you find disturbing and which don't bother you?

SPEAKING

6A Work in pairs. Read the article and answer the questions.

1 Which of the police plans do you think would be most useful for cutting crime?

2 How do you think the following groups of people would feel about the plans: the police, the local residents, parents, teenagers?

Police to install town-wide surveillance

In response to the recent surge in crime, police have announced plans to install the following security systems:

• CCTV cameras to cover the whole town

• speed cameras and number plate recognition on all main roads

• police spot checks for identity cards

• monitoring of mobile and landline telephone calls

• monitoring of social network websites

• all teenagers' mobile phones to be registered on police GPS systems

B Work in pairs. You belong to one of the four groups in Exercise 6A. Make a list of your reasons for or against the plans.

C Work in groups. Role-play a meeting between the four groups to discuss the proposed plans.

WRITING a letter of complaint

7A Work in pairs and discuss. In what circumstances would you write a letter of complaint or make an official complaint? Have you ever done this? What happened?

B Read the letter and answer the questions.

1 Who is the letter to?

2 Why is the writer complaining?

3 What does he want to achieve?

15 Maple Road
Hillhead
HH12 84L
5th February

Hillhead Local Council
1662 Parkway
Hillhead, H3 7JT

Dear Sir or Madam,

1 I am writing with regard to the Council's recent installation of CCTV cameras in our area.

2 Briefly, the problem is that despite guarantees about safeguarding the CCTV images, it is possible for anyone to view them on their home computer because the system is internet-linked and not password-protected. As a result, pictures cannot be kept secure and, in fact, myself and my car can be identified in images that were recently posted online. I regard this as a serious invasion of privacy as well as a violation of the local council promise to taxpayers.

3 I have already pursued this matter with the local police department, who have advised me to contact you immediately.

4 In order to resolve this matter I am requesting that you remove the images where I appear without delay (specific coordinates are detailed in the enclosed document), and that you take action to prevent further invasions of privacy in the future. This would include ensuring that internet-based CCTV images are pass-worded and that techniques are used to blur the pictures so that individuals are unrecognisable.

5 Please contact me within ten days of the date of this letter to confirm that these steps have been taken. If you need to contact me by telephone, you may reach me at (0141) 985-001.

6 Thank you for your prompt attention to this matter.

Yours faithfully,

Steven Jones

Steven Jones

C Write the number of the paragraph next to the correct topic.

a) explain what you have done so far *3*

b) give a time frame for action and a way of contacting you

c) state the overall reason for writing, in one sentence

d) write a polite closing comment

e) ask for specific action from the person/company you are writing to

f) give additional detail about the reason for writing

LEARN TO use formal written language

8A Match informal phrases 1–7 with formal phrases in the letter.

1 Get in touch soon to let me know that you've done something

2 To put things right, I want you to ...

3 I'm writing about

4 With best wishes

5 Thanks for dealing with this problem quickly

6 I'm sending something with this letter

7 I've already discussed the problem

B Work in pairs. Underline all the examples of the passive in the letter. Why is it used so often?

speakout TIP

A letter of complaint should follow 'The Four Cs'. It should be: concise, clear, constructive and considerate. Reread the letter. Does it follow all four of 'The Four Cs'?

9A Plan a letter of complaint.

1 Read the notes below and choose one of the situations.

2 Decide what you want to achieve in the letter.

3 Make notes on the content of each paragraph.

Situation 1

Your neighbours / new burglar alarm / alarm gone off three times / neighbours away / tried to talk to them / too busy

Write a letter of complaint to your neighbours.

Situation 2

Recently you parked car / thought it was legal / returned / parking fine / no-parking sign / behind tree

Write a letter of complaint to your local council.

Situation 3

Recently you joined online DVD store / huge increase of spam / email unusable / store did not protect contact details

Write a letter of complaint to the customer service department of the online store.

B Write the letter (120–180 words).

C Check the grammar, spelling and punctuation of your letter.

D Exchange your letter with another student. Check that he/she has:

• followed The Four Cs.

• used paragraphs well.

• used a formal style.

▶ **FUNCTION** | opinions   ▶ **VOCABULARY** | opinion adjectives   ▶ **LEARN TO** | support your viewpoint

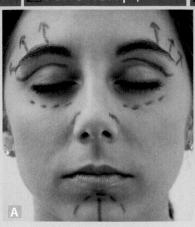

1 Statistics show that good-looking people earn 10–15% more than plain-looking people in the same job – so it makes sense that some people want to get cosmetic surgery to improve their appearance.

2 It is theft and thieves can be punished. In fact, an American woman was fined nearly $2 million for downloading and sharing songs.

3 Banning cars in the city centre has led to a 30% reduction in pollution levels and increased use of public transport. During the same period there has been a 10% reduction in shop sales although it is not certain that this is a result of the ban.

SPEAKING

1 Work in pairs. Match the newspaper extracts 1–3 with the pictures A–C. Then discuss the questions.

1 Which extract is for and which is against the topics discussed? Which one is neutral?

2 Can you think of any other reasons for and against each idea?

3 What is your own opinion about each idea?

FUNCTION   opinions

2A ▶ 2.5 Listen to three conversations. Which speaker do you agree with in each conversation?

B Listen again and make notes. What is each person's opinion? What reasons do they give?

3A Work in pairs and complete the phrases.

Giving opinions

I'm really ¹_____ it.
I'm in ²_____ of it.
The ³_____ I see it, …

Agreeing

I suppose ⁴_____.
I ⁵_____ what you mean …

Partially agreeing

You've got a ⁶_____ there, but …
I agree to ⁷_____ extent, but …

Disagreeing

I ⁸_____ disagree.
I'm not ⁹_____ sure.
I'm still not ¹⁰_____.

B Check your answers in the audio script on page 165. Which phrases show very strong or very weak opinions?

4A ▶ 2.6 Listen to the phrases and underline the stressed words. Then listen again and repeat.

B Add the phrases in the box to the correct groups in Exercise 3A.

I think …   Exactly!   I take/see your point, but …
It seems to me that …   That's right.   I agree.
I don't agree with you.   Fair enough, but …   I feel …

➤ page 130 **LANGUAGEBANK**

5A Write the conversations in full.

Conversation 1

A: I / favour / banning / smoking / all public places.

B: I / not / agree / you. / People / be / free to choose.

A: agree / some / extent, / but / what about the rights / other people?

B: way / see / freedom / choose / more important.

A: take / point, / but / passive smoking / can / very bad / you.

B: I / suppose, / but / banning / all places / too much!

Conversation 2

A: I / against / too much / violence / films / because / effect on crime.

B: not / agree/ you. / Thousands / people / watch films / but / only a few people commit crimes.

A: Okay. You / point / there, / but / seem / me even one person / be / one person too many.

B: know / what / you mean, / but / still / not convinced.

B Work in pairs and take turns. Practise the conversations using the prompts.

LEARN TO support your viewpoint

6 Look at the phrases in bold in 1–8 below. Which phrases are used:

a) to give an example?

b) for facts which you have read or heard?

c) for a fact which you have read or heard when you are not sure if it is true?

1 **Take the case of** Mike's girlfriend; she actually had some Botox injections.

2 ... some kind of surgery, you know, **such as** liposuction to get rid of fat?

3 But **it's a well-known fact that** musicians get very little money from CD sales anyway.

4 ... spend a fortune on things **like** record companies and managers and ...

5 **Apparently,** having only buses can bring in five times as many people.

6 ... **it's been shown that** buses are more polluting than cars.

7 **According to** an article I read recently, file sharing's good because ...

8 **For instance,** what about that woman in America?

7A Cover Exercise 6 and put the underlined phrases in the correct order.

A: [1]article to this according, women can't read maps and men can't listen.

B: That's just a stereotype. Men are often good at jobs that involve listening, [2]management in for jobs instance.

A: Yeah, you're right. [3]of my case the brother Take and his wife. She's a great map reader...

B: ... and your brother's good at 'female tasks', [4]cooking as listening or such to people – just not both at the same time.

A: Well, [5]well-known it's are women that fact a better at multi-tasking. It says so here.

B: No way; [6]'s shown it are that men been just as good. You shouldn't believe everything you read [7]that in like magazines.

A: I suppose not, [8]'s scientific based research it apparently on but.

speakout TIP

In a discussion, either spoken or written, develop your argument by giving reasons for your opinions as well as examples. You can also refer to your reading and research by mentioning what people or books say about an issue.

B Work in pairs and discuss. Do you agree with any of the stereotypes about men/women in the conversation in Exercise 7A? Give examples and reasons.

VOCABULARY opinion adjectives

8A Match the adjectives in the box with opinions 1–8 below.

> ~~disturbing~~   illegal   unethical   justifiable
> inevitable   inoffensive   sensible   outrageous

1 It makes me feel upset.   *disturbing*

2 It's a good idea – reasonable and logical.

3 It's going to happen sooner or later, that's for sure.

4 It's against the principles of what is right and wrong.

5 If you do it, the police might arrest you.

6 There's a good reason for it.

7 I'm totally shocked and extremely angry.

8 Maybe it bothers some people, but not me.

B Work in pairs and take turns. Student A: give one of the opinions above. Student B: close your book and reply using one of the adjectives.

A: It's going to happen sooner or later, that's for sure.

B: Yes, it's inevitable.

C Which of the adjectives in Exercise 8A can be made into their opposites by adding/removing a prefix?

SPEAKING

9A Work in pairs and choose three topics to discuss.

1 Everyone should be paid exactly the same amount for any job they do.

2 What you wear is not important.

3 Exams are a waste of time.

4 University should be free for all.

5 Friendship is more important than love.

6 It's unethical to buy extremely cheap clothes from developing countries.

B Work in groups and discuss the questions.

1 Do you agree or disagree with each statement? Why? Give at least two reasons.

2 Which adjective(s) from Exercise 8A can you use to say how you feel about each topic?

DVD PREVIEW

1 Work in pairs and discuss. Which ways of completing the statement do you agree with?

Money can't make you happy …

- but doing a job you love can.
- What a silly thing to say! Of course it can!
- but you can't be happy with no money. You need a certain amount.
- but shopping does make me feel good.
- and neither can any objects or possessions.
- but I would still like to be very, very rich!

2 Read the programme information. What do you think the scientists will say in this episode?

BBC

The Happiness Formula

People in many countries are far wealthier than fifty years ago but happiness levels have declined. As people have recognised the failure of consumerism to deliver happiness, scientists have taken an interest in what it is that does or doesn't make people happy. This six-part series explores their findings. In tonight's instalment, presenter Mark Easton finds out why the work-and-buy ethic has failed us, and what the science of happiness says about how we should change our way of life.

▶ DVD VIEW

3A Watch the DVD. What is the scientists' main point about how we should change our life?

B Work in pairs. Explain the connection between each pair of words.

1 consume	purchase
2 status	designer label
3 being in the rat race	being stuck on a treadmill
4 increase	diminish
5 assumption	evidence
8 suspect (adj)	unreliable

C Watch again and answer the questions.

1 What is the significance of '£10,000 a year'?

2 The reporter says 'the science of happiness suggests we should do the opposite'. The opposite of what?

3 Professor Jackson talks about 'assumptions that we have to re-examine'. What is one assumption he mentions?

D Work in groups and discuss the questions.

1 What do you think has stopped people from being happier as they have become wealthier?

2 What do you think people can do to change their situation?

speakout a happiness survey

4A Work in pairs and discuss. Which are the three most important 'ingredients' of happiness in the box below? Which three are the least important?

a life partner	peace and quiet	a nice car
free time	friendship	sport or exercise
money	future plans	good food music

B ▶ 2.7 Listen to a man answering questions about happiness. Which topics from Exercise 4A do they talk about? Which are the most important for him?

C Listen again and tick the key phrases you hear.

keyphrases

[Could I/Do you mind if I] ask you some questions?

Which is the [most/least] important for your happiness?

What would you say is missing from your life?

Which would you find the [easiest/hardest/most difficult] to live without?

Are you more or less happy than you were five years ago?

How happy would you say you are, on a scale of one to five (five being very happy)?

5A Work in pairs and prepare a short happiness survey using the key phrases.

B Talk to other students and ask your questions. Make notes on their answers.

C Summarise your findings to the class.

writeback tips for being happy

6A A website asked its readers for tips for being happy. Work in pairs. Read two of the responses and discuss which you agree with.

Don't read the news or watch TV

The news is filled with negative images and stories and each one contributes to your stress levels, making you feel more depressed. Following the news can also take up a great deal of your attention. Instead, use the time to do something you enjoy, such as cooking a meal, phoning a friend or going for a walk.

Get a pet

Studies have shown that people who have a dog or cat are happier and live longer. A pet can give companionship that, for some people, is almost as good as having a partner. Be realistic about what type of pet would be most suitable for you and for your accommodation. Remember, if you choose a dog you'll have to take it for walks, whereas a cat is more independent.

B Work in pairs. Use the headings below to make notes on three tips for being happy.

Tip: *Do something new every day.*

Why this helps: *simple concept – keeps your brain alert – raises your energy levels – stimulating – makes you feel happier*

How to do it: *get off the train/bus a stop early and walk home – speak to someone you don't know – do a new type of puzzle*

C Write about your tips for the website (120–200 words). Use one paragraph for each tip.

D Read other students' tips. Whose tips would work best for you?

SOCIAL ISSUES

1A Make a list of as many social issues as you can remember.

B Which social issue(s) could each statement refer to?

1 There are different types – air, water, noise – and the latter is the one that causes the most stress.

2 Women are more commonly victims of this.

3 The rate in Japan is half that in the USA, but India has the lowest rate in the world.

4 There has been a dramatic increase in suicides among Australian farmers because of this.

5 Some of the main causes are flooding, overpopulation and war.

6 It's more common among people with less money.

C Work in pairs and discuss the statements in Exercise 1B. What reasons can you think of for these situations?

PRESENT PERFECT SIMPLE AND CONTINUOUS

2A Make questions with the prompts. Use the most natural verb form: the present perfect simple or continuous, or the past simple.

1 How long / you / learn / English?

2 Your English / improve / a lot recently. What / you / do?

3 How many teachers / you / have?

4 Who / be / your favourite teacher before your current one?

5 How far / you / travel / to class today?

6 you / do / your homework for today?

7 How long / take / you / do it?

8 you / study / a lot this week?

9 you / practise / English / outside the class regularly in the past year?

10 you / ever / forget / to bring anything to class?

11 How long / try / understand the present perfect?

12 you / spend / too much time in front of your computer lately?

B Work in pairs and take turns. Ask and answer the questions.

SURVEILLANCE

3 Match sentences 1–6 to people/things a)–f).

1 It's an invasion of privacy, for personal profit.

2 They keep track of people's movements.

3 It acts as a deterrent to burglary.

4 They aren't legally accountable for their actions.

5 It measures and logs how fast you're driving.

6 It's part of a surveillance society.

a) CCTV everywhere 6

b) a speed camera

c) children

d) an alarm on your house

e) a paparazzi photo of a celebrity

f) credit card and transport card readers

THE PASSIVE

4A Change the sentences into the passive.

1 I don't like it when people call me by my nickname.

I don't like being called by my nickname.

2 My parents brought me up in a house full of pets.

3 No one has ever robbed me.

4 I hate it when people give me clothes as a present.

5 People often tell me I look like my father.

6 I've always wanted people to admire me for my intelligence.

B Tick the sentences in Exercise 4A which are true for you. Then make the other sentences true by adding or changing no more than three words.

C Work in pairs and compare your sentences.

5A Put the words in the correct order to make passive questions.

1 an / by / bitten / been / ever / you / Have / animal?

2 you / by / invited / a / like / to / celebrity / to / Would / dinner / be?

3 being / you / Do / enjoy / photographed?

4 the / want / told / if / you / always / to / truth / Do / even / it / hurts / be?

5 die / remembered / What / for / will / after / you / you / be?

B Work in pairs and take turns. Ask and answer the questions.

OPINIONS

6A Correct the mistakes in the phrases for agreeing/disagreeing.

A: [1]**I'm in favourite of** banning people from eating food on public transport.

B: [2]**I'm so sure.** What about long journeys? For instance, with kids?

A: [3]**You are a point there, but** I meant on shorter journeys.

B: [4]**Enough fair, but** I think it'd be impossible to check.

A: [5]**I'm agree to some extent, but** maybe the ticket collectors or guards could check.

B: [6]**I'm still not convincing.** Some people would carry on anyway.

A: [7]Hmm ... **I suppose**, unfortunately.

B Choose one of the topics and have a conversation. Use the phrases in Exercise 6A to help you.

- banning homework
- letting women play on men's professional sports teams
- lowering the voting age

BBC VIDEO PODCAST

Download the podcast to view people talking about the question: Does money make you happy?

Authentic BBC interviews

www.pearsonlongman.com/speakout

UNIT 3

SPEAKING
> Discuss bad habits
> Talk about the future
> Plan a niche holiday
> Describe procedures

LISTENING
> Listen to a BBC radio programme about holidays
> Listen to people describe TV game shows
> Watch a BBC programme about adventures

READING
> Read about a couple in conflict
> Read an opinion essay

WRITING
> Write an opinion essay
> Use linkers to organise your essay

BBC CONTENT
▢ Video podcast: What's the perfect way to switch off?
◉ DVD: 50 Things To Do Before You Die

UNIT 3

downtime

SPEAKING

1 Work in pairs and discuss the questions.

1 Do/Did you regularly play any games/sports? How often and why?

2 What are the benefits of playing computer games? What are the potential problems?

VOCABULARY behaviour

2A Work in pairs and match verbs 1–5 with opposites a)–e). Use a dictionary to check.

1 take care of   *b*

2 pay attention to

3 compliment someone (on)

4 get on with something

5 give in

a) put something off

b) neglect

c) be stubborn

d) ignore

e) criticise someone (for)

B Rewrite the sentences replacing the underlined verbs with one of the verbs from Exercise 2A.

                    put off

1 Do you often ~~delay~~ doing important tasks, or do you simply immediately do them?

2 Which do you think is more useful: when someone says nice things to you about your work or your appearance, or when someone says negative things to you even if they are being honest?

3 When you've got a problem, do you listen and think carefully about advice from other people or do you often take no notice of it and make your own decision?

4 If you have plants in your house, do you look after them or fail to give them attention?

5 When you argue or disagree with a friend, do you tend to refuse to change your view or are you the one who usually changes your opinion first?

C Work in pairs and discuss the questions in Exercise 2B.

It's like a drug …

JADE'S STORY

When I first met Sam, I really liked him. He was good-looking and kind but quite shy. He used to play computer games – or one in particular – quite a lot. I'd visit him at his home and he'd be sitting at the computer. Sometimes he didn't even turn round, and I thought that was strange but I soon got used to talking to his back! Anyway, three years ago we got married.

Now when he comes home from work, one of us cooks dinner, while the other looks after our son Joe. Then instead of sitting down and chatting about the day, Sam usually goes straight to his computer to play *Battle Galaxy 2525*. Whenever I try to get him to watch a movie on TV or something, he either completely ignores me or he agrees and then gets bored because he wants to go back to his game. I'm not used to that type of behaviour. It's very different from my family. I feel ignored and often ask myself why I stay with this guy.

It wouldn't be so bad if it was just with me. But whenever his parents come round he carries on playing and ignores them. Sometimes he turns round to say something but he often doesn't even know what we've been talking about. So I have to talk to them and pretend that everything's normal.

I remember once I got really annoyed and I unplugged his computer. He was furious – he said I'd 'killed' some of his friends.

READING

3A Work in pairs. Student A: turn to page 159. Student B: read the article above. Underline two words/phrases in the box that best describe how Jade sees herself. Circle two words that describe how she sees Sam.

selfish patient talkative a good parent neglected rude a good friend

B Work with a student who read the same article and compare your answers.

4A What can you remember? Answer the questions. Then read your article again and check.

1 Why did Sam and Jade like each other at first?

2 Does Sam spend enough time with Jade and Joe?

3 Why does Sam like the game so much?

4 Why are Sam and Jade both irritated when Sam's parents visit?

5 Why did Jade unplug Sam's computer? Why were they both angry afterwards?

6 How do they both feel about Joe playing on the computer?

B Work with a student who read the other article and compare your answers to Exercises 3A and 4A.

C Work in pairs and discuss. How do you think Jade and Sam can resolve the problem? Who do you think needs to change the most?

I think these virtual 'friends' of his are more important to him than me and Joe. I mean, they aren't even real! I couldn't believe it! I shouted at him that he only thinks about himself and his virtual world ... we didn't talk to each other for a whole week.

And Joe? I suppose he's used to his father being on the computer because he's never known anything different. But Sam's idea of being a good father is showing Joe how to tap on the computer keyboard. One thing's for sure, I'm never going to let Joe start playing computer games. I've threatened to leave Sam but it would be terrible for Joe and I'm sure that deep down Sam knows he's in the wrong. It's like a drug. I think he needs help.

GRAMMAR   *used to, would, be/get used to*

5 Look at sentences 1–5 and underline the correct alternative to complete the rules.

1 Jade used to visit me at my flat and she enjoyed watching me play.
2 I'd visit him at his home and he'd be sitting at the computer.
3 Joe's used to me sitting at the computer. He's never known anything different.
4 I'm not used to that kind of behaviour. It's very different from my family.
5 I thought it was strange but I soon got used to talking to his back.

Rules:
a) Use *used to* to talk about activities and states which *happen regularly in the present/ happened in the past but not usually now*.
b) Use *would* to talk about *activities/ states* in the past which no longer happen now.
c) Use *be used to* to talk about things that are *familiar/ strange* to us.
d) Use *get used to* to talk about things that *are familiar/ become familiar to us over a period of time*.
e) After *used to* and *would*, use the *infinitive/ the -ing form or a noun*.
f) After *be used to* and *get used to*, use the *infinitive/ the -ing form or a noun*.

▸ page 132 LANGUAGEBANK

page 132

PRACTICE

6A Correct the mistake in each sentence.

1 When I was a kid, I'd often quarrelled with my parents.
2 As a child, I used to eating too many sweets.
3 I'm not used to get up early, so when I have to be somewhere in the morning, I'm often late.
4 I used to saying what I think, and sometimes I upset people.
5 I get used to my mother cooking for me when I lived at home, and now I can't cook for myself.
6 I come from a big family and I don't think I'll ever get used to live on my own.
7 I didn't used to be help much around the house.
8 I would be quite a lazy student when I was younger, and I often put off finishing my homework.

B Work in groups and discuss. Which of the bad habits and behaviour above do/ did you share? Do/Did you have any other bad habits?

SPEAKING

7 Work in pairs and take turns. Say which of the habits below really annoy you and why, giving examples. Which are the worst? Can you name any others?

• blowing your nose loudly in a restaurant
• not cleaning up after yourself in the kitchen
• interrupting people when they're speaking
• pretending to listen, but not really listening
• leaving the TV on all the time
• eating on public transport

WRITING an opinion essay

8A Look at the essay title. Work in pairs and discuss the questions.

> **Most people fill their leisure time with meaningless activities. Do you agree?**

1 What do you consider a 'meaningful' and a 'meaningless' leisure activity?
2 What is your opinion of the statement?

B Read the essay. Do you agree with the writer's point of view?

1 It is said that technological development has given people more leisure time than they used to have, and that this frees them up to concentrate on pursuing their interests or improving themselves. It seems to me however, that most people spend their free time doing things that do not contribute to their development and are essentially unproductive.

2 **To start with**, the most popular free-time activities seem to be ones that people do alone. **For instance**, most people spend a large part of their time on the internet and, even when they are interacting with others, they are only doing so electronically; they are not communicating with a person, but with digital signals. **In addition to this**, when people do go out it is often to visit the shopping centre; for some families, their main time together consists of a few hours walking, filling a shopping trolley and eating at a snack bar in a shopping mall.

3 **At the same time**, there are examples of people making good use of their time. At weekends, there are parks, forests and beaches full of people doing sports or taking walks together. Some people do volunteer work for charity organisations for a few hours a week. Other people join theatre or singing groups and there are many people who enjoy reading. Sadly, however, this reflects a relatively small part of the overall population.

4 **In conclusion**, I agree that people use their free time wastefully, and I feel that the situation is getting worse. It is my hope that this might change in the future.

C Work in pairs. Identify the purpose of each paragraph.

D Underline three phrases for giving opinions. Which paragraphs do they occur in?

LEARN TO use linkers in an opinion essay

9A Complete the table with the linking words/phrases in bold in the essay.

firstly to start with	furthermore	to conclude	in contrast	for example

B Add the following phrases to the correct columns of the table.

> moreover   in the first place   to sum up   as an example
> as opposed to this

10A Choose one of the essay titles below. Work alone and make notes on the questions.
- Do you agree with the opinion?
- Why/Why not? List three points.
- What examples can you give to support your points?

> Using computers and the internet develops important skills in young people.

> Technology has created less free time rather than more.

> Leisure activities have become too expensive.

> Children need more play time in order to develop into healthy adults.

B Work in groups and discuss your opinions. Make notes on any new points you could include in your essay.

C Write a plan for your essay.

speakout TIP

One way to organise an opinion essay is as follows:
– An introductory paragraph – state the topic and give your opinion. You can start, 'Some people believe….' or use a question or a quotation.
– The main body of the essay in two or three paragraphs. Each time you give a viewpoint, give your reasons/examples.
– A conclusion where you restate your opinion using different words.

D Write the essay (120–180 words). Then check your work for accurate grammar and for use of linkers.

> ▶ **GRAMMAR** | future forms review   ▶ **VOCABULARY** | locations   ▶ **HOW TO** | talk about the future

Traveller's Tree

The BBC radio travel show *Traveller's Tree* starts with one of the fastest growing sectors in the holiday industry and the buzzword of the day: 'niche' travel, for those with particular interests who are tired of 'flopout' beach holidays.

LISTENING

1A Work in pairs and look at the photos. Which holidays appeal/don't appeal to you?

B Read the programme listing. What is the difference between a 'niche' holiday and a 'flopout' holiday?

2A ▶ 3.1 Listen to the programme. Number the niche holidays in the order you hear them.

- Thai cooking week
- Singing on the Nile
- Historical cruise
- Sri Lanka for tea lovers
- Bird watching
- Tour of Chernobyl and Pripyat
- Tour of battlefields

B Listen again. Are the sentences true (T) or false (F)? Correct the false sentences.

1 Niche holidays are being offered by more tour operators.
2 Alison Rice describes 'niche' holidays as different from activity holidays.
3 Charlie Connolly thinks the best reason for going to a place is to look at nice views.
4 At the end of a singing holiday, you make a CD to sell to the local people.
5 In Chernobyl, you don't go into the nuclear reactor.
6 The school at Pripyat near Chernobyl is empty.
7 A lot of people have posted messages on the Traveller's Tree messageboard.
8 A contributor, Dilly Gaffe, likes the idea of a niche holiday.

C Work in pairs and discuss. Would any of the niche holidays mentioned in the programme interest you?

VOCABULARY   locations

3A Match the sentence halves.

1 Australia is the least **densely populated** continent,   g
2 People who live **in close proximity to** Los Angeles airport
3 Sir Edmund Hillary and Sherpa Tenzing spent fifteen minutes at the **summit** of Everest
4 Cape Town is about **half-way between** Santiago, Chile
5 Part of Hong Kong is an island, and part is
6 The Caribbean island of Haiti was once **heavily forested**,
7 The most **remote** and **unspoilt** place in the UK is Foula,
8 Lake Baikal is located **on the edge of** Siberia

a) before heading back down the southern **slope**.
b) but it's now almost completely **barren**.
c) an island just **off the coast of** northern Scotland.
d) on a **peninsula** connected to mainland China.
e) were found to have higher than normal blood pressure.
f) and contains twenty percent of the world's fresh water.
g) with just 2.6 people per square kilometre.
h) and Perth, Australia **as the crow flies**.

B Which of the expressions in bold in Exercise 3A:

- talk about location/distance?
- are the names of geographical features?
- describe the character of a place?

C Work in pairs and take turns. Student A: close your book. Student B: make questions out of the sentences in Exercise 3A and ask your partner.
Which continent is the least densely populated?

GRAMMAR future forms review

4A Check what you know. Complete the conversations with an appropriate form of the verbs in brackets. Sometimes there is more than one possibility.

1 A: So, are you looking forward to your Nile trip?

   B: Yes, and Francesco says _he's going to learn_ (he/learn) Arabic … in four weeks!

2 A: _____ (you/do) anything interesting next summer?

   B: Yes, _____ (we/go) to New Zealand in July.

3 A: _____ (The plane/land) very early on Friday morning.

   B: When's the first tour?

   A: As soon as _____ (we get) there, I think.

4 A: It's in Thailand, and it says here, '_____ (It/likely/rain) every afternoon, but expect to walk twenty kilometres a day, rain or shine.'

   B: I expect _____ (it/be) quite hard work.

   A: I don't know. _____ (I/check) with Tess. She was over there last year.

5 A: _____ (We/go) to Ukraine this year, we haven't decided yet.

   B: Sounds interesting.

   A: Yes, and then _____ (we/stop off) in Poland to see Magda on the way home.

6 A: Mike _____ (think/go) on a trek to Machu Picchu in Peru.

   B: It's quite a hard walk, I've heard.

   A: Yeah. He _____ (hope/ask) people to sponsor him for charity.

B ▶ 3.2 Listen and check your answers.

C Match rules 1–10 with the examples in Exercise 4A.

Rules:

1 Use the present continuous for a definite arrangement often involving other people. 2A, 2B

2 Use _be going to/be planning to/be hoping to_ + infinitive or _be thinking of_ + _-ing_ for a general intention which the speaker has thought about before.

3 Use _will ('ll)_ + infinitive for a decision which the speaker has just made.

4 Use _will ('ll)_ + infinitive for predicting, often with verbs such as _think, expect_ and adverbs such as _probably, definitely_.

5 Use _be likely to_ for a probable intention or prediction.

6 Use _might/could_ + infinitive for an intention or prediction that is not certain.

7 Use the present simple for a future timetable or schedule.

8 Use the present simple for the future after conjunctions such as _when, as soon as, after, in case_.

D ▶ 3.3 Listen to the pronunciation of the future forms in connected speech. Then listen and repeat.

1 What will you do if he doesn't phone?   /wɒtəljə/

2 What are you going to do after class?   /wɒtəjə/

3 Where are you likely to be tonight?   /werəjə/

4 Who will be there?   /huːl/

5 When will you have time to talk?   /wenəljə/

6 When are you meeting them?   /wenəjə/

▶ page 132 **LANGUAGEBANK**

PRACTICE

5A Underline the best alternative in the sentences.

1 _We're going/We might go_ to Venezuela on holiday this year. I booked yesterday.

2 _We'll probably/We're going to_ go camping but we're not sure yet.

3 On Saturday, _I'm meeting/I'll meet_ some friends for lunch.

4 In the future _I'm using/I'm going to use_ English to get a better job.

5 I think it _is raining/will rain_ this weekend.

6 My last bus home _goes/is going to go_ at five past midnight.

7 There's no lesson next week? In that case _I'm staying/I'll stay_ at home and study.

8 A friend of mine is _thinking of/hoping_ travelling to China next year.

9 I always carry a torch in my bag in case _I need/I'll need_ it.

10 _I might/I'm not likely_ to live abroad in the future.

B Change five of the sentences so that they are true for you.

C Work in pairs and take turns. Student A: tell your partner your sentences. Student B: ask follow-up questions.

A: I might go to Croatia on holiday this year.

B: Sounds good. Whereabouts in Croatia?

SPEAKING

6A Work in pairs and take turns. Ask and answer questions and make notes on:

- your partner's interests and hobbies
- the type of accommodation and transport he/she prefers on holiday
- things he/she doesn't like on holiday

B Work with a new partner. Use your notes to design a niche holiday for each of your original partners. Think about the following things:

- name of niche holiday
- location
- means of transport
- length of time
- accommodation
- main activities
- other information (clothing, equipment, climate, health, preparation, items to bring)

C Tell your original partner about the niche holiday you have designed.

You're going to travel by train and horse ... It's likely to be cold and rainy, so you should bring ...

VOCABULARY PLUS uncountable and plural nouns

7A Read the email. Why is Valerie enjoying her holiday?

To: Gabriel14@mailbox.com

Hi Gabriel,

Just a quick note from the middle of nowhere …

We got off to a rough start when Marianna fell down the stairs coming off the plane (no major injuries). Then our luggage got lost, along with all of my clothes and my reading glasses, as well as our toiletries. Things are pretty basic here – you can't buy soap for instance. We're staying on the outskirts of a tiny village, in a yurt, a sort of house made of cloth and wood (see attached photo). In fact there's no concrete anywhere ... and no electricity but I can't say I miss watching the news on TV. So what do we do? Well, a bit of horseback riding during the day and we play cards in the evening. The locals are incredibly friendly. You know, I've realised that simpler is better and I don't want to come home!

Valerie

B Work in pairs and discuss. Would you enjoy this kind of holiday? Why/Why not?

8A Look at the email again. Underline six uncountable nouns and circle six nouns which are usually found only in the plural. Use a dictionary if necessary.

B Read the quiz below. Find and correct ten mistakes.

C Work in pairs and take turns. Ask and answer the quiz questions.

▶ page 150 **VOCABULARYBANK**

Travellers' quiz

1. When you travel, do you find information and accommodations by asking at a tourist office?

2. What sort of facility do you expect hotels to have?

3. Do you ask friends for advices on what to see?

4. How many luggage do you usually carry for a two-week trip?

5. Do you ever carry any sports or camping equipments?

6. Has airport security ever gone through the content of your suitcases?

7. What mean of transport do you like to travel by most – plane, train or car?

8. On holiday, what's your favourite type of sceneries?

9. Do you like looking at the remain of ancient buildings?

10. Do you always keep someone back home informed of your whereabout?

▶ **FUNCTION** | describing procedures **VOCABULARY** | common actions ▶ **LEARN TO** | use mirror questions

SPEAKING

1 Work in pairs and discuss the questions.

1 Do you enjoy watching game shows? Why?/ Why not?

2 What sort of game shows do you have in your country?

3 What do the contestants have to do?

FUNCTION describing procedures

2A Work in pairs. Look at the BBC game shows in the photos. What do you think happens in each show?

B ▶ 3.4 Listen to the descriptions of two of the shows. Were your ideas correct?

C Listen again. For each show, make notes about:

* number of contestants
* aim of game
* best thing about it
* description of set
* winner

3A Match the sentence halves to make phrases for explaining procedures.

1 The way it works is that
2 Basically, the point is not
3 What happens is
4 The first thing they do
5 The key thing is to
6 The object is for
7 After they've finished

a) that the host says 'Bring on the wall!'

b) the team to win money by answering a chain of questions correctly.

c) bank the money as you go along.

d) is answer general knowledge questions.

e) each round, they have to vote on who should get eliminated.

f) there are two teams, with two celebs on each team.

g) to get knocked into the pool.

B Which phrases from Exercise 3A are used:

1 to state the overall goal or aim?
2 to describe details of the procedure?
3 to highlight something particularly important?

C ▶ 3.5 Listen and mark the main stresses in phrases 1–7 in Exercise 3A. Then listen again and repeat.

▷ page 132 **LANGUAGEBANK**

4A Complete the description of a game.

The [1] _way_ it works [2]_____ that there are two teams of eleven players playing with a ball on a large 'field' with two goals at either end. The [3]_____ thing they [4]_____ is toss a coin and one team decides who gets the ball first. [5]_____ happens [6]_____ that the team with the ball has four chances to try to 'advance' it 9.1 metres towards the other team's goal. After [7]_____'_____ done that, they can have another four attempts, but if they don't succeed, then the other team takes possession. Basically, the [8]_____ of the game is to score points by carrying the ball across your opponents' goal line. The [9]_____ thing is to keep possession of the ball, because then the other team can't score! The winner is the team who score the most points. The name of the game is [10]_____.

B Think of a game/sport you know. Make notes on: the number of players, the equipment, the procedure, the aim.

C Work in groups and take turns. Student A: describe the game/sport but don't say the name. Other students: guess the game/sport.

LEARN TO use mirror questions

5A Look at the questions in bold and underline the correct alternative to complete the rules.

1 A: There are two teams, with two celebs on each team.

  B: **Two what?**

  A: Celebs. Celebrities.

2 A: The host says 'Bring on the wall!'

  B **He does what?**

3 A: There's a funny-shaped hole and they have to get through it.

  B: **They have to get through where?**

4 A: The host stands in the centre.

  B: **Who stands in the centre?**

Rules:

1 Use mirror questions to express surprise or clarify understanding.

2 Repeat *a part/ all* of what was said.

3 Replace the problem word or phrase with a suitable *question word/the word 'what'*.

4 Use *do/do what* to replace a verb phrase you didn't understand.

5 Use *question/statement* word order.

6 *Stress/Don't stress* the question word.

speakout TIP

When trying to understand instructions or directions, it's useful to use part of what the other person says to make the mirror question. This helps the other person see what you understood and what you didn't understand instead of asking them to repeat everything again.

B Complete the mirror questions to check the words/ phrases in italics.

1 A: You have to *sauté the potatoes*.

  B: _____?

2 A: The first player writes *an anagram of the word*.

  B: _____?

3 A: You go *to the webinar site*.

  B: _____?

4 A: Basically, the aim is to beat *the rival team*.

  B: _____?

C ▶ 3.6 Mark the main stress in the questions above. Listen and check. Then listen again and repeat.

VOCABULARY common actions

6A Work in pairs. Which of the actions in bold is related to a game/sport (G), to a machine (M) or to cooking (C)? Use a dictionary if necessary.

1 **deal** them **out**, five to each person G

2 **stir** it so that it doesn't stick to the bottom

3 **double-click** on it

4 when it **jams**, take off the cover and pull the paper out

5 **pass** it to another player in your team

6 **unplug** it when you're not using it

7 **sieve** it so that there are no lumps in it

8 **roll** it, and if you get a one, your turn's over

9 **sprinkle** it generously all over

10 **press** it halfway to focus

B What words could replace *it* or *them* in each phrase?

C Work in pairs and take turns. Cover the phrases in Exercise 6A. Student A: act out one of the actions. Student B: say the action.

SPEAKING

7A Choose one of the situations below to explain to a partner.

• the features of your mobile phone (or any gadget/ machine) and how it works.

• a hobby, game or sport you enjoy

• how to make a favourite dish

• what one of your favourite websites is and how it works

• the procedure for something practical, e.g. giving first aid

• how you do one or more of the tasks in your job/studies

B Make notes on the main points, the procedure and key things to keep in mind.

C Work in pairs or groups and take turns. Student A: describe the procedure to the other students. Other students: ask mirror questions if you don't understand something.

⟶ page 150 VOCABULARYBANK

DVD PREVIEW

1 Work in pairs and discuss the questions.

1 What's one unusual activity you've done that you think everyone should experience?

2 What's one thing you've always wanted to try, and one place you've always wanted to visit?

2A Work in pairs. Read the programme information. Who decided what the top fifty things to do are?

B Match the activities mentioned in the article to photos A–E.

BBC
50 Things To Do Before You Die

When the BBC asked its viewers what one thing they'd like to do in their lifetime, the response was overwhelming with some 20,000 members of the public sending in their ideas. *50 Things To Do Before You Die* takes the viewers on a tour through the top fifty viewer choices, from observing rare and exotic animals in their natural habitat, to travelling a historic route by train, car or jet plane, to some more extreme activities not for the faint-hearted, among them bungee jumping, husky dog sledding and wing-walking. Whether you're a hard-core traveller or an armchair tourist, you're sure to find inspiration for your next journey.

▶ DVD VIEW

3A Watch the DVD and write down the five activities. Which activity is number one?

B Mark the sentences true (T) or false (F). Then watch again and check.

1 The main thing people say they love about sledding is the scenery.

2 The presenter preferred driving the sled to sitting in it.

3 Pilots used to strap themselves to the wings at airshows.

4 Before she went wingwalking, Rebecca said she was anxious but keen.

5 She found it surprisingly easy to wave and look elegant.

6 The legendary route 66 runs from Chicago to San Francisco.

7 It was used by Americans trying to escape from the Great Depression.

8 One of the bungy jumpers likes the feeling of being stretched and bounced.

9 People have always been fascinated by dolphins' playfulness and intelligence.

10 The speakers like dolphins because they are helpful to humans.

C Work with a new partner. Order the five activities from the one you'd most like to do to the one you'd least like to do.

speakout a recommendation

4A Think about two different things you have tried that you would recommend to someone else, for example a journey, an experience with animals/ nature, a sport. For each activity, make notes on questions 1–3.

1 What was the activity?

2 How did you feel before/while/after you did it?

3 Why do you think it's worth trying?

B ▶ 3.7 Listen to someone describing an activity, and answer questions 1-3 above.

C Listen again and tick the key phrases you hear.

Keyphrases

I'm (not) the kind of person who likes [extreme activities/new situations/spicy food] but ...

The activity I'd like to recommend is/may seem [terrifying/quite boring/silly] ...

It's one of the [best/most exciting/most challenging] things I've ever done.

The thing I'll remember most is [the feeling of .../ the moment .../the exhilaration.]

I'd recommend this experience because it makes you understand [yourself/something about fear/ how wonderful X is].

D Work in small groups. Use your notes from 4A and the key phrases and tell each other about your activities.

writeabout an experience

5A Read the introduction to this web forum, and an extract from one writer's contribution. What activity is she writing about?

We're looking for true stories that will inspire others to try something they've never done before. Whether it's a place you've been, a food you've tried, a sport or an activity you've done, tell us about it in 250 words or less. Remember, your goal is to get others to try it, so tell us what's so extraordinary about it, and why it's one thing we should do in our lifetime.

Stacey: ... Each day we walked slowly through the section of the jungle where they live.

The first two days we didn't see any but I was determined to stay as long as it took and on the third day we saw an adult female hanging by one arm from a branch, eating leaves with her auburn fur glinting in the sunlight.

The thing I'll remember most is the moment our eyes met.

B Write an entry (200-250 words) for the forum.

C Read other students' entries. Which experience would you most like to try?

BEHAVIOUR

1A Add the vowels to complete phrases that describe a person's behaviour.

1 g_v_s _n easily in an argument
2 cr_t_c_s_s people openly
3 c_mpl_m_nts people on their work
4 n_gl_cts his/her friends
5 t_k_s c_r_ of his/her appearance
6 p_ts _ff doing important tasks until the last minute
7 g_ts _n w_th things and doesn't delay
8 p_ys _tt_nt__n to how he/she expresses him/herself

B Work in pairs and discuss. Which characteristics describe you, your best friend and your ideal partner?

USED TO, WOULD, BE/GET USED TO

2A Complete the study habits website forum with words from the box.

~~used~~	would	use	get	I'd	
writing	write	getting			

How do you improve your English?

Before I came to Australia, I [1] _used_ to go online every day and find a chat partner, sometimes an English person and sometimes another student.

Although I found speaking fairly easy, I wasn't used to [2] _____ in English. At home, in Germany, I used to [3] _____ lists of vocabulary and do exercises for homework.

When I first studied English I found the pronunciation very difficult but now I'm [4] _____ used to it.

In Germany I didn't [5] _____ to watch DVDs in English. [6] _____ watch the German version, but now I always try to watch the English version.

A few of us from my English class [7] _____ get together after our weekly lesson to have a coffee and practise speaking together.

I still can't [8] _____ used to English spelling. There don't seem to be any rules, but I've found an internet programme to help.

B Which tips do you think are useful?

FUTURES REVIEW

3A Work in groups. Look at the headlines from a future newspaper. Which ones do you think:

1 are likely to happen?
2 will definitely never happen?
3 could happen, but are not likely to?

a) **Italian becomes universal language**

b) **AVERAGE LIFESPAN INCREASES TO 100 YEARS**

c) **LAST WAR ENDS – WORLD PEACE ACHIEVED**

d) **INTERNET BANNED WORLDWIDE**

e) **Petrol supply exhausted – price of bicycles soars**

B Which three predictions can you confidently make about the world in twenty years' time?

I think it's quite likely that the average lifespan will increase because ...

4A Write the conversations in full using different future forms.

1 A: What / you / do / Friday?
  B: I / go / Julia's party / or / maybe / go / cinema.
  A: I / go / Julia's party / so / I / give you a lift if / want.
  B: Thanks. / I / phone you as soon as I / decide.

2 A: How / you / planning / use / your English / in the future?
  B: I / probably / try / get a job / international company. How / you?
  A: I / thinking / apply / go / American university. Who knows? I / get in!
  B: I / sure you /.

B Work in pairs. Use the prompts to practise saying the conversations.

LOCATIONS

5A Rearrange the letters to complete the phrases.

1 _densely_ (yendsle) populated
2 on a _____ (enaunpsli)
3 less than a hundred metres as the _____ (rcwo) flies
4 on a mountain _____ (oelps)
5 heavily _____ (treseofd)
6 in close _____ (timriypox) to a port
7 on the _____ (gede) of a lake
8 _____ (metero) and _____ (ulspnoit)

B Think of a place in your country for four of the phrases above. Then work in pairs and compare your ideas.

PROCEDURES

6A Underline the correct alternatives.

⦿ The Oyster Card

The best way to get around London is with the Oyster Card. [1]*Basic/Basically*, [2]*a/the* point is that you don't need a new ticket every time you travel. The way [3]*it works/it's working* is that you put credit on your Oyster Card. What [4]*does happen/happens* is that, at the entry to the underground, you swipe the card over a reader. The next thing [5]*what/that* you do is to swipe it again when you exit, and the cost is taken from your credit. The [6]*goal/main thing* is to top up your credit before it runs out. [7]*After/Afterwards* you've left London, you can pass the card on to a friend!

B Write your own tips for getting around a town/city you know using five phrases for describing procedures.

UNIT 4

SPEAKING
- Tell anecdotes
- Talk about regrets
- Talk about your reading
- Describe a TV/film scene

LISTENING
- Listen to a BBC radio programme about very short stories
- Watch a BBC drama
- Listen to people recommending books

READING
- Read stories with a moral
- Read a funny story about a saying

WRITING
- Write a story
- Describe a TV/film scene

BBC CONTENT
- Video podcast: What was the last book you read?
- DVD: Tess of the D'Urbervilles

UNIT 4

stories

READING

1A Work in pairs. Look at the pictures and titles of the stories on pages 44 and 45. What do you think they are about?

B Read the stories and check your ideas. Then write an ending for each one.

C Turn to page 158 and read the endings. How different are they from the ones you wrote?

2A Work in pairs. Guess the meanings of the words in bold in the stories in Exercise 1B.

B Check your ideas. Match meanings 1–8 with the words in bold in the stories.

1 left in a position where you can't move
2 hopeless or pointless
3 walking in a relaxed way
4 curious
5 died
6 in progress towards
7 depressed
8 because of

C Work in pairs and discuss. What is the moral of each story? Which story is most effective in your opinion?

GRAMMAR narrative tenses

3A Read the first paragraph of *Starfish* again and underline examples of the past simple; the past continuous; the past perfect and the past perfect continuous.

B Underline the correct verb form in the rules. Use the first paragraph of *Starfish* to help.

Rules:

a) Use the *past simple / past continuous* for completed actions which give the main events in a story.

b) Use the *past simple / past continuous* for actions in progress at a particular time or when another (shorter) action happened. Also use it to set the scene of a story.

c) Use the *past perfect simple / past perfect continuous* for completed actions that happened before the main events.

d) Use the *past perfect simple / past perfect continuous* for longer actions that started before other events and often continued up to them.

Starfish

A woman was feeling exhausted because she had been working all day in the city, so she decided to drive out to the sea. After she'd driven for over an hour, she arrived at a beautiful, deserted stretch of sand just as the sun was going down.

The sea was at its highest point of the day, but the tide was just beginning to go out, so she parked her car and started walking. She was **strolling** along the beach when she noticed a young man who seemed to be dancing at the water's edge. She watched him, as time and again he bent down, picked something up and then threw it into the sea.

As she drew nearer to the man, she saw on the sand thousands of starfish which had been washed onto the beach by the tide. She was amazed because she'd never seen so many starfish at once but, at the same time, she thought it was a sad and hopeless sight because the **stranded** starfish seemed sure to die when the tide went out and they dried up. Then she noticed that one by one, the young man was tossing them back into the sea. As she watched, it seemed clear to her that his efforts were **futile**, that no matter how fast or hard he worked, most of the starfish were doomed to die. **Intrigued**, the woman said to the young man, 'There are starfish as far as the eye can see. What difference can saving a few of them possibly make?'

C Work in pairs. Mark the stress on the phrases in bold. Circle and write any weak forms (/ə/ or /ɪ/).

1 A woman (was) feeling tired because she had been working all day.
/ə/

2 … thousands of starfish which had been washed onto the beach.

3 Two old men were staying in the same hospital room.

4 He had been put in the bed right next to the window.

D ▶ 4.1 Listen and check. Then listen and repeat.

➠ page 134 **LANGUAGE**BANK

HOSPITAL WINDOW

Two old men, both very ill, were staying in the same hospital room. One man, Walter, had been suffering from a serious illness for a few months. He had been put in the bed right next to the window and, during the afternoon, he was allowed to sit up for an hour or two. The other man, Frank, had been in hospital for only a week and was in a bed some way from the window.

Owing to his illness, Frank had to spend all his time flat on his back. Needless to say, this made him feel very **low** because he could never sit up or see outside. So every afternoon, while Walter was sitting up, he used to tell his roommate everything happening outside the window. He would describe a park with a beautiful lake: ducks and swans were swimming in the water, children were sailing their model boats and couples were walking amongst the trees. He always made these images of the outside world come to life, and Frank looked forward to the hour or two every day when Walter would bring the beauty of the world into their bare hospital room. He realised that more than any doctor or medicine, Walter's descriptions saved him from depression and helped him **on the road to** recovery.

One day, sadly, Walter **passed away**. Shortly afterwards, the nurse asked Frank if he wanted to move to the bed next to the window.

PRACTICE

4A Work in pairs. Complete the story below with the correct form of the verbs in brackets.

One afternoon, Socrates ¹_____ (stand) outside the gates of Athens when he ²_____ (notice) a traveller who ³_____ (stare) at him for a long time. Socrates ⁴_____ (ask) the man why he ⁵_____ (come) to Athens. 'I am thinking of moving to Athens,' he said. 'What is it like to live here?' Socrates ⁶_____ (look) at him. 'First, would you tell me what it was like in your home city?' The man replied, 'Oh, it was awful. Everyone stabs you in the back and wants to make money from you.' Frowning, Socrates ⁷_____ (tell) him, 'Well, you will find the same thing here. I suggest you go somewhere else.'

Socrates ⁸_____ (stand) there a few hours more when another man ⁹_____ (approach) him. This man too ¹⁰_____ (just arrive) in Athens and he ¹¹_____ (consider) moving to the city. He too asked Socrates, 'Can you tell me what it is like to live here?' Socrates asked, 'First, would you tell me what it was like in your previous home city?' 'Where I come from the people all work together and help each other', said the man. 'Kindness is everywhere and you are never treated with anything but complete respect.' 'Well,' ¹²_____ (reply) Socrates, 'you will find the same thing here. Welcome to Athens.'

B Work in pairs. What is the moral of the story?

VOCABULARY   sayings

5A Work in pairs and match the halves of the sayings. What do you think they mean?

1	Every cloud g	a) there's hope.
2	What goes around	b) do as the Romans do.
3	Where there's smoke	c) twice shy.
4	Once bitten,	d) when we come to it.
5	When in Rome	e) there's fire.
6	Where there's life	f) comes around.
7	Nothing ventured,	g) has a silver lining.
8	Let's cross that bridge	h) nothing gained.

B Complete the conversations with one of the sayings in Exercise 5A.

1 A: Shall I enter the talent show?
   B: Oh, go on! After all, _____.

2 A: Did you eat snake in China?
   B: Yes, you know what they say: _____.

3 A: Joe was fired but now he's found an even better job!
   B: Really? Well, _____.

4 A: You should buy your new phone online.
   B: No, last time my card details were stolen. _____.

5 A: Since my accident, Pam's been so helpful.
   B: You were always there for her. _____.

6 A: Alain said he wasn't dating Kim.
   B: Well, I've seen them together, and _____.

7 A: What happens with our picnic if it rains?
   B: I think it's unlikely but anyway, _____.

8 A: The company can't survive another year!
   B: Look, we're still in business and _____.

speakout TIP

People often use only the beginnings of a saying and expect the listener to understand the full idea, e.g. *What goes around …* or *When in Rome …* or *Let's cross that bridge later*. Look at B's sentences in Exercise 5B. Which part of each saying could you leave out?

C Work in pairs and discuss. Do you have similar sayings in your language? What other common sayings do you have?

SPEAKING

6A Choose an experience in your life that illustrates one of the sayings in Exercise 5A.

B Prepare to tell your story. Write down eight to ten key words to help. Think about the verb forms you want to use.

C Work in groups and take turns. One student: tell your story. The other students: guess the saying it illustrates.

WRITING a story

7A Read the story opposite. Did the ending surprise you? Why?

B Read the story again and answer the questions.

1 How does the writer link the beginning and end of the story?

2 Which paragraph sets the scene? Which verb forms are used to do this?

3 Which paragraphs develop the story? Which verb forms are used to do this?

4 Where does the writer include his feelings and what he learnt from the incident?

LEARN TO use adverbs

8A Work in pairs and circle ten *-ly* adverbs in the story in Exercise 7A.

B Write the adverbs in the correct category in the table.

adverbs of manner (describing how an action happened)	
attitude markers (expressing the writer's attitude to something in the story)	*apparently*
time markers (referring to time)	

C Match meanings 1–5 with adverbs from the table.

1 The writer thinks something is normal and not surprising (two adverbs) *naturally,*

2 In a sad and disappointed way

3 The writer has heard something is true but he's not completely sure about it

4 In a clumsy and uncoordinated way

5 After a long time (two adverbs)

speakout TIP

To make a story more interesting, use a range of different adverbs. When you write the story in Exercise 9A, try to include at least two of each type of adverb.

9A Choose one of the following tasks and write a story (120–200 words) for a magazine. Use a saying as a title.

• an experience that illustrates a saying

• an experience that disproves a saying

• your story from Exercise 6A

B Check your story for accuracy of verb forms and spelling and for use of adverbs of manner, attitude and time.

▮▮▶ page 151 **VOCABULARY**BANK

If at first you don't succeed ...

1 They say 'If at first you don't succeed … try, try again.' But I'm not so sure that's always true.

2 A few years ago, I was visiting some friends in France, on the coast of Brittany. These friends were all avid windsurfers and apparently most of them had been windsurfing since childhood, or so it seemed because they were all quite good at it. So, on my first day there, we all went to the beach and I got my first chance to try out the sport. I watched them for a while and tried to see how they did it.

3 Finally, my turn came, so I waded into the cold sea water, pushing the board in front of me hopefully and stood up on it. Stupidly, I wasn't paying attention to the waves, so when a small wave came, I slipped awkwardly and fell in the water. My friends laughed from the beach; naturally I felt embarrassed, but I was determined to succeed. I stood up again on the board, this time keeping my eyes out for the waves, and I was able to stand without falling in. Then came the next step: pulling up the sail. I began to pull the sail up by the cord attached to it, lost my balance and fell in. I climbed up again, started to pull the sail up and fell in again.

4 I must have done this at least fifty times and, by now, fortunately, my friends had left the beach because they'd got tired of laughing at me. Eventually, I began to feel cold – unsurprisingly, as I'd been falling in and climbing out of the water for an hour – and I came out of the water, defeated.

5 I walked back to my towel dejectedly and in my mind rewrote the saying: If at first you don't succeed … give up!

▶ **GRAMMAR** | *I wish, If only, should have* ▶ **VOCABULARY** | *multi-word verbs (1)* ▶ **HOW TO** | *talk about regrets*

A LIFE IN SIX WORDS

In the 1920s, the American author Ernest Hemingway bet ten dollars that he could write a complete story in just six words. He wrote: 'For Sale: baby shoes, never worn.' He won the bet.

An American online magazine has used the Hemingway anecdote to inspire its readers to write their life story in just six words, and they've been overwhelmed by the thousands who took up the challenge. They have published the best in a book, which they have given the title of one of the submissions: *Not Quite What I Was Planning.* The online magazine editor, Larry Smith, appeared on *Today,* BBC Radio 4's early morning current affairs programme.

Today then invited its listeners to send their own six-word life stories to the BBC website.

LISTENING

1A Work in pairs. Read the text and discuss the questions.

1 What do you think Hemingway's six-word story is about?

2 Why is Larry Smith appearing on *Today*?

3 Where does the title of the book come from?

4 Do you think you could write your life story in six words?

B ▶ 4.2 Listen to the interview with Larry Smith and answer the questions.

1 What does his magazine website believe about story writing?

2 What surprised him about the response to the six-word life story challenge?

3 What feeling do a lot of the stories express?

C Listen again and complete sentences in the six-word stories you hear:

1 Not quite _what I was planning_ .

2 Wasn't born _____ , _____ ,

3 Found _____ . _____ .

4 Never _____ .

D Work in pairs and discuss. Which of the stories above sounds most interesting? What do you think happened in this person's life?

GRAMMAR | *I wish, If only, should have*

2A Work in pairs. Look at the six-word stories from the BBC website. What does each person want to change about their life?

1 Wrong era, wrong class, wrong gender.

2 Really should have been a lawyer.

3 Born London, lived elsewhere, died inside.

4 Any chance I could start again?

5 Worry about tomorrow, rarely enjoy today!

6 Aspirations compromised by procrastination, then children.

B Match sentences a)–f) with stories 1–6 above.

a) I wish I could do it all again.   *4*

b) If only I weren't so anxious.

c) I wish I'd been born twenty years later.

d) If only I hadn't given up on my dreams.

e) I should have stayed where I was happy.

f) I shouldn't have become a doctor.

C Complete the rules. Use the sentences in Exercise 2B to help.

Rule:

To express regret about the present or future use *If only / I wish* + _____

To express regret about the past, use:
If only / I wish + _____ or:
should(n't) + _____ + _____

D ▶ 4.3 Listen to the sentences from Exercise 2B and underline the stressed words. Then listen and repeat. Pay attention to the weak forms in *should have* /ʃʊdəv/.

▶ page 134 **LANGUAGEBANK**

PRACTICE

3A For each pair of sentences, complete the second sentence so that it means the same as the first.

1 I'd really like to have a new laptop.
I wish *I had a new laptop*.

2 I regret growing up in a small family.
I wish _____.

3 I'm sorry I didn't learn another language.
I should _____.

4 I'm not very sociable.
If only _____.

5 I regret not travelling more when I was younger.
I should _____.

6 I never learnt how to touch-type.
If only _____.

7 I often lose my temper with people.
I wish _____.

8 I can't cook very well.
I wish _____.

9 I gave up doing sport a while ago and I regret that.
I shouldn't _____.

10 I regret not spending more time with my grandfather.
If only _____.

B Tick the sentences in Exercise 3A which are true for you. Change the others so that they are true.

I wish I had a ~~new laptop~~ car.

C Work in pairs and take turns. Student A: say your sentences from Exercise 3B. Student B: ask follow-up questions.

A: I wish I could cook.
B: Do you? Why's that?

VOCABULARY regrets

4A Put sentences a)–f) in the correct order to complete the forum entry.

What's your greatest regret?

a) I actually turned down an offer to teach English abroad in my gap year. Now I realise that it was **a missed opportunity.**

b) Lately **I've had second thoughts** about becoming a lawyer   1

c) Every time I remember that, I **kick myself** for not having jumped at the chance.

d) It's my fault in the end, and **it's a pity** that I didn't listen to my father's advice. He was a lawyer and he always said I shouldn't become one.

e) To make things worse, my best friend from university is teaching abroad, and **I'm gutted** every time I get a postcard from him.

f) **With hindsight,** I think it's the wrong job for me and I should have gone into teaching or something more 'human'.

B Work in pairs and answer the questions.

1 Which phrases in bold mean:
a) I regret? (4 phrases) *I've had second thoughts about,*
b) when I look back now? (1 phrase)
c) a chance I didn't take? (1 phrase)

2 Which two phrases are very informal?

3 Which phrase is followed by:
a) *that?*
b) *about* + noun/*-ing* form?
c) *for* + (*not*) *-ing* form?

C Write your own entry for the website forum. Use at least four of the phrases.

D Work in pairs and takes turns. Tell your partner about your regret and give each other advice.

SPEAKING

5A Work in pairs. Do any of the six-word stories below describe your life? Why/Why not?

1 If only I had turned left.
2 No A Levels but a millionaire.
3 Alas, Mr Right never turned up.
4 Wasted my whole life getting comfortable.
5 Started slowly then dashed to line.
6 Ditched the map, found better route.

B Write your own six-word story about an aspect of your life.

C Work in groups and take turns. Ask and answer questions about your stories.

VOCABULARY PLUS multi-word verbs

6A Underline the multi-word verbs in stories 1–4 below. Then match each verb with meanings a)–f).

1 Alas, Mr Right never turned up.

2 Gave up chocolate, took up running.

3 Loved Sonia. Settled down with Elena.

4 Set up company. Money ran out.

a) started (a hobby or habit)

b) was completely used up

c) arrived

d) started (a business)

e) started living a quiet life, e.g. got married and had children

f) stopped (a hobby or habit)

B Work in pairs. Look at the extracts from the *Longman Active Study Dictionary*. Which verb:

1 can sometimes be used without an object?

2 must be used with an object?

3 can be separated with an object?

4 can be followed by a preposition?

> **set up** *phr v* **1** to start a company or organisation [=establish]: **set sth ⇔ up** : *She left the company to set up her own business.*

> **run out** *phr v* **1 a)** to use all of something, so that there is none left; **+of** *We've run out of sugar* | *I'm running out of ideas.* **b)** If something is running out, there will soon be none left. *We'll have to make a decision soon - time is running out.*

⸜ speakout TIP

A dictionary gives useful information about multi-word verbs, including: the meaning, an example, whether the verb takes an object, whether the verb and its particle can be separated. In the extracts above, how does the *Longman Active Study Dictionary* show these features?

7A Look at the photos in the article on the right. What do you think this man's life has been like?

B Read the text and answer the questions.

1 What was his first job?

2 What almost prevented him from appearing on TV?

3 What makes him a particularly good traveller?

Sir David Attenborough

was born in London in 1926 and **grew up** in Leicester. He was **brought up** alongside two brothers and two adopted sisters. As a child he collected stones and fossils, and **went on** to read geology and zoology at Cambridge University.

After a short time in the Royal Navy, Attenborough **was taken on** by a publishing company, editing children's science textbooks. He didn't **take to** the work and, in 1952, he joined the newly formed BBC television Talks Department. Ironically, the woman who hired him didn't want him to appear on camera because she thought his teeth were too big – she believed this would **put** viewers **off**, so he initially worked as a producer.

In 1954, he made the first of his famous *Zoo Quest* series, which, over the next ten years, took him to wild places all around the world. He then became Director of Programmes at the BBC but **stepped down from** this position in 1973 and also **turned down** the job of Director General in order to return to his first love, making programmes.

As the presenter of such landmark documentary series as *Life on Earth* and *Life in Cold Blood*, Attenborough is perhaps one of the most travelled men ever. He has a reputation for stamina and also for his ability to **get over** jet lag. 'I am perfectly able to fly to Australia and film within three hours of arrival,' he says.

As the years **go by**, Attenborough remains one of the most recognisable faces on TV screens all over the world, and millions have him to thank for bringing a passion for nature into their lives.

C Read the article again and match meanings 1–10 with the multi-word verbs in bold.

1 be hired

2 recover from

3 be raised

4 refuse

5 spend your childhood

6 start to like

7 pass (talking about time)

8 make someone dislike

9 resign

10 do something after doing something else

SPEAKING

8A Make notes for a life story about someone you know – a famous figure, a family member or an acquaintance. Use at least five of the multi-word verbs from Exercise 8.

B Work in pairs. Student A: tell your partner about the person but stop when you get to each multi-word verb. Student B: try to guess the multi-word verb.

A: He caught malaria on holiday, but he soon …

B: Got over it?

⮕ page 151 **VOCABULARYBANK**

VOCABULARY reading

1A Work in pairs. Look at the words in the box and answer questions 1–5. Use a dictionary if necessary.

> novel   blog   lyrics   gossip magazine   manga
> biography   autobiography   e-book   poetry
> online encyclopaedia   manual   website forum

Which things:

1 can only be read on a computer screen?

2 often include rhymes?

3 are about real people's lives?

4 aim to give factual information?

5 almost always contain pictures, photos or diagrams?

B Work in pairs. Make a list of other things to read.

C Work in pairs and take turns. Student A: tell Student B the kinds of things you like reading and give examples. Student B: ask questions.

A: I enjoy gossip magazines. My favourite is '¡Hola!'
B: Why do you like it?
A: It's just a really easy read after a long day ...

SPEAKING

2A Work in pairs and discuss the questions.

1 In your country, are there any books that are considered important to read?

2 Why might somebody lie about having read certain things? Would you ever do this?

B Work in pairs. Read the article and answer the questions.

1 Why do people lie about their reading?

2 What sort of reading do men, women and teenagers think is important?

Many lie over books 'to impress'

Nearly half of all men and one-third of women have lied about what they have read to try to impress friends or potential partners, a survey suggests.

A poll of 1,500 people found that men were most likely to do this to appear intellectual or romantic. The men polled said they would be most impressed by women who read news websites, Shakespeare or song lyrics. Women said men should have read Nelson Mandela's autobiography or Shakespeare.

About four in ten of the 1,500 said they had lied about what they had read to impress friends or potential partners – forty-six percent of men and thirty-three percent of women. Among teenagers, the figure rose to seventy-four percent, with most saying they would pretend to have read social networking pages or song lyrics.

FUNCTION expressing likes and dislikes

3A Work in pairs. Look at the three books in the photo. Have you read any of them or do you know anything about them?

B ▶ 4.4 Listen to the conversation and complete the table. For each person write (✓) if they liked it, (✗) if they didn't like it or (–) if they haven't read it. Which book does Amy decide to take?

1 *The Girl With the Dragon Tattoo* Amy Barbara ✓ Carl	
2 *Life of Pi* Amy Barbara Carl	
3 *Pride and Prejudice* Amy Barbara Carl	

C Listen again and make notes about the reasons why they liked or didn't like each book.

D Work in pairs and discuss. Which of these books would you choose to read? Why?

5A Rewrite the sentences using the words in brackets. Make sure the meaning is the same.

1 I liked the plot of *The Da Vinci Code*.
(What / liked) <u>What I liked about The Da Vinci Code was the plot.</u>

2 Reading e-books on my computer hurts my eyes.
(I / stand) _____

3 Gossip magazines aren't my favourite thing to read.
(I / fan) _____

4 I really like reading anything by Stephen King.
(I / into) _____

5 The best thing is that lots of different people contribute to the forum.
(What / like)_____

6 I can't get interested in *Manga* or other types of comics.
(I / into)_____

7 I like the way his lyrics sound so natural.
(thing / is)_____

B Think of one thing to read that you really like/liked and one that you don't/didn't. Write three positive and three negative sentences about the things. Use the phrases in Exercise 5A.

C Work in pairs and take turns. Student A: read your three sentences. Student B: guess what Student A is talking about.
A: What I hate is that they use complicated language.
B: A manual?

➡ page 134 **LANGUAGEBANK**

LEARN TO summarise a plot

6A ▶ 4.6 Listen and complete the summary of *The Girl with the Dragon Tattoo*.

It's about a Swedish journalist, Mikael Blomkvist who [1]_____ by a retired businessman who [2]_____ him to investigate the disappearance of a favourite niece about forty years previously. The only clues he [3]_____ come from old photos and newspaper clippings of the day she disappeared. Blomkvist [4]_____ by Lisbeth Salander, the 'girl with the dragon tattoo', a mysterious young woman who [5]_____ punk clothes and who [6]_____ a genius with computers. As the two of them [7]_____ the shocking truth, they [8]_____ their own lives in increasing danger.

B Work in pairs and answer the questions.

1 Which verb forms are used in the summary?

2 Why do you think these verb forms are used?

3 Do you use the same verb forms when you summarise the plot of a book or film in your language?

4A Put the words in the correct order to make sentences. Then check in the audioscript on page 168.

1 I'm / novels / fan / big / detective / of / a

2 really / I / it / main / What / character / the / was / about / liked

3 not / I'm / on / novels / keen / detective / that

4 get / couldn't / it / just / into / I

5 stand / couldn't / I / it

6 really / I'm / fantasy / into / not

7 thing / it / the / love / The / I / writing / about / is

B Work in pairs and answer the questions.

1 Which phrases mean *I don't/didn't like*?

2 Look at sentence 2. How is it different in form from *I really liked the main character*? Which word/idea is emphasised?

3 Look at sentence 7. How is it different in form from *I love the writing*? Which word/idea is emphasised?

4 Which of the phrases can be made negative (or positive) to express the opposite meaning?

C ▶ 4.5 Underline the main stresses in sentences 1–7 in Exercise 4A. Listen and check. Then listen and repeat.

SPEAKING

7A Choose a book you like and make notes about: the main events in the story; why you liked it; why the other students should read it.

B Work in groups. Persuade the other students to read your book.
Has anyone read 'Cien Años de Soledad' by Gabriel García Márquez? I think it's called 'A Hundred Years of Solitude' in English. It's about …

DVD PREVIEW

1 Read the programme information and answer the questions.

1 Where is the story set?

2 What two things do the female characters have in common?

3 How do you think Angel 'saves' the four women?

BBC Tess of the D'Urbervilles

This film of Thomas Hardy's 19th century novel tells the tragic story of Tess, the daughter of uneducated peasants in rural Wessex, the semi-fictional setting for many of Hardy's novels. In this episode, Tess and three other dairymaids* are all in love with Angel Clare, the son of a local clergyman. On their way to church one Sunday, the four dairymaids find their way blocked by a flood, but fortunately Angel arrives to save them.

* **dairymaid** – traditional female farm worker involved with the production of milk.

▶ DVD VIEW

2A Watch the DVD. How did each woman feel when she was crossing the water? Tick two adjectives for each person.

1 1st woman: eager / nervous / pleased

2 2nd woman: nervous / thrilled / awkward

3 3rd woman: expectant / excited / happy

4 4th woman: agitated / eager / contented

B Watch again. Who says each sentence? What do they mean by it?

1 There's nothing in it Retty.

2 A nice easy one this time.

3 You wouldn't mind, would you, if I tried?

4 I've undergone three quarters of the labour just for this moment.

5 That's not what I meant at all.

C Work in pairs and discuss the questions.

1 Why do you think this type of costume drama is popular?

2 Is it a kind of drama you like to watch? Why/ Why not?

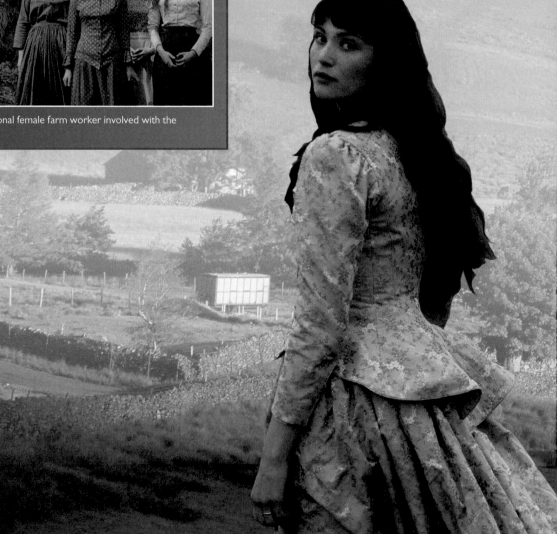

speakout a favourite scene

3A ▶ 4.7 Listen to a description of a favourite scene in a TV programme called *Fawlty Towers*, and answer the questions.

1 One of the characters is Basil Fawlty, who runs a hotel. Who is the other one?
2 What happens?

B Listen again and tick the key phrases you hear.

> ### keyphrases
>
> I've seen [it/this] X times and [I never get tired of it/I can't get enough of it/it's my absolute favourite].
>
> It's a(n) [amazing/very moving/really cool] scene.
>
> It always [makes me laugh/cry/sends shivers up my spine].
>
> It's like a lesson in [comic acting/timing/directing].
>
> My favourite scene is the scene [when... / with...]
>
> It's very cleverly done.
>
> If you've never seen it, you really should.

C Think of a favourite scene in a TV programme or film. Write notes on:

- the point in which it appears in the programme/film (what has happened to set the scene?)
- the moment itself (what happens exactly?)
- why you like it.

D Work in pairs. Tell your partner about your favourite TV/film scene.

writeback a description of a scene

4A Read the magazine article. What type of film is it? Have you seen it?

My favourite film moment

I loved one bit in _____. The whole film is about watching how the original crew get together. My favourite moment comes when Spock is in charge of the Starship Enterprise because the captain has left the ship. He makes an important decision about something and Bones, the doctor, comes up to him and asks if he can have a quiet word. He pulls Spock aside and says 'Are you out of your Vulcan mind?' Spock just looks at him and raises an eyebrow.

Bones's accent, his expression, and the way he delivers that line are all exactly the same as in the original TV series. It's not a classic moment in the film by any stretch of the imagination, but it shows how much effort was put into finding people who were similar to the original cast. It's a way of honouring the original. There were a few other moments like that in the film, but for some reason that's the one that sticks in my memory. I laugh out loud every time I remember it.

B Write a description of a favourite TV/film scene for a magazine. Don't include the name of the programme/film.

C Read other students' descriptions and write the type of programme/film and, if you know it, the name.

SAYINGS

1A Work in pairs. Look at the prompts. What are the sayings?

1 bridge – come

2 ventured – gained

3 Rome – Romans

4 bitten – shy

5 life – hope

6 smoke – fire

7 goes – comes

8 cloud – silver

B Which sayings are paraphrased below?

1 We should deal with that only when necessary.

2 We're not dead yet, so a solution isn't impossible.

3 You always get what you deserve in the end.

C Choose three other sayings and paraphrase them. <u>Don't</u> use any of the words in the original.

D Work in pairs and take turns. Student A: read your paraphrased saying. Student B: guess the 'real' saying.

NARRATIVE TENSES

2A Complete the first part of the story with the verbs in brackets in a correct narrative tense.

He ¹_____ (be) an old man with big hands and a limp, and he ²_____ (live) in the same house all of his life. The house ³_____ (fall) apart and he ⁴_____ (not paint) it for years, so it ⁵_____ (look) as if it would collapse at any moment. We ⁶_____ (walk) past his house every day, and he ⁷_____ (always work) in his garden and he ⁸_____ (always say) hello. One day, I ⁹_____ (come) home alone – in fact, I ¹⁰_____ (never walk) home alone before. I ¹¹_____ (look) up and ¹²_____ (see) the man at his window. He ¹³_____ (watch) me, and I felt as if he ¹⁴_____ (watch) me for a long time. Then he ¹⁵_____ (come) out of the house …

B Work in pairs and write an ending to the story.

EXPRESSING REGRET

3 Read the email extract and correct one word in each phrase in bold.

You know me – I'm never one to have regrets – but this has been the worst month of my life! Remember that job I applied for? I really wanted it but they gave it to someone else and **I was absolutely stomached.** However, they offered me a different position so I took it but, when I went home, I **had second decisions** about taking it – something didn't seem quite right about it.

Well, **it's a sadness** that I didn't listen to my instincts because it turned out to be a disastrous decision. I hate the new job. On top of that, the day after I started, I got another offer of a job abroad that I really wanted, so that was a real **missed possibility.** Now **I'm hitting myself** for taking the first job that came along. **With looking back,** I realise I should simply have been more patient!

I WISH, IF ONLY, SHOULD HAVE

4A Look at the list and complete the sentences.

My wish list

1 I didn't finish university. I wish …

2 I spent too little time with my friends in secondary school. If only …

3 I didn't travel very much when I was younger. I should …

4 My partner doesn't like the same kinds of music as me. I wish …

5 I have a boring desk job. If only …

6 I don't have enough time for sport. I wish …

B Write your own wish list. Write three sentences about the past and three about the present. After each one write: *I wish …* , or *If only …* , or *I should …* .

C Work in pairs and take turns. Student A: read out one of the sentences on your list. Student B: try and complete the sentence.

A: *I didn't study English when I was younger. I should …*

B: *You should have studied English?*

EXPRESSING LIKES AND DISLIKES

5A Complete the phrases with words from the box.

| get | that | into | stand | what |
| fan | thing | | | |

1 I'm really _____ …

2 _____ I love about it is …

3 I'm not _____ keen on …

4 The _____ I like most about it is …

5 I just can't _____ into …

6 I'm a big _____ of …

7 I can't _____ …

B Work in pairs. Take turns to say the past form of each phrase.

A: *I was really into …*

B: *What I …*

C Choose a TV programme that you watched when you were younger. Make notes about what you liked and disliked using the phrases in Exercise 5A.

D Work in pairs and take turns. Tell each other about your programmes.

When I was about ten, I was really into cartoons and I was a big fan of a cartoon from the US called …

BBC VIDEO PODCAST

Download the podcast to view people discussing the question:

What was the last book you read?

Authentic BBC interviews

www.pearsonlongman.com/speakout

UNIT 5

UNIT 5

5

ideas

the new limited edition fragrance bottle
BE DELICIOUS

BBC
speakout DVD

► **GRAMMAR** | articles ► **VOCABULARY** | change; compound nouns ► **HOW TO** | talk about change

A Car

B Nuclear power

C Fast food

F Mobile phone

D Cigarettes

E Weapons

G TV

THE WORLD'S WORST INVENTIONS

Fast food and speed cameras rank among the most hated inventions of all time. But what *really* gets you worked up? Thousands of votes were cast on the BBC website and the results, published by the BBC science magazine, *Focus*, make for a surprising read.

1 _____
Bombs, guns, biological _____, you name it – innovations that go bang or cause bodily harm were the most widely frowned upon in our survey. Nuclear _____ were the worst offender, getting eleven percent of the total vote. They've only been used twice in warfare – in 1945, the US dropped the bomb 'Little Boy' on the Japanese city of Hiroshima, followed three days later by 'Fat Man' which fell on Nagasaki.

2 _____
A surprising silver medal for the gadget that's revolutionised communication – _____ have been available in the UK since 1985 and have been widely used since the late 1990s. Almost three quarters of Britons now own one. Despite health scares linking _____ usage to brain tumours, most studies have found there is no increased risk. Maybe it's those annoying ring tones that have put _____ here.

3 _____
_____ accidents are rare but can have devastating effects. _____ plants have higher construction and operating costs than their fossil fuel counterparts, and are supported by large subsidies courtesy of the taxpayer. Waste storage is also a concern but supporters promote _____'s green status as it produces no carbon dioxide directly.

4 _____
The _____ haters out-voted the petrol users. Developed in the late 1880s, the modern _____ was initially the toy of the wealthy, but falling prices have made it a key part of family life. The motor industry is now booming – 63 million _____ and light trucks were produced globally in 2005. But a green fuel is unlikely to take over from petrol soon, so the _____ continues to add to our growing carbon footprint.

5 _____
Cancer-causing chemicals in _____ mean that men who smoke are twenty-two times, and women twelve times, more likely to develop lung cancer than those who don't. Smoking is also linked to other cancers and heart attacks. Pregnant smokers are at greater risk of giving birth to underweight babies. The World Health Organisation says up to twenty-nine percent of British men and nineteen percent of women smoke.

6 _____
Many of us are doubtless surprised by this one. But it's actually reality _____ that's the main offender with three percent of the total vote. Making its debut in 1948 with *Candid Camera* in America, reality _____'s popularity has risen in the 21st century; in the US there are two _____ channels devoted to it. Why it's so unpopular is anyone's guess.

7 _____
Americans are the ultimate _____ eaters, spending an estimated $142 billion (£73 billion) on it in 2006. But it seems our days of carefree consumption of fatty, cholesterol-rich food may be numbered, as we gradually wake up to the health risks. In 2002, some obese US teenagers filed a lawsuit against McDonald's accusing the _____ chain of fattening them up. A judge later threw out the lawsuit.*

***threw out the lawsuit** – decided there was no basis for any legal action

READING

1 Work in pairs and look at the photos. Why do you think the inventions are on the 'World's worst inventions' list? Write down one reason for each.

2A Read the article and complete headings 1–7 with the inventions in the photos.

B Read the article again. Which inventions do sentences 1–7 refer to?
1 It's more dangerous to men than women. *smoking cigarettes*
2 Research hasn't shown them to be dangerous.
3 It's more expensive than traditional sources.
4 Americans consume the most.
5 It's not clear why it's unpopular.
6 It was voted the worst idea of all.
7 At first only rich people had one.

C Find words/phrases in the text which mean:
1 disliked (invention 1)
2 be extremely destructive (invention 3)
3 given by (invention 3)
4 increasing and becoming very successful – about a business (invention 4)
5 replace (invention 4)
6 first arriving (invention 6)
7 limited (invention 7)
8 start to realise and understand something (invention 7)

D Work in groups and discuss. Can you think of any other inventions that have been as damaging as the ones on the list? Agree on one idea and tell the class why.

GRAMMAR articles

3A Check what you know. Complete the sentences with *a(n)*, *the* or *–* (no article). Then check your answers in the article in Exercise 2A.
1 _____ World Health Organisation says up to twenty-nine percent of _____ British men and nineteen percent of _____ women smoke.
2 In 2002, some obese US teenagers filed _____ lawsuit against McDonald's accusing _____ fast food chain of fattening them up.
3 But it's actually _____ reality TV that's _____ main offender with three percent of _____ vote.
4 Developed in _____ late 1880s, _____ modern automobile was initially _____ toy of _____ wealthy.
5 In _____ America, _____ reality television's popularity has risen in the 21st century; in _____ US there are two television channels devoted to it.

B Circle the correct alternative to complete the rules. Use the sentences in Exercise 3A to help.

Rules:
1 Use *a(n)/the/–* with plural and uncountable nouns when you are talking about things in general.
2 Use *a(n)/the/–* with singular countable nouns when you are not talking about a particular thing, or when you mention something for the first time.
3 Use *a(n)/the/–* with any type of noun when you and your reader/ listener know which particular thing you are talking about, for example because it is unique or it has been mentioned before.
4 Use *a(n)/the/–* with a singular countable noun or an adjective to talk about things in general.
5 Use *a(n)/the/–* with most place names.
6 Use *a(n)/the/–* in fixed phrases such as *in _____ 1960s, in _____ beginning*.

C ▶ 5.1 Circle *the* where it is pronounced /ðə/ and underline it where it is pronounced /ðiː/. Then listen and check.
1 **The** interesting thing is that many of **the** people who hate it are **the** ones who watch it.
2 **The** automobile has done less well since **the** economic crisis.
3 Those who voted for **the** car mentioned **the** harm it does to **the** environment as **the** biggest problem.

D Complete the rule with *vowel* or *consonant*.

Rule: *The* is pronounced /ðiː/ when the next word starts with a _____ sound, and /ðə/ when the next word starts with a _____ sound.

➡ page 136 **LANGUAGEBANK**

PRACTICE

4 Complete the text with the correct articles.

Bicycle chosen as best invention

[1] _____ humble bicycle has won [2] _____ UK national survey of [3] _____ people's favourite inventions.

Listeners to BBC Radio 4's *You and Yours* programme were invited to vote in [4] _____ online poll looking at [5] _____ most significant innovations since 1800.

It was [6] _____ easy victory for [7] _____ bicycle which won more than half of [8] _____ vote. [9] _____ radio came second with eight percent of the vote, and the electro-magnetic induction ring – the means to harness electricity – came third.

Despite the fact that you can find them everywhere, [10] _____ computers gained just six percent of the vote and [11] _____ internet trailed behind with only four percent of all votes cast. There were more than 4,500 votes cast in total.

People chose the bicycle for its simplicity of design, universal use and because it is [12] _____ ecologically sound means of transport.

VOCABULARY change

5A Work in pairs. Match 1–8 with a)–h) to make sentences.

1 The internet has **transformed** the way people g
2 The microscope **altered** people's
3 The overuse of pesticides has **damaged**
4 The mobile phone has **had a beneficial effect on** elderly people's
5 The overuse of antibiotics has **had a detrimental effect on** people's
6 Audio email has **enhanced** blind people's ability to
7 High speed travel has **distorted** people's
8 The microwave oven **revolutionised**

a) food preparation
b) understanding of the make-up of matter.
c) quality of life.
d) resistance to disease.
e) the environment.
f) sense of distance.
g) access information.
h) communicate via the internet.

B Look at the verb phrases in bold in Exercise 5A and decide which phrases: mean changed in a big way; are positive; are negative.

C Work in pairs. Which three statements in Exercise 5A do you most agree with? Give reasons.

D Work in groups and take turns. Explain your choices and reasons.

SPEAKING

6A Choose two commonly-used inventions. Make notes about why they are important.

B Work in pairs. Compare your ideas and agree on the most important invention.

C Work with another pair. Try to persuade them that your invention is the most important.

> Previously, people used to …

> Without the … we couldn't … we'd have to …

D Work in groups. Discuss all the inventions and agree on the order from most to least important.

A Wrist radio

B Ring pull   **C Bottle cap**   **D Jet pack**

VOCABULARY *PLUS* compound nouns

7A Work in pairs and look at the pictures above. Which inventions do you think were the least/most successful?

B Complete the encyclopaedia entries with the names of the inventions in the photos.

The ¹_____ was expected to be a major **breakthrough** for transport but in the **trade-off** between safety and efficiency, safety won. The **outlook** for its future remains poor.

The ²_____ was expected to revolutionise communication but had a serious **drawback**: it could not be used over a long range and communication **breakdowns** were common.

As glass bottles were replaced by cans, the ³_____ needed a replacement that was easier to use and the **outcome** was the ⁴_____. The **downside** of the move to cans was a huge increase in rubbish volume.

C Match definitions 1–6 with the words in bold above.

1 compromise or balance between two things   *trade-off*
2 expectations of what will happen
3 the failure of a system
4 a new discovery or development
5 disadvantage or weakness (2 words)
6 the result of something

8A Complete the information with examples from the entries in Exercise 7B. More than one answer is sometimes possible.

Compound nouns are usually made of two words. They can be written as separate words, e.g. *bottle top*, or a single word, e.g. ¹_____, or they can be written with a hyphen, e.g. ²_____. The plural is made by adding an *s* to the end, e.g. *breakdowns*. Several common compound nouns are made of a verb + preposition, e.g. ³_____, or a preposition or adverb + verb, e.g. ⁴_____. If you understand both parts of the compound, you can often guess the meaning.

B ▶ 5.2 Listen to seven sentences. Write the compound noun in each sentence in your notebook and underline the stress. Where does the stress usually come?

C Work in pairs and choose three inventions. Write an encyclopaedia entry for each one using two of the compound nouns above. Write *they/it* instead of the invention.

They were an important breakthrough in the twentieth century. They give us relatively clean energy but they also have some serious drawbacks, including the danger of a major breakdown.

D Exchange entries with other pairs and guess the inventions.

⇒ page 152 **VOCABULARYBANK**

▶ **GRAMMAR** | conditionals (1)   ▶ **VOCABULARY** | advertising   ▶ **HOW TO** | talk about advertising

LISTENING

1A Work in pairs. Complete the questionnaire on the right and make notes on your answers.

B ▶ 5.3 Listen to the radio programme and check your answers to the questionnaire.

2A Work in pairs and underline the alternative to complete what the expert said. Use a dictionary to check any new words. Then listen again and check.

1 Each machine would sell two hundred cans per day, unless the market was *too small/crowded/saturated*.

2 *Choice/Advertising/Hunger* makes people want things.

3 People are expected to think, 'If there are two similar products at different prices, I'll buy the *cheaper/more expensive/bigger* one.'

4 We intuitively feel that if something *is advertised/costs/appears on TV* more, it's better.

5 To make it so shiny, a food *chef/stylist/handler* has painted the meat with *oil/ink/ketchup* or maybe lacquer.

6 8.20 is a very *good-/aggressive-/sad-* looking time.

7 Blue is linked more to intellect and *technology/precision/speed*.

8 Seventy-five percent of young *people/children/women* prefer purple to all other colours.

B Work in pairs and discuss. Which statements in Exercise 2A surprised you most?

What's your advertising IQ?

1 Imagine there's a Coke machine in the centre of town. It sells a hundred cans of Coke a day. Pepsi comes in and puts a machine right next to the Coke machine. After that, how many cans would each machine sell?

2 You want to introduce a new product to the market, for example a new lipstick. The product you want to compete with sells for five euros. Should you price your product above or below your competition?

3 What special ingredients are used to make a hamburger look so delicious in advertisements?

4 What time does a watch or clock nearly always show in adverts, and why?

5 Which colour (blue, green, orange, purple, red or yellow) is best to use in an advert for:
a) high-tech products?
b) drugs and medical products to indicate safety?
c) energy drinks, games and cars?
d) toys?
e) food?

6 Why do you rarely see the colour blue in a food commercial?

GRAMMAR conditionals

3A Match sentences 1–4 with conditional forms a)–d).

1 If you price your product just above the competition's price, you'll end up with a bigger share of the market.

2 If something costs more, it's better.

3 If I were to introduce a new lipstick on the market, should I price mine above or below the competition?

4 If a watch showed 8.20, it wouldn't sell as well.

a) Zero conditional: *if* + present simple, present simple

b) First conditional: *if* + present simple, *will/ can/could/may/might/should* + infinitive

c) Second conditional (A): *if* + past simple, *would/should/could/might* + infinitive

d) Second conditional (B): *if* + *were to* + infinitive, *would/should/could/might* + infinitive

B Work in pairs and complete the rules.

Rules:

1 a) Use the _____ conditional to talk about hypothetical present or future events or situations.

b) Use the _____ conditional to talk about something that is likely to happen in the future as a result of an action or situation.

c) Use the _____ conditional to talk about something that is always or generally true as a result of an action or situation.

2 In formal English, *if* + _____ + infinitive can be used for hypothetical situations.

C Look at examples a)–c) and find three conjunctions which mean *if and only if*, and one which means *if not*.

a) Yes, it's fine to look at <u>as long as</u> you don't eat it.

b) Each machine would probably sell two hundred cans a day <u>unless</u> the market was saturated.

c) People will pay more <u>providing/provided</u> the difference is small.

4A ▶ 5.4 Listen and write sentences 1–5 in your notebook.

B Underline the two main stresses in each sentence, one in each clause. Listen again and check. Then listen and repeat.

▌▶ page 136 **LANGUAGEBANK**

PRACTICE

5A Underline the correct alternatives in the text.

If you wanted a new product to reach the maximum number of people for the minimum cost, what [1]*would/will* you do? The answer is launch a viral advert – a video that people can email so that it spreads like a virus and gives your product free publicity. It works like this: your company makes a video and then, [2]*providing/unless* this viral advert reaches a 'susceptible' user (one who likes the idea), that user [3]*will/would* send the advert to others, thus 'infecting them'. [4]*As long as/Unless* each 'infected' user shares the idea with more than one other user, the number of users [5]*grows/would grow*. So, [6]*provided/unless* an advert is novel or entertaining enough, it [7]*will spread/spread* across the Web like a virus at no extra cost to the advertiser. If you [8]*send/were to send* out a viral advert that didn't catch on, it would go nowhere – people would simply delete it. [9]*Unless/As long as* adverts are funny, smart or edgy, they [10]*won't/will* have any effect.

B Work in pairs and discuss. Have you ever sent or received a viral advert or video? What's your favourite/least favourite TV or internet advert at the moment?

SPEAKING

6A Read the guidelines on creating a viral advert. What product is being advertised in the example?

How to create a viral advert

STEP 1: Make a video of a person or animal in an odd place, for example a businessman trapped on the branch of a tree, using both hands to balance.

STEP 2: Introduce a problem, e.g. a mosquito attacks him but he can't swat it as he can't let go of the tree.

STEP 3: Bring in an unexpected solution, e.g. a gorilla swings in on a vine, lands on the same branch and hands the businessman a spray.

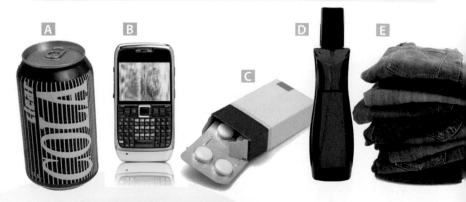

B Choose a product from the photos and create your own thirty-second viral advert, following the guidelines above.

C Work in groups and take turns. Describe your viral advert but don't say what product you chose. Can the other students guess?

VOCABULARY advertising

7A Complete questions 1–10 with a word from the box.

> commercials pop-ups brands
> endorse/promote campaigns
> logos influence slogans cold calls
> advertise makes jingle

1 Are there too many TV _____ in programme breaks?

2 'Just do it!' and 'The world's local bank' are memorable _____. What others do you know?

3 What are the most popular _____ of car in your country? What's your favourite?

4 Which are the most popular sports equipment _____ in your country?

5 Do you think celebrities should _____ a particular product?

6 What does an image of an apple with a bite taken out of it mean to you? What other _____ do you know?

7 What type of advertisement would _____ you to try a new food or drink product?

8 Do you ever find yourself singing a particular _____ for a product or a radio station?

9 Can you recall any particularly successful advertising _____?

10 If you wanted to sell a product, where would you _____?

11 How do you feel about website _____? Do they work?

12 What do you say when someone _____ you in the evenings?

B Work in pairs and answer the questions in Exercise 7A.

➠ page 152 **VOCABULARYBANK**

WRITING a report

8A What influences you when you buy a new gadget? Write a list of factors and put them in order of importance.

I always go for the latest model because it makes me look trendy.

B Work in groups and compare your ideas.

9A Look at the chart below which shows the results of a survey on why men, women and teenagers choose a particular smartphone. What is the most and least important factor for each group of people?

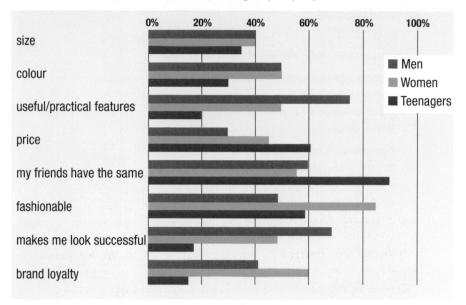

B Read the report written by a student on the survey results and answer the questions.

1 Which factors are mentioned?

2 The student has made one factual error. What is it?

3 What is the purpose of each of the first three paragraphs in the report?

> The bar chart shows the results of a survey of students and employees in our language school in relation to their reasons for buying a particular mobile phone.
>
> First of all, comparing the results for men and women, it can be seen that some factors affect both groups more or less equally. For example, there is no difference in how much size and colour influence their choice of phone, and the results for 'my friends have the same one' show only a slight variation.
>
> There are, however, significant differences in the results for other factors. The usefulness or practicality of a phone's features is far more important for men than for women, as is the price and how much it makes the owner look successful. On the other hand, women place greater importance on brand loyalty.
>
> The results for teenagers showed an interesting contrast to those for men and women. First of all ...

LEARN TO make written comparisons

10 Read the report again and complete tasks 1–3.

1 Circle three phrases for saying that two things are the same or nearly the same.

2 Underline four phrases for talking about differences.

3 Put a box around four linking phrases

11A Work in pairs. Look at the chart and make notes on five points you could make about teenagers.

B Complete the report by continuing the last paragraph. Write 100–150 words. Include at least six of the phrases in Exercise 10.

▶ **FUNCTION** | suggesting ideas   ▶ **VOCABULARY** | adjectives   ▶ **LEARN TO** | show reservations

READING

1A Work in pairs and discuss: What do you understand by 'brainstorming'? What is it used for?

B You are going to read about the rules of brainstorming. Before you read, discuss what the underlined words in sentences 1–5 might refer to.

1 <u>It</u>'s more important than quality.

2 Sometimes <u>it</u> leads you to the perfect solution.

3 <u>It</u>'s the worst thing you can do in a brainstorm.

4 It's important to notice who <u>they</u> are and make sure they get a chance to contribute.

5 One person does <u>this</u> or the ideas are lost.

C Read the rules and check your ideas.

fruit?

The five rules of brainstorming

1 Quantity is more important than quality. Let's say you're looking for a way to get kids to love vegetables. At the brainstorming phase, you don't want just one **brilliant** idea, you want five, ten, dozens to choose from, including some **weird** and **obscure** ones. So the goal of brainstorming is to produce as long a list as possible.

2 No idea is too **predictable** or **absurd**. In fact, sometimes these ideas somehow lead you to the perfect solution.

3 Zero judgment. At this point you can't say an idea is **dreadful** or **unrealistic** or just too **ambitious**, because what you need is just ideas, ideas, ideas. The worst thing you can do in a brainstorm is to criticise an idea.

4 Everybody's equal. You have to spot the shy people and encourage them. There's no hierarchy, it only works if you work as a team.

5 Keep a record. Write the ideas down – each and every one. Have one person as a secretary and they just write whatever anyone says.

VOCABULARY adjectives

2A Match definitions 1–8 with the adjectives in bold in the interview above.

1 strange   *weird*   5 obvious

2 awful   6 not obvious

3 impractical   7 senseless

4 aiming very high   8 clever; excellent

B Work in pairs and take turns. Student A: choose a definition from 1–8 above. Student B: agree, using an adjective from the interview.

A: It's strange.

B: Yes, it's a weird idea.

FUNCTION suggesting ideas

3A You are going to listen to a brainstorm on ways to make children like eating fruit and vegetables. Before you listen, work in pairs and write three ideas.

B ▶ 5.5 Listen to the first part of the brainstorm. Are any of your ideas included? What other ideas do they give?

4A ▶ 5.6 Listen to the second part. Which ideas are rejected and why? Which one is chosen in the end?

B Listen again and complete the phrases.

1 How _____ about this idea?

2 What _____ a competition?

3 Would _____ the gardening campaign?

4 How does the recipe idea _____ you?

5 It _____ if we could get kids into vegetarianism.

6 _____ try combining the two ideas.

C Work in pairs and practise saying the phrases in Exercise 4B. Remember to start the intonation quite high when you are proposing ideas.

How do you feel about this idea?

D Put the words in the correct order to make reactions to the ideas.

1 not / It's / enough / original

2 complicated / I / to / think / set / it's / up / too

3 me / grab / doesn't / It

4 we're / think / wrong / track / I / on / the

5 idea / I'm / campaign / and / the / between / viral / torn / that

6 go / Let's / that / with

▰▰▶ page 136 **LANGUAGEBANK**

5A Work in pairs and look at the ideas for getting people to walk to work. Which ones do you think are best?

Getting people to walk to work

- put articles in popular newspapers
- get celebrity spokesperson to promote idea
- get doctors to promote idea
- organise 'Walk to Work Week' (WWW)

B Work in pairs and complete the sentences in the flow chart.

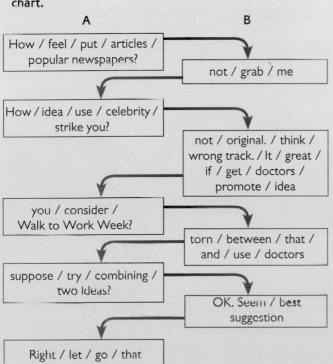

A

| How / feel / put / articles / popular newspapers? |

B

| not / grab / me |

A

| How / idea / use / celebrity / strike you? |

B

| not / original. / think / wrong track. / It / great / if / get / doctors / promote / idea |

A

| you / consider / Walk to Work Week? |

B

| torn / between / that / and / use / doctors |

A

| suppose / try / combining / two ideas? |

B

| OK. Seem / best suggestion |

A

| Right / let / go / that |

C Work in pairs and practise the conversation. Use the flow chart to help.

LEARN TO   show reservations

6A Work in pairs. Cross (✗) the negative comments and tick (✓) the one that is neutral.

1 _____, that could be a problem.
2 _____, it wouldn't be my first choice.
3 _____, I think it's too complicated to set up.
4 _____, it's all wrong.
5 _____, I think we're on the wrong track here.
6 _____, I was thinking of that myself.

B Look at the audio script on page 169 and write the missing words/phrases in comments 1–6 above.

C Which one signals a *very* negative comment?

speakout TIP

We often use short phrases before making negative comments in order to prepare the other person in situations where their feelings might be hurt or they may feel uncomfortable about a comment. Some phrases (*to be honest*, *actually*, *as a matter of fact*) can also signal a positive or neutral comment, depending on the intonation and context.

7A ▶ 5.7 Listen to the phrases and pay attention to the intonation. Do they signal a positive (+) or negative (−) comment?

B Listen again and repeat the phrases. Pay attention to the intonation.

SPEAKING

8A Work in groups. Choose one of the topics below and brainstorm at least five ideas.

- How to encourage people to learn a foreign language
- How to get people to visit a particular country or city
- How to make men interested in shopping
- How to make football appeal to women
- How to encourage young people to be more polite to older people

B Look at your list of ideas and choose the best one. Give reasons for rejecting the other ones.

C Tell the class your best idea and briefly describe two other ideas you rejected.

We considered the idea of ... but we decided against it because ...

In the end we chose to ...

DVD PREVIEW

1A Work in pairs. Read the programme description and decide if the statements are true (T) or false (F).

1 Celebrity guests present their ideas.
2 The ideas are generally both funny and clever.
3 The audience decides which ideas are 'genius'.

BBC Genius

Can an idea be both silly and genius at the same time? That's what the BBC programme *Genius* is all about. Each week, members of the public present their wild and wacky ideas for a new product or service. Presenter Dave Gorman and a celebrity guest humourously grill each inventor to get to the bottom of the invention, and help the celebrity guest decide whether the idea is truly genius or not. Tonight's suggestions include a new type of choir where each chorister has very little to do!

B Look at these ideas from the programme. What are the benefits and drawbacks of each one? Which is the most 'genius' idea?

* Sell socks in threes instead of pairs.
* Set up a 'democrobus' bus service where the passengers decide where the bus goes.
* Have genetically engineered 1 metre-high mini-elephants as pets.
* Send food direct to houses via taps for those times when you don't want to cook.

▶ DVD VIEW

2A Watch the DVD and answer the questions.

1 Who gets invited to the show?
2 What is Dan Haythorne's invention?
3 What did the show add to his invention to make it work?

B Which of these do you think are good tips for presenting an idea?

Presentation tips

* Prepare and practise your first and last sentences.
* Don't over-prepare. Be spontaneous, and respond to the audience.
* Make eye contact with your audience.
* Include humour.
* Use visuals to create interest and direct the audience's focus away from you.
* Speak clearly; don't mumble.
* Never show your back.
* Dress appropriately.

C Watch the DVD again and tick the ones you think Dan Haythorne follows.

speakout a business idea

3A Work in pairs. Student A: turn to page 160. Student B: turn to page 163. Either choose one of the business ideas from your lists, or think of an idea of your own to present to your classmates.

B Prepare your presentation. Discuss questions 1–3 below and make notes.

1 What is the product called?

2 Why is it such a good idea?

3 Where will it be sold?

C ▶ 5.8 Listen to two students presenting their idea and answer questions 1–3 above.

D Listen again and tick the keyphrases you hear.

---

keyphrases

We would like to introduce to you an idea that...

What makes our idea special is that it's not just [new/healthy/practical]

We anticipate (sales of 1000 units in the first year)

We envisage this product being sold [in supermarkets/on TV/via the internet]

We have particular expertise in the field in that we have...

We think that (product name) will be a hit with [single people/families/kids] in particular

We differentiate ourselves from the competition by ...

In the future, we are planning to develop a [businessman's/lightweight/sweetened] version

Our track record shows that we can...

4A Join another pair and take turns. Pair A: Practise your presentation. Pair B: give advice on improving the presentation. Use the tips in Exercise 2B to help.

B Present your product to the class and listen to the other presentations. Vote on the best one.

writeback a product leaflet

Do you have trouble getting out of bed in the morning?[1]

FlipBed is the answer! Just set the FlipBed clock and go to sleep knowing that you won't have to get out of bed in the morning. FlipBed will flip you out of bed![2]

- The whole bed turns over at the time you set the alarm for.
- Speed can be adjusted for slow and fast flip.
- Couples version available.
- Satisfaction guaranteed: If you oversleep once, we'll give you your money back![3]

for more information go to www.flipbed.com.[4]

5A Look at the leaflet extract and discuss. Would you buy such a product? Why or why not?

B Match 1-4 in the leaflet with the features below.

_____ A list of 3-4 things to give detail and make you feel that the product is rich in features

_____ Details of where to go for more information or to buy your product

_____ A question posing an everyday problem to get the reader's attention

_____ A short description answering the question

C Write a leaflet for your product. Include all of the features listed above.

D Look at other students' leaflets. Which one do you think is the most effective? Why?

CHANGE

1A Rewrite sentences 1–4 using the correct form of one of the words/ phrases in the box.

> ~~distort~~ revolutionise damage have a beneficial effect on

1 It has altered people's feeling about violence in real life.

It has distorted people's feeling about violence in real life.

2 It has enhanced the quality of life of people in the developing world.

3 It's had a detrimental effect on family relationships.

4 It completely transformed the way people think about war.

B Work in pairs and discuss. What could 'it' be in each sentence above?

ARTICLES

2A Complete the quiz questions with *a/an*, *the* or no article (–).

> *** * FUN AND GAMES * ***
>
> 1 ___ [1]game of ___ [2]BASKETBALL was invented by:
> (a)___[3] teacher in America.
> (b)___[4] Chinese general Zhao Tuo.
> (c)___[5] prisoners of war in Korea.
>
> 2 Originally, basketball was played by throwing … into a fruit basket.
> (a)___[6] first peach of the season
> (b)___[7] football
> (c)___[8] apples
>
> 3 WINDSURFING was first developed by:
> (a)___[9] Ukrainian sailor.
> (b)___[10] American.
> (c)___[11] Head of ___ [12]Australian Imperial Navy.
>
> 4 It was developed:
> (a) in ___[13] 14 BC.
> (b) during ___[14] First World War.
> (c) in___[15] 1960s.
>
> 5 SCRABBLE was developed by a former architect who was:
> (a)___[16] unemployed.
> (b)___[17] designer of the Eiffel Tower.
> (c)___[18] blind.

B Work in pairs and answer the quiz questions. Then check your answers on page 160.

CONDITIONALS

3A Underline the correct alternatives in the article.

Seducing shoppers

[1]*Provided/Supposing* you wanted to sell something in a shop; exactly where [2]*would/do* you place it to encourage people to buy it? And if you [3]*might/could* move your competitors' products to a poor location, where [4]*would/could* that be? Nowadays, placement of goods in a shop is a whole science.

For example, if there [5]*are/would be* two similar products, identical in quality but different in price, the shop [6]*will put/put* the more expensive one on the shelf you see first, and put the cheaper one around the corner. That way, [7]*provided/imagine* you want to buy the product, you [8]*put/would put* the expensive one in your basket; and then, even if you [9]*were to/would* see the cheaper one later, you probably [10]*wouldn't/won't* go to the trouble of swapping it. Similarly, if a product is on the bottom shelf, consumers [11]*are/would be* less likely to buy it (they're often too lazy to bend over [12]*unless/if* they're quite short).

B Work in pairs and discuss:

1 Which of the ideas in the article in Exercise 3A do you think are true?

2 What makes you decide to buy one brand over another?

3 What makes you buy something that you hadn't planned to buy?

ADVERTISING

4A Add the vowels to the groups of words.

1 _dv_rt_s_, pr_m_t_, _nd_rs_
2 sl_g_n, saying, phrase
3 m_k_, br_nd, l_g_
4 persuade, manipulate, _nfl_ _nc_
5 _dv_rt, c_mm_rc_ _l, c_mp_ _gn

B What do the three words in each group have in common?

SUGGESTING IDEAS

5A Find and correct ten mistakes in the students' conversation.

A: It's be great if we could have the class party at a four-star hotel.

B: I think it's much ambitious and expensive. How much do you feel about the school cafeteria?

C: That doesn't grabbing me. What does Pizza Hut strike you?

A: I think we're on the wrong truck here. That's not enough elegant.

B: OK. Supposed we try the Four Seasons or the Hilton?

A: Yeah, I'm tearing between the two, but the Four Seasons is closer.

C: OK. Let go with that.

B Cover the conversation and try to memorise the phrases.

C Work in groups and plan a party for your class.

1 Brainstorm the place, kind of food, activities/games, live music and dress. Remember the rules of brainstorming – just say ideas and write them down but don't criticise.

2 Discuss the different ideas and come to an agreement for each.

BBC VIDEO PODCAST

Download the podcast to view people discussing the question:

If you could start a business, what would it be?

Authentic BBC interviews

www.pearsonlongman.com/speakout

UNIT 6

SPEAKING
> Talk about different ages
> Discuss generations
> Talk about your future

LISTENING
> Listen to a BBC programme about letters to your future self
> Listen to a call-in about life's milestones
> Watch a BBC programme about living longer

READING
> Read a web forum about different age groups
> Read a letter written by someone to his future self

WRITING
> Write a letter to your future self
> Write a forum comment

BBC CONTENT
⌾ Video podcast: What was the best period of your life?
◉ DVD: How To Live Longer

UNIT
6

age

> The time of my life   p68

> Future me

> So what you're saying is ...p74

> How to Live to 101   p76

SPEAKING

1 Work in pairs and discuss. What are the advantages and disadvantages of being the ages in the box?

| 10 | 15 | 20 | 30 | 45 | 65 |

VOCABULARY age

2A Match the words/phrases in bold in questions 1–8 with meanings a)–h).

1 If someone looks young **for his or her age**, is that good or bad?

2 When is someone **in his or her prime**?

3 If you tell a twenty-five-year-old man, '**Act your age!**' what kind of thing might he be doing?

4 At what age do people generally **come of age** in your country: seventeen; eighteen; twenty-one?

5 Do you think most eighteen-year-olds are too **immature** for university?

6 At what age do you think a person has the **maturity** to make a decision about marriage or a career?

7 At what age is a person **elderly**?

8 Does **age discrimination** affect people looking for jobs in your country?

a) behave in a more adult way   *3*

b) 'old' (said in a more polite way)

c) in the best period of their life

d) treating people unfairly based on age

e) reach the age when legally an adult

f) in relation to how old they are

g) wisdom that comes with age

h) childish

B Work in pairs and discuss the questions in Exercise 2A.

▸ page 153 **VOCABULARYBANK**

READING

3A Read the website forum entries and complete each one with one of the ages in the box in Exercise 1.

B Work in pairs and compare your answers.

C Read the forum entries again and answer questions 1–6. In some cases there may be more than one answer.

1 Who feels much more confident?

2 Who's enjoying more freedom?

3 Who's afraid of something in the future?

4 Who has no financial worries?

5 Who exaggerates his or her achievements?

6 Who only sees the positive aspects of their life?

D Work in pairs and discuss. What are the best and worst things about being your age?

Q What's the best and worst thing about being your age?

A This year's been good because my parents have begun to trust me more. They say I can stay out late now – even six months ago I wasn't allowed to go out on a weeknight, and at weekends I had to phone them every hour to say where I was. So that's the best thing, I guess, and, of course, that I can hang out with friends. The worst thing about being _____ is not having enough money. Like, last Friday, I couldn't pay for my own cinema ticket because I didn't have the cash, so I had to borrow from my friend.

B By _____, the best thing is you appreciate your friends and family and every moment you spend with them, you don't take anything for granted. All of my friends are still healthy and active, so we can do a lot of things together, such as travel, and we're lucky enough to have the money to do it. I must admit that if there is a worst thing it's the fear of growing older and that, one day, I won't be able to do the things I want to. I don't think of myself as elderly ... I'm still middle-aged. As they say, 'Old age is always ten years older than you are.'

C The best thing about being _____ is living away from home! I live in a hall of residence and although we're supposed to attend lectures, I only go when I feel like it. To be honest, I prefer going out and enjoying myself. I do some reading for lectures and I study, but I know I ought to do more. So far it's been enough. I managed to pass my first set of exams, though it wasn't easy. The only bad thing for me is that I don't look my age, I still look quite young for my age, and girls think I'm immature, so I haven't managed to find a girlfriend yet.

D   The thing I find most difficult about being _____ is that I feel obliged to give everyone the impression that I'm successful. Older people keep telling me I'm in my prime, that I should enjoy this period of my life, so I pretend I have a good job, that I'm happy, but it's just a pretence. In fact, so far my working life hasn't been all that satisfying. And my friends seem to do the same, you know, trying to outdo each other. But the best thing I reckon is that there's plenty of time ahead of me, time to get things right.

E   I think the best thing is that I don't have to work and I don't need to worry about money. The worst thing? Homework! The teachers make us do two hours homework a day and we have to do four hours at the weekend. Oh, and my mum's always yelling at me for being noisy, she's always saying, 'Tina, act your age!' I tell her 'Mum, I *am* acting my age, I'm only _____!' Anyway, Mum says I mustn't write any more now 'cos I've got to do my maths. Then maybe she'll let me watch some TV. I'm never allowed to do anything fun before I finish my homework.

F   When I look back at the past, at how insecure I felt fifteen or twenty years ago, I have to laugh, because one thing I appreciate now is how comfortable I feel in my own skin. I've outgrown the need to seek other people's approval – I guess that's part of the maturity that comes with age and experience. I'm happy with the things I've achieved: my professional life has been OK, my marriage is fine, we don't have kids yet but I'm not in a panic about that. So, I'm _____ and I feel pretty content. I don't have a worst thing, or at least I can't think of one.

GRAMMAR modal verbs and phrases

4A Check what you know. Underline the modal verb in each sentence. Then put it in the correct place in the table.

1   They say I <u>can</u> stay out late.
2   We can do a lot of things together, such as travel.
3   I study, but I know I ought to do more.
4   The best thing is I don't have to work.
5   Mum says I mustn't write any more now.
6   We have to do four hours of homework at the weekend.
7   I had to phone them every hour to say where I was.
8   Older people keep telling me that I should enjoy this period of my life.

obligation (strong)		prohibition	
obligation (weak)		permission	can
lack of obligation		ability	

B Match the phrases in bold in sentences 1–8 with rules a)–h).

1   I **don't need to** worry about money.
2   One day, I **won't be able to** do the things I want to.
3   Although we**'re supposed to** attend lectures, I only go when I feel like it.
4   I **managed to** pass my first set of exams, though it wasn't easy.
5   I **feel obliged to** give everyone the impression that I'm successful.
6   The teachers **make** us do two hours homework a day.
7   Maybe she'll **let** me watch some TV.
8   I'm **never allowed to** do anything fun before I finish my homework.

Rules:

Use this phrase when:

a) you should do something but you don't really want to.
b) you mustn't do something.
c) you don't have to do something.
d) you talk about ability in the future. It's the future of *can* or *can't*.
e) someone says you have to do something.
f) someone says you can do something; it's OK to do it.
g) you think you have to do something. It's more formal.
h) something was difficult but you succeeded in doing it.

5A ▶ 6.1 Listen and write the sentences you hear.

B Underline the stressed word(s) in the positive and negative forms. Then listen and repeat.

➤ page 138 **LANGUAGEBANK**

PRACTICE

6A Complete the sentences with a modal verb or phrase. In some cases there is more than one possibility.

1 Parents _should_ be strict with babies or they _____ to control them later.

2 The worst thing about school was that I _____ do what I wanted to.

3 A good thing about being a child was that my parents often _____ me stay over at my friends' houses.

4 When I was younger, I _____ help clean our apartment but I never did.

5 The best thing about being an adult is that no one can _____ you do something if you don't want to do it.

6 The worst thing about being a parent is that you just _____ get the flat tidy and then the family messes it up again!

7 When I am older and richer I _____ afford an apartment in the city centre.

8 One good thing about being retired is that you _____ work any more.

B Change the sentences to give your opinion. Then compare with a partner.

SPEAKING

7A Make notes on your answers to questions 1–3 below.

1 Are most of the people you spend time with your age or a different age? Why?

2 How is your generation different from older and younger generations? What sort of misunderstandings or conflicts does this cause?

3 Is the 'generation gap' greater or smaller than it used to be? Why?

B Work in groups and discuss the questions.

VOCABULARY _PLUS_ word formation

8A Complete the sentences with the noun form of the verbs in brackets.

1 By sixty-five, you have more _____ of your friends. (appreciate)

2 I'm happy with my _____. (achieve)

3 My _____ is to go out and enjoy myself. (prefer)

4 Young people ignore the _____ of older people. (advise)

B Complete the table with the noun form of the verbs in the box.

~~appreciate~~ achieve pretend advise react involve judge oblige impress interfere practise prefer encourage

-ion	-ment	-ence	-ice
appreciation			

9A Underline the stressed syllable in verbs and nouns 1–8.

1 appreciate – appreciation
2 oblige – obligation
3 achieve – achievement
4 encourage – encouragement
5 prefer – preference
6 interfere – interference
7 advise – advice
8 practise – practice

B ▶ 6.2 Listen and check. Then listen and repeat.

C Complete the rules with _-ence_, _-ion_, _-ice_ or _-ment_.

Rules:
1 Nouns ending _____ and _____ have the same stress as the verb.
2 Nouns ending _____ have the stress on the next to last syllable.
3 Nouns ending _____ have no fixed pattern.

◖ speakout TIP

Learning different forms of a word will help make your speech and writing more expressive and interesting. Rewrite this sentence replacing the underlined verbs with the noun form and making any other necessary changes: _We were discussing which film to see but neither of us could decide and in the end we just argued about it._

10A Complete the sentences with a verb or noun.

1 It's more important to imp_____ other people.

2 It's easier to ignore obl_____.

3 Your rea_____ time is quicker.

4 You are more open to taking adv_____.

5 You tend to jud_____ other people more harshly.

6 You sometimes make a pre_____ of knowing more than you do.

7 You understand that it's important to pra_____ what you preach.

8 Fewer people int_____ in your everyday decisions.

9 Enc_____ from other people is particularly important.

10 You have a pre_____ for expensive things and a high level of comfort.

B Work in pairs and discuss. Which sentences above do you think are true for younger people and which are true for older people?

▶ page 153 **VOCABULARYBANK**

▶ **GRAMMAR** | future perfect & continuous ▶ **VOCABULARY** | optimism/pessimism ▶ **HOW TO** | talk about plans

LISTENING

1A Think about your life over the next year. Write one thing you will definitely do / will probably do / aren't likely to do / definitely won't do.

B Work in pairs and compare your answers.

2 Read the programme information. Would you like to receive a letter from your younger self? Why/Why not?

3A ▶ 6.3 Listen to a woman reading a letter she wrote to herself four years ago. Is her letter optimistic?

B Listen again and underline the correct alternative.

At sixteen, Laura expected her twenty-year-old self to be ...

1 *unchanged/ different.*
2 *abroad/ in the UK.*
3 *with/ without* a partner.
4 *with/ without* children.
5 *happy/ unhappy.*
6 *working/ studying.*

Letters to myself

The idea is simple: write a letter to yourself, and futureme.org will keep it and send it back to you at a point in the future – you pick the date. You will get a glimpse of the person you used to be and discover if you have met the expectations and hopes of your younger self. In this BBC radio programme, people read aloud and comment on their letters.

C ▶ 6.4 Listen to the second part of the programme and answer the questions.

1 How does Laura see her sixteen-year-old self now?
2 Is she happy with the way her life has turned out?

GRAMMAR future perfect and continuous

4A Look at sentences a) and b) from Laura's letter. Which one talks about:

1 things that will be completed before she opens the letter?
2 things that will be in progress around the time that she opens the letter?

a) I'll have changed so much.
b) I bet when I get this, it'll be raining.

B Complete the rules.

> Rules:
> 1 To talk about something that will finish before a specific time in the future, use *will* + _____ + _____.
> 2 To talk about something that will be in progress at or around a specific time in the future, use *will* + _____ + _____.

C Underline the correct alternative in the sentence and explain your reason.

In ten years' time, I expect *I'll be owning/ I'll own* a flat.

5 ▶ 6.5 Listen to the sentences in Exercise 4A. Underline the stressed words and mark the weak forms of *have* /əv/, and *be* /bɪ/. Then listen and repeat.

▶ page 138 LANGUAGEBANK

PRACTICE

6A Complete the questions with the correct form of the future perfect, future continuous or future simple.

1 By the end of the day, do you think _____ (you/receive) more than fifty emails?
2 At 9p.m. tonight, _____ (you/watch) TV? If so, what?
3 Do you reckon _____ (you/fall) asleep by midnight tonight?
4 Do you think _____ (you/drink) twenty cups of coffee or tea by the end of the week?
5 This time next year, _____ (you/still/study) English?
6 Do you think _____ (you/pass) any English exams by then?
7 Do you reckon _____ (you/still/like) the same kind of music a few years from now?
8 In twenty years' time, _____ (you/live) in the same town, do you think?

B Work in pairs and discuss the questions in Exercise 6A. Use words/phrases from the box in your answers.

> Possibly   That's pretty unlikely   Yes, definitely
> That's quite likely   I doubt it   No, definitely not
> Perhaps   I expect so   I don't suppose so

Glass half full or half empty?

1 How do you feel about your English?

a) It's going well.

b) You **have your ups and downs**.

c) You're stuck and **going nowhere**.

d) You're always **taking one step forward, and two steps back**.

2 This weekend, you're going to a party where there will be a lot of people you don't know. How do you feel?

a) You're **looking forward to** it.

b) You **have mixed feelings**.

c) You feel neither positive nor negative.

d) It's **the last thing you feel like doing**.

3 Your partner rings you and asks to meet as soon as possible because he/she has something important to tell you. What do you think?

a) You **look on the bright side** and think it'll be fantastic news.

b) You think it'll just be news, nothing particularly positive or negative.

c) You imagine it'll be terrible news.

d) You're **dreading** it because you're sure he/she wants to break off your relationship.

4 When you think about the next year or two in your life, how do you feel?

a) quite **upbeat** about it

b) cautiously hopeful

c) rather **cynical** about things getting any better

d) quite **gloomy** about the prospects

5 How does the future in general make you feel?

a) It **fills you with** great **optimism** and hope.

b) It looks **promising** to you.

c) It has its fair share of positive and negative prospects.

d) It **fills you with despair**.

VOCABULARY optimism/pessimism

7A Work in pairs and read the quiz. Try to guess the meaning of the words/phrases in bold or check in a dictionary.

B Work in pairs and take turns to complete the quiz questions.

C Read the key on page 160 and work out your partner's score. Do you think the analysis is accurate?

8A Replace the phrases in bold in questions 1–8 with a phrase from the quiz.

1 What's one thing you **feel positive and negative about at the same time**?

2 What's one experience you**'re thinking about in the future and feeling good about**?

3 What's one relationship or job you have that **sometimes goes well and sometimes doesn't**?

4 What's one experience coming up soon that you **are really worried about**?

5 What's one thing in your life at the moment that you feel **positive** about?

6 Is there one event in your country recently that **makes you feel hopeful**?

7 Can you remember an event in your country that **made you feel pessimistic**?

8 What's one profession you feel **suspicious and distrustful** about?

B Work in pairs and take turns. Ask and answer the questions in Exercise 8B.

SPEAKING

9A Think about your hopes and plans for the next five years. Make notes on the topics in the box below.

> work or studies   achievements   travel
> relationships   children   living situation

B Work in pairs and discuss your ideas.

A: What have you put for 'achievements'?

B: Well, in five years' time, I hope I'll have become fluent in English. I'd like to be working abroad somewhere, maybe Australia. How about you?

WRITING a letter

10A Read the letter from Greg to his future self. Which two words/phrases below describe his personality best?

- a pessimist
- a workaholic
- a family man
- a realist
- an optimist
- a dreamer

Dear FutureMe,

1 _____ I'm writing **to** see how you're doing and **because** you might appreciate a friendly message from the past.

2 _____ You'll probably be working in your father's business, you might even be managing one of his hotels yourself by then. I hope very much you'll be enjoying the work but I also hope you went into it because you wanted to and not because you were expected to. Are you still doing everything because of family pressure to conform?

3 _____ You could have started that band you were always talking about with Sammy and maybe you'll have made a million dollar album and will be rich and famous. Yeah, I like the sound of that! But somehow, I doubt it.

4 _____ I hope by now you will have quit smoking and will have found some great person to settle down with. Maybe you'll have some kids – make sure you spend enough time with them **so that** they'll actually <u>want</u> to spend time with you when you're older. Don't work all hours of the day and night **in order to** make money. Remember to keep in touch with your old friends **so as to** have people around you who know what you're really like (and don't mind). Why don't you phone up one of them now **for** a chat?

5 _____ Well, that's another story. I wish I could be there with you to see what it's like. Did they do something to sort out the environment? Did the global downturn end up being a good thing for some people, or for the world? Who are the great world powers now?

Look after yourself,

Greg

B Put sentences a)–e) in the correct places in the letter.

a) Maybe your life will have turned out quite differently.

b) And what about the rest of the world?

c) Here I am in 2010 and there you are in 2020.

d) Here's some advice and good wishes from 'present me':

e) These are the things I expect you'll be doing.

LEARN TO use linkers of purpose

11A Work in pairs. Look at the linkers in bold in the letter and answer the questions.

1 Which linkers are followed by:

a) an infinitive? *to*

b) a subject + modal verb?

c) a noun?

2 Which two linkers are often used in more formal situations?

3 How do you change the underlined linkers to make the sentences negative?

Make sure you keep practising <u>in order to</u> forget your English.

Send emails and phone your friends <u>so as to</u> lose touch with them.

B Join the sentences from other letters using the linkers in brackets.

1 I'm writing to you on my twenty-first birthday. I never want to forget how happy I was. (so that)

I'm writing to you on my twenty-first birthday so that I never forget how happy I was.

2 I wish I could get a letter back from you. Then I might know what to do next. (because)

3 I hope you took a year off. You wanted to take a round-the-world trip. (for)

4 If you haven't found a partner yet, try to do so soon. Otherwise, you might find yourself alone and lonely in your old age. (so that)

5 I imagine you're still doing sport every day. You always thought you could impress people that way. (so as to)

6 I guess you have to be optimistic. Otherwise, you wouldn't always dream about being rich and famous in the future. (to)

7 Make sure you read this every day. You need to remember how you used to be. (in order to)

8 If you're not happy in your job, try something else. You'll regret wasting years of your life doing something you don't enjoy. (in order not to)

12 Write a letter (120–180 words) to your future self to be opened five years from now. Make sure you mention:

- why you're writing.
- what you imagine you'll be doing.
- what you hope for your future self.
- advice for your future self.
- questions about changes that will have happened.

▶ **FUNCTION** | persuading   ▶ **VOCABULARY** | collocations   ▶ **LEARN TO** | ask for clarification

VOCABULARY collocations

1A Underline the correct alternative.

1 *making/doing* a part-time job
2 *owning/belonging* a mobile phone
3 *wearing/putting* make-up
4 *keeping/staying* home alone
5 *getting/making* your ears pierced
6 *going/using* social networking websites
7 *having/signing up* your own credit card
8 *driving/riding* a scooter
9 *babysitting/taking care* for a toddler
10 *journeying/travelling* solo
11 *staying/keeping* up as late as you want
12 *being in charge/running* your own business

B Work in pairs. Which of the activities above can you see in the photos?

C Work in pairs and discuss. At what age do you think it's appropriate for someone to do activities 1–12?

D Tell the class any activities/ages you disagreed about.

FUNCTION persuading

2A ▶ 6.6 Listen to a radio phone-in and tick the three activities in Exercise 1A that the people discuss.

B Listen again and make notes about the callers' problems and the DJ's opinions.

problem	DJ's opinion

C Work in pairs and check your answers.

D Work in pairs and discuss. What's your opinion about each of the situations from the phone-in?

3 Match examples 1–4 with meanings a)–d).

1 Is that an important part of growing up?
2 That's an important part of growing up.
3 Surely that's an important part of growing up.
4 Isn't that an important part of growing up?

a) an opinion
b) a genuine question – the listener can answer *yes* or *no*
c) an opinion where the speaker is inviting the listener to agree with them
d) a strong opinion where the speaker thinks the listener *should* agree with them

4A Complete the questions from the phone-in.

1 _____ the parents' responsibility. (Surely/it/be)
2 _____ that the world used to be a safer place? (you/not agree)
3 _____ what every generation says. (Surely/that/be)
4 _____ that just normal nowadays? (not be)
5 _____ it's just a stage he's going through? (you/not think)
6 _____ to be like her friends? (she/simply/not want)

B ▶ 6.7 Listen and check.

C Listen again and repeat. Pay attention to the intonation.

Surely that's what <u>every</u> generation says.

Doesn't she simply want to be like her <u>friends</u>?

▶ page 138 **LANGUAGEBANK**

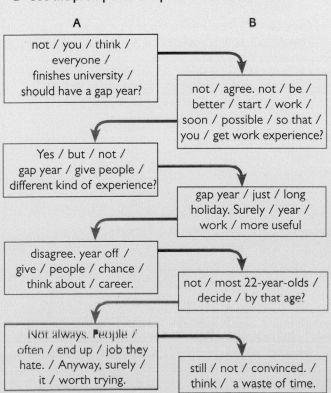

5A Work in pairs. Do you know anyone who has had a 'gap year' either before they went to university or between university and work? What do you think of the idea?

B Use the prompts to complete the conversation.

A

B

> not / you / think / everyone / finishes university / should have a gap year?

> not / agree. not / be / better / start / work / soon / possible / so that / you / get work experience?

> Yes / but / not / gap year / give people / different kind of experience?

> gap year / just / long holiday. Surely / year / work / more useful

> disagree. year off / give / people / chance / think about / career.

> not / most 22-year-olds / decide / by that age?

> Not always. People / often / end up / job they hate. / Anyway, surely / it / worth trying.

> still / not / convinced. / think / a waste of time.

C Work with a new partner and take turns to practise the conversation. Use the flow chart to help.

LEARN TO ask for clarification

6A Read the extract from the radio phone-in. Find two phrases where people ask for clarification of an idea.

DJ: So I gather your point is whether she's too young to have a mobile.

Vince: Yeah, yeah, that's right.

DJ: Er, surely it's the parents' responsibility to set some sort of guidelines ahead of time.

Vince: So what you're saying is I should have given her some rules?

B Read the audio script on page 170 and find three other phrases to ask for clarification.

speakout TIP

Asking for clarification of an idea by putting it into your own words is useful not only to check that you understand, but also to 'buy' time while you think about how to react.

C Complete statements 1–6 with your own ideas.

1 The biggest problem with young people today is …
2 It's not fair that …
3 I think it was a mistake to …
4 I get upset when I see an elderly person …
5 One thing I learned from my parents …
6 If I regret anything, it's that …

D Work in pairs and take turns. Student A: read out your statements from Exercise 6C. Student B: ask for clarification using any of the phrases below.

- If I've got it right …
- I gather your point is (that) …
- So what you're saying is (that) …
- So, in other words, …
- So what you're getting at is (that) …

A: *It's not fair that people with money can get the best education.*

B: *So, in other words, education should be free?*

A: *That's right, and …*

SPEAKING

7A Work in pairs. For each statement, think of two points that support the opinion and two points against it.

- Thirteen is too young to join a social networking site.
- A seventeen-year-old boy shouldn't be allowed to get a tattoo.
- An eighteen-year-old who has just passed his driving test isn't ready to drive the family car alone.

B You are going to take part in a radio phone-in. Student A: turn to page 159. Student B: turn to page 160. Student C: turn to page 162.

DVD PREVIEW

1 Work in pairs and discuss the questions.

1 Who is the oldest person you know or have known?

2 What do you think they would say is the secret to a long life?

2A Match 1–8 with a)–h) to make collocations.

1 keep	a) some gentle exercise
2 follow	b) into monotonous routines
3 do	
4 don't fall	c) a sensible diet
5 avoid	d) mentally active
6 stay	e) a positive attitude
7 maintain	f) healthy
8 don't become	g) depressed
	h) stress

B Work in pairs and discuss. Which two factors do you think are the most important for a long life?

3 Read the programme information. Which three places are mentioned and what do they have in common?

BBC
Horizon: How to Live to 101

The quest to live longer has been one of humanity's oldest dreams, but while scientists have been searching, a few isolated communities have stumbled across the answer. On the remote Japanese island of Okinawa, in the Californian town of Loma Linda and in the mountains of Sardinia people live longer than anywhere else on earth.

A group of scientists have dedicated their lives to trying to uncover the secrets of these unique communities. Tonight's documentary travels to Okinawa to meet some of its long-living and remarkably healthy inhabitants.

▶ DVD VIEW

4A Watch the DVD. What are the two main reasons mentioned for why Okinawans live such long lives?

B Are the statements true (T) or false (F)? Watch the DVD again and check your ideas.

1 Okinawa has double the percentage of people over a hundred that Britain and America has.

2 The Okinawans think a lot about the effect of their lifestyle on their longevity.

3 Bradley and Craig have been studying the Okinawan diet for 20 years.

4 Their diet is rich in antioxidants and protein from meat and eggs.

5 The Japanese saying *hara hachi bu* means eat about a thousand calories a day.

6 Bradley sees the attitude towards eating as different from in the west.

C Watch the DVD again and underline the word you hear.

1 Unaware of the latest diet or lifestyle *fad/ fashion*, Mr Miyagi has developed his own way of *defying/ fighting* the ageing process.

2 The explanation for this extraordinary *miracle/ phenomenon* begins in the most ordinary of places.

3 They've identified a number of crucial *qualities/ properties* that guard the Okinawans from disease.

4 You go and you load up at the all-you-can-eat restaurant and you walk away with this *swollen/ bloated* feeling.

D Work in pairs and discuss. How easy do you think you would find it to live on Okinawa? Is there anything you would find difficult?

speakout a debate

5A Look at the topic for a debate. Work in pairs and write one idea in favour of the statement and one idea against it.

Age discrimination should be illegal at work.

B ▶ 6.8 Listen to part of the debate. Which speaker do you agree with most?

C Listen again and tick the key phrases you hear.

> **keyphrases**
>
> The first point I'd like to make is that ...
>
> I would like to start off by saying that ...
>
> I would like to support the point made by ...
>
> Going back to what [Junko] said
>
> I would like to pick up on the point made by ...
>
> In [answer/reply] to the point made by ...

6A As a class, choose one of the topics for a debate.

1 Junk food can shorten lives and should be made illegal.

2 Politicians should be young – younger adults understand the changing world better.

3 Children should take care of their parents when they get old.

B Work in pairs either for or against the statement. List at least four points to support your opinion.

C Work in groups and debate the topic. At the end, have a vote.

writeback a forum comment

7A Read the forum comment and discuss in pairs. Do you agree with the writer?

> I grew up in a traditional society, where my grandparents lived with us and were always in the house. When I came to this country, it surprised me how unusual it was for three generations to live together. I accept that most young people's lifestyles don't fit with those of grandparents. However, in my opinion, we are fully responsible for taking care of our ageing parents and grandparents. My reasons are that:
>
> • our parents and grandparents invested a lot in caring for us, and it's our duty to do the same for them.
>
> • elderly people can experience loneliness and helplessness. If we care about someone, we should protect them from these feelings.
>
> • it's more expensive and wasteful for people to live in separate homes.
>
> I feel strongly that everyone should reconsider the way they live, and move towards a more traditional family structure, even in a modern context.

B Number parts a)–d) in the order they occur in the forum comment.

a) summary statement

b) reasons for opinion

c) statement of opinion

d) personal background

C Choose one of the topics from Exercise 6A and write a forum comment giving your point of view.

AGE

1A Add the vowels to complete the sentences.

1 Society, not families, should take care of the _ld_rly.

2 People _n th_ _r pr_m_ should simply enjoy life and not work.

3 The key sign of someone c_m_ng of _g_ is when they earn enough money to pay their own rent.

4 It's embarrassing when an older man or woman dresses too young f_r h_s or h_r _g_. People should dress and act th_ _r _g_.

5 _g_ d_scr_m_n_t_ _n is necessary in certain types of jobs.

6 M_t_r_ty comes from experience, not from age.

B Work in pairs and discuss. Which sentences do you agree with?

MODAL VERBS AND PHRASES

2A Underline the correct alternatives in the website forum.

My worst job

My current job is the worst ever. I'm a waiter in an amusement park restaurant and the manager [1]*makes/ lets* us dress up as animals. The bear costume is the worst because it's so heavy and when I'm wearing it I [2]*can't / 'm not able* to see properly to write down the orders. I can't believe some of the things children [3]*are allowed to / should* do. We [4]*don't have to / aren't supposed to* get angry with them but I'm sure one day I [5]*can't / won't be able* to keep my temper and will do something awful! Thankfully, we [6] *don't have to/ aren't allowed* wear the costumes for more than two hours at a time and I can tell you, it's a relief to take them off in the breaks. Fortunately, because of the masks, my friends [7]*don't need to / oughtn't to* know that I spent my summer holidays dressed as a bear! Once, I [8]*could / managed to* serve two of my friends without them realising it was me!

B Work in pairs and discuss. What's the worst job you've ever had or that you can imagine?

FUTURE PERFECT AND CONTINUOUS

3A Complete the sentences with the correct form of the words in brackets.

1 Ten minutes from now, I _____ here any more. (not sit)

2 In two hours' time, the class _____. I _____ English. (definitely finish/probably not speak)

3 This Sunday at noon, it _____ warm with plenty of sunshine. (be)

4 A year from now, all of us in this group _____ on a weekly basis. (still communicate)

5 By 2020, the internet _____ by an alternative technology. (replace)

B Work in pairs and discuss. Which of the sentences above are true?

C Work in pairs and write five predictions about yourself/a classmate/a country/a famous person/the world.

D Work with another pair and discuss your ideas.

OPTIMISM/PESSIMISM

4A Correct twelve mistakes in the words/phrases in bold.

I've **had my downs and ups** at work, but I will never forget my first job: teaching French to a group of sixteen-year-olds in a state school. I **had fixed feelings** about taking the job, since I was very young myself, but I'd learned to always **look on the light side of things**. I went in the first day feeling **beat-up** and really **looking backward to** meeting my group. I was in for a surprise, as my group was the most difficult bunch of sixteen-year-olds imaginable – **cynic** about the past and **gloom** about their future. I taught them every morning and for a long time I truly **dread** those lessons. No matter what I tried, I always felt I was **taking two steps forward and one step back**. Then, one day, a **promise** thing happened, and from my **despaired** I was suddenly **filed with optimism**. One of the students brought a …

B Work in pairs and discuss. How do you think the story ended?

PERSUADING

5A Complete the conversation by adding the missing words from the box to the phrases in bold.

what	surely	isn't	agree
can	clearly	shouldn't	

A: **Don't you that** everyone should be vaccinated against flu?

B: **But** people ought to be able to choose for themselves.

A: **Why? Anyone see that** the community needs to be protected and that means everyone has to be vaccinated.

B: **But** parents decide what they think is best for their children? **What** about some of the side effects of vaccination?

A: **So you're saying is that** you think parents know more than the medical profession?

B: **But it obvious that** it's the companies who make the vaccines that are actually making money?

A: **Well**, we'll have to agree to disagree.

B Practise the conversation above in pairs. Look only at the phrases in bold to help.

C Work in pairs. Use the phrases in bold in Exercise 6A to discuss the following topics.

1 People who drink and drive should never be allowed to drive again.

2 The ideal world language is _____, not English.

3 Everyone should do one day a week of community service work.

BBC VIDEO PODCAST

Download the podcast to view people talking the question:

What was the best period of your life?

Authentic BBC interviews

www.pearsonlongman.com/speakout

UNIT 7

SPEAKING
> ❯ Talk about 'must-see' TV
> ❯ Express strong reactions
> ❯ Retell a news story

LISTENING
> ❯ Listen to an expert talking about hoax photographs
> ❯ Listen to people talking about recent news stories
> ❯ Watch a BBC programme about live news

READING
> ❯ Read about five 'must-see' TV programmes
> ❯ Read an essay on celebrities and the media
> ❯ Read about hot topics for tabloids

WRITING
> ❯ Write a discursive essay
> ❯ Write a newspaper article

BBC CONTENT
> 🎧 Video podcast: What kind of news stories interest you?
> 💿 DVD: The Funny Side of the News

UNIT 7

media

VOCABULARY television

1A Work in pairs. Think of one similarity and one difference between the TV programmes. Use your dictionary to help if necessary.

1 a wildlife programme – a reality show
2 a costume drama – a soap opera
3 a sketch show – a sitcom
4 a documentary – a docudrama
5 a series – a serial
6 a thriller – a detective series
7 a game show – a quiz
8 a current affairs programme – the news

B Work in pairs and discuss. Which of the programme types above do you like most/least? Give some examples.

READING

2 Work in pairs and look at the photos of five BBC TV programmes. What types of programme are they? Would you watch them?

3A Read the magazine article about five TV programmes and match the programmes with photos A–E.

B How do you know sentences 1–10 are false? Underline the relevant phrase or sentence in the article.

1 *EastEnders* is a typical soap opera.
2 It doesn't take risks with topics.
3 *Top Gear* is a very serious programme.
4 It is recorded entirely in the studio and on the test track.
5 The dancers on *Strictly Come Dancing* are professionals.
6 The judges choose who is in the dance-off.
7 Paxman is the only *Newsnight* presenter.
8 Guests on *Newsnight* enjoy being 'Paxoed'.
9 Doctor Who is an evil character.
10 The programme is only popular in the UK.

C Match meanings 1–8 with the correct words/phrases in the article.

1 was broadcast *(EastEnders)*   aired
2 arguments *(EastEnders)*
3 done only once *(Top Gear)*
4 attractive and exciting *(Strictly Come Dancing)*
5 famous *(Strictly Come Dancing)*
6 thorough and full *(Newsnight)*
7 been criticised *(Newsnight)*
8 is popular with all ages *(Doctor Who)*

4 Discuss. Which of the programmes would you most like to watch?

Check it out

What's on the Beeb?

If you think Brits spend **a good deal of** time around the coffee machine talking about the weather, you'd be wrong. They're actually discussing the latest episode of *EastEnders* or *Top Gear*. Want to join in? Then check out **a few** must-see shows on the Beeb, as the BBC is affectionately known by its viewers.

EastEnders

EastEnders first aired in February 1985 and since then has remained one of the top-rated programmes in the UK. Set in a fictional east end London square and its surroundings, this award-winning soap opera follows the domestic and professional lives of a group of local residents. There are **plenty of** typical storylines: family life, rows, romance and business troubles, but the show's writers also aim for greater realism than is found in most soaps. During its long run, the show has tackled **quite a few** issues previously unseen on mainstream UK TV, such as racism, unemployment and drug abuse.

Top Gear

If your idea of heaven is James Bond fantasy car rides, **lots of** crazy challenges and **no** rules, this is the series for you. With its humorous style and easy relationship between the three presenters (Jeremy Clarkson, Richard Hammond and James May), **each** programme regularly attracts 350 million viewers worldwide. A recurring feature is 'The Power Lap', where the Stig (a mysterious white-suited figure) completes a lap around the track to test a car's performance. *Top Gear* is also famous for one-off exploits such as when the four men raced across London: May in a Mercedes, Hammond on a bicycle, the Stig on public transport and Clarkson in a speedboat.

newsnight

Strictly Come Dancing

This reality show has it all: show-stopping dances, celebrities, glamorous dresses, big band music, a popular host and **plenty of** viewer participation. Sixteen famous contestants with **little** or **no** experience of dancing pair up with internationally renowned professional dancers. They learn everything from the traditional ballroom waltz to Latin dances such as the tango or salsa. The couples then perform in front of a live audience **every** Saturday night to impress the viewers and judges and keep their places in the competition. Each week, after the viewers' vote, the bottom two couples face each other in a dance-off where the judges decide who will leave the show. The show, which regularly attracts audience figures of over ten million in the UK, has been exported to thirty other countries.

Newsnight

Newsnight is a current affairs programme famous for its in-depth reporting, hard-hitting interviews and intelligent analysis. Its main presenter, Jeremy Paxman, has won **several** journalistic awards and is regularly praised for being tough, but he has also come under fire for being aggressive with interviewees. Very **few** politicians enjoy the experience of being 'Paxoed' – on one famous occasion, he asked a senior politician the same question an astonishing twelve times. *Newsnight* is on daily at 10.30p.m.

Doctor Who

There are **few** fictional characters who are as well known as Robin Hood or Sherlock Holmes, but 'The Doctor' is one. He is a mysterious alien who travels through space and time, righting wrongs and fighting monsters such as his ongoing enemies, the robotic Daleks, all with **a little** help from various companions. Equally famous is his time-ship, the 'Tardis', which looks from the outside like an old fashioned police box but has **lots of** room on the inside. Twelve actors have played the Doctor over the lifetime of the series, which has been running off and on since 1963. *Doctor Who* has cross-generational appeal and millions of fans worldwide. One not to miss.

GRAMMAR quantifiers

5A Check what you know. Which of the quantifiers in bold in the article refer to: all; a lot; a moderate or a small number/amount; zero?

B Underline the correct alternative to complete the rules. Use the article to help.

> Rules:
> 1 Use *a good deal of, little, a little* + *countable/uncountable* noun
> 2 Use *each, every* + *singular/plural* countable noun
> 3 Use *a few, quite a few, several* + *singular/plural* countable noun
> 4 Use *plenty of, lots of, most, no* + *plural/plural or uncountable* noun

C In sentences 1–4 below, do the quantifiers *few* and *little* mean *some* or *not many/not much*?

1 Check out <u>a few</u> must-see shows.
2 Very <u>few</u> politicians enjoy the experience.
3 Sixteen celebrities with <u>little</u> or no experience of dancing.
4 I always try to spend <u>a little</u> time watching the news each day.

6A ▶ 7.1 Listen and write sentences 1–4 in your notebooks.

B Draw links between final consonants and initial vowels in the quantifiers in connected speech.

1 All_of_us are from Spain.

C Listen and check. Then listen again and repeat.
➡ page 140 **LANGUAGEBANK**

PRACTICE

7A Find and correct one mistake in each sentence.

1 I watch very little sports programmes.
2 Every programmes have a commercial break every ten minutes.
3 The weekend schedules usually include few talent shows, at least three or four.
4 You can watch a good deal of popular programmes online.
5 I like each programmes about hospitals or emergencies.
6 I once spent quite few days watching a box set of the series *Lost*.
7 I think a large number of TV has been dumbed down.
8 We have plenty detective shows; we don't need more.
9 Lots the best shows are US imports, such as *The Wire*.
10 I think little news is OK but not 24-hour news non-stop.

B Make the sentences true for you/your country.

C Work in pairs and compare your answers.

SPEAKING

8 Work in pairs. Read the information and discuss:

- which surprises you the most?
- which is the most worrying?
- which is reassuring or is a good idea?

> The average young person living in the USA watches television twenty-five hours a week.

> Forty-seven percent of nine-year-olds in Ireland have a TV in their bedroom.

> Some experts say that television helps children develop a richer vocabulary.

> A sociologist has stated that children who don't watch TV have difficulty relating to their schoolmates.

> Children's television shows contain about twenty violent acts per hour.

> By the time the average child finishes elementary school, he or she will have witnessed eight thousand murders on TV.

> TV advertising aimed at children is banned in Sweden.

9A Work in groups and discuss the questions.

1 How many hours of TV do you watch a week? Is it more or less than when you were a child?
2 How many televisions are there in your home?
3 Have you watched TV in English? Which programmes?
4 Which do you think is the more important function of TV – to entertain or to educate? Why?
5 Do you think TV violence makes people more violent in real life?
6 How do you think parents should control what young children see on TV?

B Tell the rest of the class what you found out in your discussion.
Quite a few of us watch more than twenty hours of TV a week.

VOCABULARY *PLUS* multi-word verbs

10A Underline the eight multi-word verbs in quotes 1–5. Which of the BBC programmes in the box might the quotes come from?

EastEnders   Top Gear   Strictly Come Dancing   Doctor Who   Newsnight

1 " The company has just brought out a new electric version of their popular 408 range. This model has several appealing features, and should help them to break into the fast-growing 'green' market.

2 " The latest news from the summit meeting is that negotiations have broken down. Both the Chinese and Americans are pulling out of the talks and sending their representatives home.

3 " Marvellous! You're my favourite couple! And that dress! It takes me back to my teenage days and memories of dances on Saturdays!

4 " No time to talk! It turns out that the captain is one of them – one of the aliens. He completely fooled me. That means we're in serious trouble. Run!

5 " I came across this old mate of mine, Brenda, in the market. I hadn't seen her for ages so we had a good old chat. Anyway, she was telling me she'd got a divorce from her husband. I don't know how she put up with him for so long – he was always coming home drunk …

B Match meanings 1–8 with the multi-word verbs in Exercise 10A.

1 happen in the end   *turn out*
2 fail or end unsuccessfully
3 meet by chance
4 introduce (a product) or make something available
5 make somebody remember
6 tolerate
7 enter something with difficulty
8 end somebody's involvement or quit

C Look at the multi-word verbs in sentences 1–8. Are the meanings similar (S) or completely different (D) from those in Exercise 10B?

1 Hundreds of people **turned out** to hear his speech. *D*
2 My car's in the shop, it **broke down** on the way to work today.
3 She **comes across** as a confident person but, in fact, she's not.
4 You seem so happy. This new job **brings out** the best in you.
5 I **take back** everything I said about Tom, he's actually really nice.
6 I missed the last bus. Could you **put me up** for the night?
7 Someone **broke into** my flat and stole my passport.
8 I missed the train, it was **pulling out** when I got to the station.

11A Work in pairs. Use six of the multi-word verbs to write either a story for a TV drama, soap opera or thriller, or a report for a current affairs, documentary or news programme.

B Tell other students about your story or report. Which one do you think would make the best TV programme?

▶ page 154 **VOCABULARYBANK**

▶ **GRAMMAR** | reported speech   ▶ **VOCABULARY** | reporting verbs   ▶ **HOW TO** | report what someone says

A   Plane crosses road in China.

LISTENING

1 Look at photos A–C. Do you think the news events really happened or are they hoaxes?

2A ▶ 7.2 Listen to the interview and check.

B Listen again and make notes on the answers to the questions.

1 Why does the studio guest want to remain anonymous (hide his identity)?

2 What do the police pay him to do?

3 What feature in each photo makes him think the photo could be a hoax?

3 Work in pairs and discuss the questions.

1 Do you know any hoax photos or news stories?

2 Are hoax photos that make fun of celebrities or public figures offensive or simply funny?

GRAMMAR   reported speech

4A Check what you know. Match sentences 1–4 with functions a)–c).

1 I asked you before the show if you'd ever earned money for your hoax work.   c

2 You said that you often work with the police.

3 Sometimes the police ask me to decide if the photograph is a hoax.

4 A friend told me he had seen it with his own eyes a number of years before.

a) reporting a statement

b) reporting a request

c) reporting a question

B For the sentences in Exercise 4A, write the exact words each person said in their original conversations.

1 *'Have you ever earned money for your hoax work?'*

C Work in pairs and answer the questions. Use the sentences in Exercise 4A to help.

1 What usually happens to verb forms when we report what people say?

2 Why does the verb form stay the same in sentence 2?

3 What is the difference in word order between reported and direct questions?

4 When do we use *if* in reported questions?

5 Which form do we use to report a request?

6 What happens to time phrases such as *ago, yesterday, today, next week*?

▐▐▶ page 140 **LANGUAGE**BANK

B   Suitcase from plane found in tree.

C   Man risks 900 metre drop in Grand Canyon.

PRACTICE

5A Work in pairs. Complete the conversation between the man in photo C (M) and a park official (P). Use your own ideas.

1 P: Are you feeling …?

2 M: Yes, I'm …

3 P: Why did you …?

4 M: I wanted …

5 P: Did you realise …?

6 M: No, not until …

7 P: Have you ever …?

8 M: Well no, but once I …

9 P: Would you mind coming …?

10 M: First, I'll just phone …

B Write the conversation in reported speech. Then check your answers with your partner.

The park official asked the man [1]_____ and the man said that [2]_____. Then the official asked [3]_____ and the man told him [4]_____. Next, the official wanted to know [5]_____ and he explained that [6]_____. Finally, the official asked the man [7]_____ and the man said [8]_____. So then the official asked the man [9]_____ and he replied that [10]_____.

VOCABULARY reporting verbs

6A Work in pairs and read the dialogues. Who are the people and what are the situations?

1 A: It was YOU! You told the media about our private life!
   B: I've never spoken to anyone.
   A: That's it! I'm going to divorce you!
   B: No, please. Please don't. It really wasn't me.
   A: OK, OK, I won't – for now.

2 A: I can't allow you to do it. You could hurt yourself badly.
   B: Too bad – I'm going to do it anyway. You can't stop me.
   A: All right but you have to stop if you get any symptoms.
   B: OK … right. I'll take care, honestly.

3 A: Yes, that's right. It wasn't real. It was meant to be a joke.
   B: Well, we'd like to meet and discuss it.
   A: Look, I'm really sorry. I'll come back on the programme to explain.

B Match conversations 1–3 above with news reports A–C.

A

CANYON PHOTO A HOAX

Amateur photographer, Daniel Martinez, has ¹_____ that the photo of himself jumping over part of Copper Canyon in Mexico was a hoax. The photo shows him jumping 2.5 metres over a 1 kilometre drop and first appeared on the Good Morning Show on Channel 5. Apparently, he has ²_____ for causing the problem and the show's producer has ³_____ meeting him to discuss the issue. Martinez has ⁴_____ to go on the programme this week to explain but is …

B

MARATHON CHAMP TO RUN

Champion runner Freida Leitner has said she will run in this week's marathon against her trainer's advice. It has been reported that her trainer, Ben Kramer, at first ⁵_____ to let Leitner run because of a back injury but she has ⁶_____ on taking part. Apparently the two had a serious argument but Kramer eventually ⁷_____ to allow her to take part and we understand that she has ⁸_____ to take care and to withdraw at the first sign of strain. Leitner …

C

MODEL ON SPLIT

In an exclusive interview, model Sharon LaMar has told *GossipPlus* that her problems with rapper Demon-X are his fault. 'He ⁹_____ me of telling the media about our private life but I've never spoken to anyone before now. I ¹⁰_____ saying anything and then he ¹¹_____ to divorce me!' So are the rumours about a possible split true? 'I ¹²_____ him to change his mind and try and make the marriage work,' said a tearful Sharon as …

7A Complete the news reports above with the reporting verbs in the box. Use the conversations in Exercise 6A to help.

accuse apologise persuade insist suggest agree
promise deny admit refuse threaten offer

B Look at the reporting verbs. Which verb patterns follow each reporting verb?

• infinitive with *to*:
• *-ing* form:
• object + infinitive with *to*:
• (object) + preposition + *-ing* form: *accuse sb of doing sth*

8 Work in pairs and take turns. Student A: read one of the conversations in Exercise 6A. Student B: report the conversation.

A: *'It was YOU! You told the media about our private life!'*

B: *He accused her of telling the media about their private life.*

9A Complete the questions with the correct form of the verb in brackets.

QUESTIONS OF TRUST

Situation 1

A colleague has a photo of you at an office party doing something embarrassing. He threatens to show it to your boss unless you pay him a small sum of money. Would you:

a) talk to your boss and admit *acting* (act) stupidly?

b) deny _____ (do) anything wrong and tell your colleague to do whatever he wants?

c) agree _____ (pay) the money since it's a small amount, just to avoid trouble?

Situation 2

Someone shows you a printout of an email written by your best friend. It's full of negative comments about you and also contains a few secrets that you told your friend. Would you:

a) accuse your friend _____ (betray) you?

b) refuse _____ (believe) that the email is real, and do nothing?

c) insist _____ (see) the original email so you can check its authenticity?

Situation 3

A year ago, you promised to take a friend out to dinner for her birthday at an expensive restaurant. She's just reminded you, but now you don't really have the time or money. Should you:

a) promise _____ (take) her but next year?

b) persuade her _____ (go) to a cheaper restaurant?

c) tell her the situation and apologise _____ (break) a promise?

Situation 4

Your boss has offered to give you a bonus if you write a report that will have her name on it and that she will take full credit for. Would you:

a) offer _____ (do) it but only if she gives you credit too?

b) suggest _____ (ask) someone else?

c) say no and threaten _____ (report) your boss to *her* boss?

B Work in pairs. Take turns to ask and answer the questions in Exercise 9A.

WRITING a discursive essay

10A Look at statements 1–3. Write one reason for and one reason against each statement. Give examples.

1 The media should be free to examine the private lives of public figures.

2 Positive images of celebrities in the media have a good effect on people.

3 The internet is the most reliable source of news and information.

B Work in groups and compare your ideas.

11A Read the essay and answer the questions.

1 Which of the topics in Exercise 10A is it about?

2 Do you agree with the writer's point of view?

3 Can you think of a good title for the essay?

These days the media is full of stories of celebrities' private lives: their relationships, rows, problems with weight and so on. In fact, the public seems to have a never-ending appetite for this type of gossip.

It could be argued that celebrities invite publicity, for instance by giving interviews or welcoming the media into their homes, despite knowing this will leave them open to public attention. Therefore, it is hypocritical for them to complain when the media shows interest in other aspects of their lives. Also, celebrities are influential role models to many people and because of this, their private lives should be open to public examination. Additionally, the public have the right to know about the rich and famous since it is our money that supports them, through sales of tickets, DVDs and music downloads.

However, there are several reasons why celebrities deserve a certain level of privacy. Firstly, while some people actively seek fame, others do not. For example, a person might want to be a great tennis player but not wish to suffer media intrusion into their or their family's private lives. Secondly, although reporters might claim an item is 'in the public interest' often, in fact, they are more interested in selling a sensational story than in investigating something of genuine importance. Lastly, the unwelcome attentions of reporters and photographers can put celebrities under great stress or sometimes even in danger. Just think of Michael Jackson or Princess Diana.

On balance, I believe that celebrities have the right to the same kind of privacy as anyone else. Just because, on some occasions, they invite interest, often in order to publicise their work or please their fans, this does not mean that, on other occasions, they should not be able to say 'no'.

B Read the essay again and underline the correct alternative.

1 The introductory paragraph *explains why the topic is of interest / gives the writer's opinion about the topic.*

2 Paragraph two gives points *for / for and against* the idea.

3 Paragraph three gives points *against / for and against* the idea.

4 The conclusion *asks the reader's / gives the writer's* opinion.

LEARN TO use linkers of contrast

12A Look at sentences 1–4. Circle the linker which is used to show a contrasting idea.

1 Celebrities invite publicity (despite) knowing this will leave them open to public attention.

2 While some people seek fame, others never want or plan for it.

3 Although a reporter might claim that a story is 'in the public interest', often they are more interested in selling a sensational story.

4 However, there are a number of reasons why celebrities deserve our sympathy.

B Work in pairs and answer the questions.

1 What punctuation follows *However*?

2 Which form follows *despite*?

3 In sentences 1, 2 and 3, which is the main clause?

4 Do the linkers in 1, 2 and 3 introduce the main clause or the subordinate clause?

C Use the linkers in brackets to connect the ideas in two different ways.

1 some celebrities are good role models for young people / others set a negative example
(however, although)

2 anonymously published internet news is unreliable / many people rely on it as a main source of information
(despite, while)

3 false reports of celebrity deaths are common / some people still believe them
(while, however)

4 the scandal damaged his reputation / he still has millions of fans
(although, despite)

13A Write notes for the four sections of a discursive essay on one of the other topics in Exercise 10A.

speakout TIP

A discursive (or 'for and against') essay is different from an opinion essay. In an opinion essay, the writer starts out by stating his/her opinion; in a discursive essay, the writer gives a balanced view and in the conclusion can either state his/her opinion or give a summary of both sides of the argument. Check the notes you have made to see that your introduction and conclusion are appropriate.

B Write the essay (250–300 words).

VOCABULARY | the press

1A Read the headline of the article below. What do you think the six topics are? Then read the article and check your ideas.

Six topics that keep the tabloids in business

In an age when **broadsheet** newspapers are seeing a serious drop in **circulation**, tabloid newspapers are in no danger of dying out. There are six topics that always guarantee sales:

1 Scandal – more than any other topic, it's scandal that fuels **tabloid** sales. The public loves glimpses into the lives of the rich, famous and powerful.

2 Money – everyone wants more, and some people will stop at nothing to get it. Many tabloids have a **columnist** dedicated to writing **features** about money.

3 Babies – whether it's because they were born in a taxi or can speak two languages from birth. It seems we can't get enough of them.

4 Animals – flip through any tabloid and you'll find a heart-warming story about a brave dog, or a cat that's befriended a mouse.

5 Royalty – hardly a day goes by that a 'royal' doesn't make an appearance somewhere in the tabloids.

6 Winners – from lottery winners to Olympic gold medallists, a winner on the front cover guarantees a high **readership**.

Bold headlines, appealing photos, low prices and colour **supplements** also make tabloids the perfect bait for a commuter seeking some escape from real life. The tabloids aren't afraid to be **biased** and show their opinion, most strikingly in the **editorial page**, which tends to be direct and aggressive in stating the editors' position on major issues. The public want excitement and **sensationalism**, and tabloids deliver.

B Read the article again. Which types of stories would you read?

2A Match meanings 1–10 with the words in bold in the article.

1 the section of the newspaper that gives the paper's opinion *editorial page*

2 special reports or articles about a topic

3 the (number of) people who read a newspaper

4 someone who regularly writes a section of a newspaper, under the same title or topic

5 an extra section of a newspaper which can be pulled out, often a magazine

6 a serious newspaper, usually printed on large sheets of paper

7 giving a single point of view, unfairly

8 reporting news to make it sound as exciting as possible

9 the number of newspapers sold in a day or week

10 a popular newspaper, half the size of a standard newspaper, with few serious stories

B Work in pairs and discuss the questions.

1 Which paper in your country is the most sensationalist/biased?

2 Which sections do you read: the main news story, foreign news, sports coverage, features, the editorial, magazines or colour supplements?

▥▶ page 154 **VOCABULARY**BANK

A **Scientists Find Life On Moon**

B **Pop Star Love Triangle**

C **Prince Protests Parking Penalty**

FUNCTION | adding emphasis

3A Work in pairs and look at tabloid headlines A–F above. What do you think the stories are about?

B ▶ 7.3 Listen to the conversations. Which headlines do they talk about?

C Listen again. What is surprising in each story?

4A Work in pairs. Underline the phrases that the speakers use to add emphasis.

1 <u>The amazing thing is</u> the two winners are from the same town

2 That's absolutely incredible!

3 Yeah, it's such an amazing coincidence.

4 There's no way I would have guessed that.

5 I suppose it does look like bacteria now I come to think about it.

6 That *is* incredible.

7 Why on earth would they do that?

8 He's the one who's always talking about reducing car use.

9 That's so hypocritical.

10 Sometimes he can be such an idiot

B ▶ 7.4 Work in pairs and mark the main stresses in the sentences in Exercise 4A. Listen and check. Then listen and repeat.

▥▶ page 140 **LANGUAGE**BANK

D

NEWBORN FOUND IN RUBBISH BIN

E

EUROMILLION WINNERS

F

LIONS SAVE GIRL, 12

5A Rewrite the sentences to add emphasis using the words in brackets.

Conversation 1

A: I'm ⟨so⟩ angry with you. Why didn't you tell me about the party? (so)

B: But I told you. A few minutes ago. (did)

A: That's helpful! How am I supposed to get ready in time? (really)

B: But you said you never want to go to parties. (one)

Conversation 2

A: Dave was good-looking but she was crazy about Will. (absolutely)

B: It's sad. Dave adores her. (the sad thing)

A: Yeah, and he's really kind; a nice man. (such)

B: What shall I say if he asks me about Will? (earth)

Conversation 3

A: I'm quitting my job. It's a bore. (such)

B: I think you'll regret it. (do)

A: You always say I should do what I want (one)

B: But you shouldn't just quit. (way)

B Work in pairs and add two more sentences to each conversation. Add emphasis to one of your sentences in each conversation.

C Cover and practise the conversations.

LEARN TO make guesses

6A Work in pairs and try to complete the sentences. Then check your ideas in the audio script on page 171.

That ¹_____ _____ one of the biggest prizes ever.

It's ²_____ to say, but I ³_____ it's some sort of painting

It ⁴_____ be a computer image.

I ⁵_____ it does ⁶_____ like bacteria now I come to think about it.

⁷_____ they heard her crying.

B Which words in 1–7 above could be replaced with words in the box?

hard   seem   perhaps   think   might   's surely   reckon   imagine

🗣 speakout TIP

We often use *'d* (would) + verb to sound less sure or less direct when guessing, making a suggestion or giving an opinion. Which category are the following sentences: *I'd recommend the red wine; I'd agree that it's technically possible; I'd imagine she's married?*

7A ▶ 7.5 Listen to the sound. What do you think it is? Write down two ideas.

B Use the prompts to discuss the sound.

A: What / you / think / it / be?

B: hard / say / but / I / imagine / it / be (your first idea)

A: I / think / sound / like (your first idea)

B: suppose / could / be (another idea)

A: Or / might / be (another idea)

B: Well / reckon / it / be (final decision)

C ▶ 7.6 Listen to five more sounds. Practise the conversation after each one.

SPEAKING

8A Work in pairs and look at the categories. What do you think the top five are for each category?

The top five ...

* most dangerous animals (page 161)
* countries with the tallest people (page 158)
* cities for art lovers (page 159)
* friendliest countries (page 162)

A: I'd imagine the most dangerous animal is a lion. What do you think?

B: I'm not sure. I suppose it could be but ...

B Work in groups and take turns. Student A: choose a category and look at the answers. Ask the other students to guess, then give them the correct answers. The other students: guess, then react to the correct answers using the phrases in Exercise 4A to help you.

A: OK, what do you think the top one is?

B: We think tigers.

A: No, they're not on the list. The top one is _____.

C: I can't believe that! Why on earth would _____ be considered dangerous?

DVD PREVIEW

1A Work in pairs and discuss the questions.

1 Do you watch the news? How would you describe the newscasters: serious or funny?

2 Why do you think TV viewers enjoy seeing newscasters and reporters making mistakes?

B Look at the programme information and match the underlined words/phrases with 1–8 below.

1 hesitate or make mistakes when you are speaking
   stumble over your words

2 happen suddenly and cause damage

3 a small problem with a machine

4 continuous

5 a machine that shows the words the TV presenter has to say

6 a mistake

7 go wrong (for a machine)

BBC
The Funny Side of the News

The Funny Side of … is a BBC series that looks at all the things that can go wrong on TV, from talent shows to wildlife programmes. Tonight it takes a look at TV news. As serious as news can be, mistakes and <u>blunders</u> are unavoidable. And with the introduction of 24-hour <u>rolling</u> news, mistakes have become more frequent and more visible with newsreaders <u>stumbling over their words</u> and endless <u>technical hiccups</u>. From the <u>autocue</u> <u>malfunctioning</u> to the wrong guest being brought into the studio for an interview, disaster is waiting to <u>strike</u> at any moment.

▶ DVD VIEW

2A Watch the DVD and make notes on which blunder:

• you found the funniest.

• you didn't find funny or didn't understand.

B Watch the DVD again. Number the blunders in the order they appear in the programme. Some have more than one example.

Malfunctioning equipment /

People stumbling over their words

The wrong guest in an interview

An accident on a live programme

C Complete extracts 1–5 from the DVD. Then listen again and check.

1 It's one of the few things on television these days that really is live. So if it starts going _____, you're going to see it.

2 The _____ about rolling news _____ that you have to fill an awful lot of time …

3 I'm afraid we obviously have the wrong guest here. That's deeply _____ for us.

4 But the undisputed _____ of the wrong guest division is the BBC news 24 incident _____ the charming but inappropriate Guy Goma.

5 It goes to _____ just how much the public love a good news blunder.

D Work in pairs and discuss. Which incident do you think was the most embarrassing for the newsreader?

speakout a news story

3A ▶ **7.7** Listen to someone retelling a news story about a man who swapped a paper clip for a house. Number the things he traded in order.

a paper clip   *I*   an empty house

a snow globe   a door knob

a pen shaped like a fish   a part in a film

B Listen again and tick the phrases you hear.

> ### keyphrases
>
> Did you [hear the story/see the news] about … ?
>
> I [heard this story/read this article] about …
>
> Apparently what happened was …
>
> According to [the report/the guy on the news] … ?
>
> The [weird/strange/interesting thing] was …
>
> I don't remember all the details, but …

C Think about a recent news story. Make notes and think about which key phrases you can use.

D Work in groups and tell each other your stories. Ask follow-up questions and take notes.

writeback a newspaper article

4A Read the article and write down the two things that the man traded that are mentioned in the article, but not in the recording.

MAN TRADES PAPER CLIP FOR HOUSE

A Canadian man has made internet headlines by trading a paper clip for a house. Blogger Kyle Macdonald became bored with his work one day and had the idea of swapping a red paper clip on his desk for a house.

His first trades were for very small objects – a pen, a door knob, later a neon sign – but step by step the 26-year-old built up to items of larger and larger value. His big breakthrough came when he swapped an afternoon with rock icon Alice Cooper for a snow globe. People who were following his trades thought he had made a big mistake by giving away something of such great value for a less desirable article, but as it turned out, a film director who collected snow globes wanted this one so much that he offered the Canadian a part in a film.

This swap gave the enterprising trader the opportunity he needed for the final trade when a mayor of a small town offered him an empty house in exchange for the film part. The whole process took one year and fourteen trades.

B Read the article again and do the tasks.

1 Underline three different words (synonyms) for *thing(s)*.

2 Circle five different ways to refer to the man in the story apart from *he* or *his*.

C Write an article (150–200 words) about one of the stories your group told in Exercise 3D. You may need to invent some details.

TELEVISION

1A Find fourteen kinds of TV programme in the wordsnake.

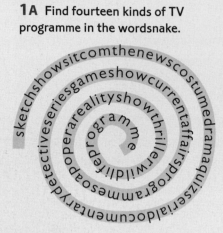

sketchshowsitcomthenewscostumedrama
series gameshowcurrentaffairsquiz
reality show thriller wildlife programme
detective soap opera
documentary serial

B Work in pairs. Which type of programme would you choose if you wanted to:

* laugh?
* learn something?
* just relax and watch real people?
* catch up on the news?
* test your knowledge?

QUANTIFIERS

2A Work in pairs and underline the correct alternative. The sentences are about two people.

1 *Both/Few* of us enjoy airports.
2 *None/Neither* of us plays a musical instrument.
3 We remember *a large amount of/ quite a few of* our dreams.
4 Both of us take *a few/a little* sugar in our coffee.
5 We both got *hardly any/very few* sleep last night.
6 *Neither/Both* of us is allergic to anything.
7 We like *all/every* type of music.
8 *Each/Both* of us has a pet.
9 We spend *several/a great deal of* hours in the gym every week.
10 We both like having *few/a few* minutes' sleep in the afternoon.

B Which sentences are true for you and your partner? Change any that are not true.

A: Do you enjoy airports?
B: No.
A: Me neither. OK, so neither of us enjoys airports.

REPORTED SPEECH

3A Rewrite the sentences in reported speech.

1 Last week, an interviewer asked me, 'What's your biggest weakness?'
2 The other day, a complete stranger walked up to me and asked, 'What have you been doing lately?'
3 Once, I was trying on trousers and the shop assistant asked, 'Would you like to try a bigger size?'
4 Every day, my flatmate says, 'Could you do the dishes?' and then says, 'I'll do them next time.'
5 At the end of a first date, the girl asked me, 'So when do you want to get married?'
6 At 3a.m., my phone rang, and the person asked, 'Are you sleeping?'

B Which question would make you feel most uncomfortable?

REPORTING VERBS

4A Complete the questions with the correct form of a verb in the box. Add any necessary words.

| help   go   quit   lend   make |
| do   pay x2   be x2 |

1 When was the last time you offered _to help_ someone?
2 Do you find it easy to admit _____ a mistake?
3 Would you ever agree _____ a friend money?
4 If someone was visiting your town, where would you suggest _____?
5 Have you ever refused _____ a bill?
6 Would you always apologise _____ late?
7 Have you ever threatened _____ your job?
8 Should a man insist _____ when he invites a woman out for a meal?
9 Have you ever been accused _____ too serious?
10 Do you often promise _____ something and then simply forget?

B Work in pairs and discuss the questions above.

ADDING EMPHASIS

5A Find and correct the mistakes. There is one extra word in each sentence.

1 My hometown is such a so boring place.
2 I so do think that some people are very generous.
3 It's completely very ridiculous that people have such short holidays.
4 Why on the earth am I learning English?
5 There's no the way that I would ever borrow money from a friend.
6 My teacher was the one who she had the most influence on me when I was young.

B Work in pairs and take it in turns. Student A: read one of your sentences. Student B: continue the conversation using some of these follow-up questions:

> How do you mean?

> In what way?

> Why (not)?

> For example?

> What makes you say that?

BBC VIDEO PODCAST

Download the podcast to view people discussing the question:

What kind of news stories interest you?

Authentic BBC interviews

www.pearsonlongman.com/speakout

UNIT 8

SPEAKING
> Talk about behaviour
> Talk about using time
> Deal with awkward situations
> Describe a family ritual

LISTENING
> Listen to a BBC programme about people's daily rhythms
> Watch a BBC documentary about body language

READING
> Read three articles about life-changing decisions
> Read about saving time

WRITING
> Write an informal article
> Write about a ritual

BBC CONTENT
> Video podcast: What kind of behaviour gets on your nerves?
> DVD: The Human Animal

UNIT
8

behaviour

> **It's a tough call** p92

> **Body clock** p95

> **Have you got a minute?** p98

> **The Human Animal** p100

READING

1A Match photos A–C to the headlines.

B Look at the photos and read the headlines. What do you think happened in each situation? Write two sentences about each one.

C Read the articles and check your ideas.

Hiker risks life

Chamonix, France – A hiker who risked his own life to save the lives of two stranded hikers says he would do the same thing again.

Akira Sakamoto was among a number of hikers caught in the snowstorm on Mont Blanc late on Sunday afternoon, and was in the middle of his descent when he came upon two fellow hikers. Tamas Konig and Sandor Petres had stopped their own descent, too exhausted to continue, and had built a make-shift shelter in the snow to try to survive the night.

Sakamoto had two choices – to carry on and send up a rescue party from the bottom, or to stay and help them even though this could mean he put his own life in serious danger. 'It was obvious that they couldn't survive the night,' said Sakamoto. 'And I wasn't sure I could get a rescue party in time. So I stayed with them.'

Sakamoto used a rain poncho to protect the three of them from moisture, and made them huddle together to minimise the loss of body heat. The three shared Sakamoto's remaining food.

'In doing so, Akira probably saved their lives,' a park spokesman said on Thursday. 'If he had left them there, they wouldn't be alive now.'

The three were evacuated by helicopter in the morning and treated for hypothermia at a local hospital before being discharged.

Mother turns son in to police

Wellington, New Zealand – Sandra Matthews called it the toughest day of her life, but she felt she had no choice after seeing the CCTV footage on the TV news showing her son robbing a local shop.

'I wanted to talk to Simon first before I contacted the police, but I couldn't get in touch with him,' said Ms Matthews. 'So I just walked into the police station and turned him in.'

The heartbroken mother told police that it was her son Simon, 21, who security cameras showed pointing a gun at the manager of the shop and stuffing cash into a bag. It was the second of two robberies there this month. Police found Matthews hiding at a friend's house later that day and arrested him.

Ms Matthews also apologised to shop manager Carl Ruiz. 'I just felt so bad. It must have been a real shock for him,' she said.

'He's my son, and I love him, but I didn't see any other option except to turn him in,' Sandra said. 'I couldn't call myself a good mother if I hadn't.'

'I admire her,' a family friend said. 'If I were in the same situation, I'd find it difficult to turn my son in.'

Couple ordered to return cash

Birmingham, UK – A couple who found a winning lottery ticket and cashed it in were ordered to pay back the money.

Dorothy Millet, 59, bought the Euromillions ticket at a local shop on 31 May, and dropped it later that day in the post office. Alan and Megan Beecham found the ticket and cashed it in at the same post office. They immediately spent half of the €50,000 prize money on a new car and other luxuries.

'When Alan showed me the ticket, we talked about what to do,' said Megan. 'It wasn't an easy decision, but we felt as if we had found the money and it was ours.'

'Maybe it wasn't the best decision,' Alan added. 'But the temptation was too great.'

'If I'd been paying attention, I wouldn't have dropped the ticket,' said Millet. 'It's just part of my routine so I didn't pay attention to where I put it.'

The lottery company used computer records to find out that the ticket had been cashed in at their main office. Millet used the receipt to prove that she had purchased the winning ticket.

'If she hadn't saved the receipt, we might never have recovered her money,' a spokesman for the lottery company said.

2 Match statements 1–8 with the people mentioned in the articles.

1 His mouth was covered but I recognised him from his eyes.

2 I just thought we were lucky, that's all. I didn't think it was illegal.

3 We had no idea the weather could change like that.

4 It's happened to us before – the last time was just a few days ago.

5 I was so angry at myself that I couldn't sleep all night.

6 That's why we always tell people to keep the receipt in a separate place.

7 I didn't really think seriously about leaving them there.

8 She shouldn't have done it.

3 Work in pairs and discuss. Who had the most difficult decision: Sakamoto, Sandra Matthews or the Beecham couple? Do you think you would have behaved in the same way?

GRAMMAR conditionals

4A Look at the sentences and underline all the verbs.

1 If I were in the same situation, I'd find it difficult to turn my son in.

2 If she hadn't saved the receipt, we might never have recovered her money.

3 If I'd been paying attention, I wouldn't have dropped the ticket.

4 If he had left them there, they wouldn't be alive now.

B Work in pairs and answer the questions about sentences 1–4 above.

1 Do they refer to real or imaginary situations?

2 Does each sentence refer to the past, to the present/future or to both?

C Complete the rules with the words in the box.

> modal (would, might) (x2)   past perfect   have   infinitive
> past simple   past participle   past perfect continuous

Rules:

1 In the *if* clause:
• use the _____ to talk about the present or future.
• use the _____ or the _____ to talk about the past.

2 In the main clause:
• use _____ + _____ to talk about the present or future.
• use _____ + _____ + _____ to talk about the past.

5 ▶ 8.1 Listen and match the words in bold in sentences 1–4 with the weak forms a)–d). Then listen again and repeat.

1 I **would have** done the same.   a) /maɪtəv/

2 I **might have** behaved differently.   b) /kʊdəntəv/

3 I **wouldn't have** been so brave.   c) /wʊdəntəv/

4 I **couldn't have** done what he did.   d) /wʊdəv/

▶ page 142 **LANGUAGEBANK**

PRACTICE

6A Complete the email with the correct form of the verbs in brackets.

To:	Shaun

Dear Shaun,

I haven't heard from you since I lost my job. I've tried to phone you but you don't answer and my emails keep getting returned. Everybody believes I was the one stealing laptops. Now I think I made a big mistake.

If I ¹_____ (not work) late that evening, I ²_____ (not see) you stealing the laptops. I ³_____ (might speak) to you first if the boss ⁴_____ (not ask) me about it early the next morning. I ⁵_____ (tell) him it was you if you ⁶_____ (not be) such a close friend. Unfortunately, the boss knew I was hiding something and sacked me. If I ⁷_____ (be) a better liar I ⁸_____ (might not lose) my job. I have one question for you: if you ⁹_____ (know) that I was going to get fired, ¹⁰_____ (you tell) the truth – that you were the thief?

Nick

B Work in pairs and compare answers. What would you have done in Nick's situation?

VOCABULARY collocations

7A For each word web cross out the verb that does NOT collocate with the noun.

postpone
put off   do
a decision
come to   arrive at

go against
stick to   betray
one's principles
follow   make

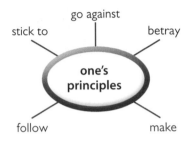

analyse
compare   weigh up
the pros and cons
decide   examine

analyse
argue   weigh up
a situation
assess   examine

B Complete the definitions using appropriate verbs from the word webs in Exercise 7A.

1 If you _____ or _____ a decision, you choose to do one thing or another.

2 If you _____ or _____ a decision, you delay, perhaps because you're not sure what to do.

3 If you _____ or _____ your principles, you are faithful to what you believe is right.

4 If you _____ or _____ your principles, you do something that you don't believe is right.

5 If you _____, _____, _____ or _____ the pros and cons, you think about the relative importance of the advantages and disadvantages of a situation.

6 If you _____ or _____ a situation, you look at it in detail.

7 If you _____ or _____ a situation, you judge the overall situation.

8A Read the extracts from a web forum below. Complete the texts with verbs from Exercise 7A. More than one answer is possible.

> I was buying some food at the local supermarket. It came to $9.50 so I gave the cashier $20 but she gave me $100.50 in change. Obviously she thought she had given me a $10 note. I ¹_____ the situation – I needed money badly, it was her mistake. Should I ²_____ my principles and keep the money even though I knew she would have to pay the missing cash back herself? In the end, I ³_____ a decision …

> It was the final school exams – really important for my future. I had studied hard all year and felt well prepared. Then, the night before the exam, one of my classmates sent me an email with the answers to the exam in an attachment. I'm a good student and I don't cheat. But this was an important exam. I ⁴_____ the pros and cons: open the attachment and guarantee a good result or ⁵_____ my principles and do the exam without cheating. I ⁶_____ the decision by going to bed early. In the morning, it was clear to me what to do …

B Work in pairs and discuss. What would you have done in each situation?

SPEAKING

9A Think of some real-life situations where it was difficult for you or someone you know to decide how to react, e.g. a job you were offered and took/didn't take.

B Work in pairs and take turns. Ask and answer questions 1–6 about each situation.

1 Where did it happen?

2 What happened leading up to the situation?

3 How did you/he/she feel?

4 What did you/he/she do?

5 What else could you/he/she have done?

6 Do you/Does he/she regret the action now or would you/he/she do the same again?

C Work in groups and take turns. Student A: describe one of the situations and what happened. The other students: say whether you would have done the same.

▶ **GRAMMAR** | – *ing* form & infinitive (I)   ▶ **VOCABULARY** | feelings (2)   ▶ **HOW TO** | talk about attitudes to time

VOCABULARY feelings

1A Work in pairs and discuss. Are you a morning person or an evening person?

B Read the quiz and find words/phrases in bold in the quiz that mean:

1 clear-headed and focused (x3)   *alert*
2 the opposite of fast asleep
3 tired or not having much energy (x2)
4 feel anxious or fearful
5 full of energy (x2)
6 hate deeply
7 don't mind
8 what you might do when afraid, disgusted or embarrassed

C Work in pairs and do the quiz.

2A Choose six of the words/phrases in bold and write a sentence that either a *lark* or an *owl* might say.

B Work in pairs and take turns. Student A: read out one of your sentences. Student B: guess whether a *lark* or an *owl* would say it.

A: I cringe when the alarm clock goes off.

B: Owl!

▶▶▶ page 155 **VOCABULARY**BANK

LISTENING

3 What do you think people might say about why they like or dislike being a *lark* or an *owl*? Work in pairs and write two ideas for each.

4A ▶ 8.2 Listen to the BBC radio programme. Were any of your ideas mentioned?

B Who made statements 1–8? Write lark (L) or owl (O). Then listen again and check.

1 It is just so peaceful and so beautiful.
2 I stay there until the absolute last second.
3 I do look at other people walking their dogs, or walking along with a bounce in their step and I just think, 'Where does it come from?'
4 You've wasted the best part of the day.
5 It's just quite a nice feeling of being awake and nobody else is there.
6 That's when I'm really thinking straight.
7 Anybody mentions 'party' to me and I cringe.
8 David and I always joked before we had children that it would be great because he would be great in the morning and I would be great in the evenings.

C Work in pairs. Which of the speakers in the programme did you agree with the most?

Are you a lark or owl?

Answer the questions and find out which kind of person you really are.

1 You have to get up at six o'clock in the morning to catch a flight. You get out of bed feeling …
   a) **bright and breezy**.
   b) **groggy**.
   c) exhausted.

2 What time of day are you **at your sharpest**?
   a) 10a.m.
   b) 1p.m.
   c) 10p.m.

3 When do you feel **at your lowest ebb**?
   a) Monday morning
   b) Friday evening
   c) Sunday night

4 You're on your way to an all-night party. You …
   a) **have a sense of dread**.
   b) hope it'll be fun.
   c) **have a spring or a bounce in your step**.

5 Your alarm clock has just gone off! You …
   a) love it and are **wide awake** straightaway.
   b) are**n't that fussed**.
   c) **despise it with a passion** – you usually turn over and go back to sleep.

key

Mostly As: Good morning! You're clearly a lark, a person who is most efficient and **alert** in the morning. The downside is that you wilt like an unwatered flower by early evening and **cringe** at the thought of going out after nine.

Mostly Bs: Hi there! Getting up early might not be your favourite thing in the world, but you do it if you have to and you can't imagine why some people make such a fuss about it. You're not fond of staying up late but feel your routine is normal and wonder why everyone can't be like you.

Mostly Cs: Good evening! You're a real night owl and you're not really **on the ball** until it starts to get dark – that's when you come alive and you feel most energetic. Your ideal schedule would be sleeping in until noon and doing all your work and socialising after dinner.

GRAMMAR -ing form and infinitive

5A Check what you know. Cross out the incorrect forms in the sentences.

1 Would you rather ~~being/to be~~/be up for the sunrise every morning?
2 Does it take an army of alarm clocks to make you *waking/to wake/wake* up before 9a.m.?
3 I'm an owl, coming to life late in the evening and capable of *dancing/to dance/dance* till dawn.
4 I despise *getting up/to get up/get up* with a passion.
5 Should I just *eating/to eat/eat* more vegetables …?
6 … or should I get up earlier *being/to be/be* more awake?
7 Late evening is best for me *being/to be/be* focusing rather than partying.
8 *Being/To be/Be* a late riser can cause problems.
9 Do you tend *sleeping/to sleep/sleep* late?
10 Perhaps this will let larks *understanding/to understand/understand* why owls are the way they are, and vice-versa?

B Work in pairs. Look at sentences 1–10 above and complete the table.

	-ing form, infinitive or infinitive with *to*	example sentence
after a preposition	-ing	3
to express purpose		
after *let someone* or *make someone*		
as part of a semi-fixed phrase, e.g. *it's good/better/best* and *it's the best time*		
as a subject or object (or part of one of these)		
after modal verbs		
after certain verbs e.g. *enjoy, not mind, despise, avoid, keep, consider, imagine, end up*		
after certain verbs e.g. *want, would like, tend, prepare*		
after *had better* and *would rather*		

C ▶ 8.3 Work in pairs. Complete the sentences with the correct form of the modal verbs in brackets. Then listen and check.

1 I don't want _to have to_ tell you again. (must)
2 I hate _____ get up in winter. (must)
3 I don't seem _____ start the computer. (can)
4 I enjoy _____ watch the sunrise. (can)

6 Listen again and mark the stressed words and weak forms in the verb phrases. Then listen and repeat.

1 <u>don't</u> want to have to <u>tell</u> you <u>again</u>.
        /tə/   /tə/

➡ page 142 **LANGUAGEBANK**

PRACTICE

7A Complete the questions and answers to the Time Doctor, using the correct form of the verbs in brackets.

Ask the Time Doctor

Q: What is the best time of day ¹_____ (do) exercise?

A: Late afternoon or early evening is good for ²_____ (undertake) sport or other physical activity. Avoid ³_____ (exercise) too early in the day when your muscles aren't properly warmed up as you're more likely to hurt yourself.

Q: Does ⁴_____ (eat) a big lunch make you ⁵_____ (feel) tired?

A: Yes, but not because of ⁶_____ (digest) food. It's because your body temperature tends ⁷_____ (dip) in the early afternoon and this makes you feel sleepy. If your boss doesn't mind you ⁸_____ (put) your head down for twenty minutes after lunch, it can really raise your energy levels.

Q: My teenage son would rather ⁹_____ (do) all his homework late at night. Isn't that the worst time?

A: If ¹⁰_____ (can remember) things long-term is his aim, then, in fact, late evening is the best time, so ¹¹_____ (study) then is a good idea. Still, if he's preparing ¹²_____ (take) an exam, he might consider ¹³_____ (get) up early ¹⁴_____ (study) for it, as short-term memory and immediate recall are strongest then.

B Work in pairs and discuss. Did anything in the Time Doctor's answers surprise you?

SPEAKING

8A ▶ 8.4 Listen to people talking about their attitudes to time. Which opinions do you agree with (✓)?

Speaker 1 _____   Speaker 4 _____
Speaker 2 _____   Speaker 5 _____
Speaker 3 _____   Speaker 6 _____

B Work in groups and discuss: What differences are there in your attitudes? Which differences are personal and which are cultural?

VOCABULARY PLUS idioms

9A Look at the extracts from the *Longman Active Study Dictionary*. What information is given?

> **time** **for the time being** for a short period of time, but not permanently: *You can stay here for the time being.*

> **kill** **kill time/an hour etc** *informal* to spend time doing something that is not important while you are waiting for something else to happen

❝ speakout TIP

In the *Longman Active Study Dictionary*, idioms are shown in bold and are organised under the first or second key word in the idiom. How does your dictionary show the two idioms above?

B Work in pairs. Look at the phrases/idioms and underline the word you would look up in a dictionary.

1 We were **pressed for time**.

2 We had to **cut it short**.

3 He's **biding his time**.

4 She arrived **in the nick of time**.

5 It happens **once in a blue moon**.

6 I've tried **time after time**.

7 We had to **make up for lost time**.

8 They're **dragging their feet** on a decision.

C Work in pairs. Student A: turn to page 161. Student B: turn to page 158.

D Work in pairs and take turns. Ask your partner to guess the meaning of your phrase/idiom. Then explain it.

10 Work in pairs. What would you say in these situations? Use the words in brackets.

1 You need to stop a conversation. (cut)

   Sorry, I'll have to cut this short.

2 Your friend is taking too long to decide which job to take. (drag)

3 You're telling a police officer why you were speeding. (make up for)

4 You've told your PA many times to check her spelling and she still hasn't. (after)

5 You're telling someone why you can't talk to them now. (pressed)

6 You're telling a doctor how rarely you fall ill. (once)

7 You're expressing relief at just catching the train. (nick)

8 You're telling someone why you're delaying a decision. (bide)

⫸ page 155 VOCABULARYBANK

WRITING an informal article

11A Read the article and choose the best title.

a) Time is money   b) Pressed for time?   c) Killing time

Have you ever felt you don't have enough hours in the day? Or that you'd give anything for a whole day to catch up with yourself? Well here are some ideas that work for me.

First of all, make a to-do list every day and prioritise ruthlessly. The trick here isn't making the list; that's the easy part. No, the trick is prioritising. I look at my list and put a star next to anything that's really urgent. Then I put '2' next to anything that will just take a couple of minutes. I actually do these quick tasks before I get on with the urgent ones; it's a bit like clearing off the top of your desk before sitting down to write that important letter.

Second, know which is the most productive time of day for you and do your work or study then. One of the shocking discoveries I made about myself is that if I get up at 5a.m, I can do a day's work and even fit breakfast in before 9.30. Of course, if you're an early bird it can be difficult to accomplish tasks that involve phoning 'night owls', but that's what email's for!

Finally, don't let your inbox run your life. I just realised recently how frequently I interrupt my real work to check my inbox and respond to the most trivial of emails. So now I only open it when absolutely necessary and this saves me hours. If your work depends on you being constantly accessible by email, then you can't do this; but be honest and ask yourself, 'Am I an email addict?'

With these simple, practical techniques, you'll become more effective, less stressed and be able to win some 'me-time' for yourself.

B Underline the correct alternative and give a reason.

1 The article is probably for a *student magazine/serious newspaper*.

2 The aim of the article is to *describe/give advice*.

3 The topic sentence is at the *beginning/end* of the three main paragraphs.

LEARN TO use an informal style in articles

12A Work in pairs and read the guidelines. Are they true (T) or false (F)? Find examples in the article.

In an informal article you should:

1 give personal examples

2 use the pronouns *I* and *you*

3 avoid contracted forms

4 use conversational language

5 use linkers to help structure the article

6 use questions to the reader

7 avoid multi-word verbs

8 use the passive where possible

B Work in pairs and brainstorm a list of main ideas for an article about:

• the perfect study plan

• what to do when you're bored

• tips on how to waste time

C Choose the best three ideas and discuss ideas for opening/closing paragraphs. Then write the article (250–300 words).

VOCABULARY manner

1A Look at the pairs of adjectives. Are they similar (S) or different (D) in meaning? Use a dictionary to check.

1 supportive – unhelpful
2 diplomatic – tactful
3 sensitive – sensible
4 confrontational – collaborative
5 aggressive – assertive
6 direct – focused

B Work in pairs. Which adjectives above describe your manner when:

• you break bad news to someone?
• a friend is down or in trouble?
• making a complaint?
• you work on a project with someone?
• you are driving or cycling?
• trying to sort out a problem between two friends?

I think I'm tactful but also quite direct if I have to break bad news to someone.

C Which adjectives in Exercise 1A become opposites by adding/removing a prefix/suffix?

supportive   unsupportive

SPEAKING

2A Work in pairs. Look at situations 1–3 and photos A–C. What would be the best way to handle each situation? How might the person react?

1 A flatmate of yours keeps borrowing money and never pays you back.
2 You're the manager of an elegant restaurant and a waitress has come in with blue hair.
3 Your colleague has loud, personnal conversations on the phone when you're trying to work.

B Work in pairs. Read the tips and discuss: Which do you agree/disagree with? Would you add anything to the list?

Tips for talking things through

Sometimes we have to raise topics with a friend, colleague or even our boss which we find embarrassing or awkward. Following these five tips will help smooth the process and minimise hurt feelings.

» 1 Say clearly why you want to talk to them at the start and stay focused.
» 2 Give the message clearly. Be specific.
» 3 Don't tell them what other people say or think.
» 4 Get their point of view. Give them space to say what they think and feel.
» 5 Suggest a solution (if they don't).

A

FUNCTION handling an awkward situation

3A ▶ 8.5 Listen to the conversation. Tick the tips in Exercise 2B that the man follows.

B Listen again. Are the statements true (T) or false (F)? Correct the false statements.

1 Liz owes Jim a small amount of money.
2 She wants to pay him back immediately.
3 She doesn't always keep her promises.
4 Jim wants her to pay a set amount of money each week.

4A Complete phrases 1–5. Then look at the audio script on page 172 and check.

Preparing the ground

There's something I've been [1]_____ to talk to you about.

Giving the message

It's [2]_____ that …

I hope you don't [3]_____ this the wrong way, but …

I don't want you to get the wrong idea, but …

Getting the other person's point of view

Do you know [4]_____ I mean?

Do you see where I'm coming from?

How does that [5]_____?

B ▶ 8.6 Listen and underline the stresses in the phrases. Does the voice rise or fall at the end of each phrase? Why?

1 There's something I've been meaning to talk to you about.
2 I hope you don't take this the wrong way, but …
3 I don't want you to get the wrong idea, but …

C Listen again and repeat.

➡ page 142 **LANGUAGEBANK**

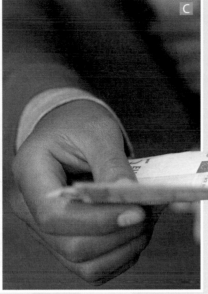

LEARN TO soften a message

6 ▶ **8.7 Listen to the sentences and add the extra words or sounds you hear.**

1 It's not that. I hope you don't take this the wrong way, but it's just that this isn't the first time I've lent you money and you haven't paid it back. I know it's not a lot, just small amounts each time but it adds up quickly. I dunno. Do you know what I mean?

2 Actually, you've said that once before. I don't want you to get the wrong idea, but it never happened. And it makes things awkward. It makes me feel annoyed. Do you see where I'm coming from?

🗣 speakout TIP

Fillers can help you sound less confrontational and allow thinking time. Some fillers (e.g. *um, er, well, you know, I mean, kind of*), are used anywhere you would pause. Modifiers (e.g. (*just*) *a bit, slightly, quite*) often come before an adjective and soften even a very strong message (e.g. *I'm just a bit concerned = I'm VERY concerned*).

SPEAKING

7A Work in pairs. For each situation below, write the first two sentences of the conversation.

1 You've been driving your colleague to work for over a month. He/She has never offered you money for petrol.

2 Your neighbour leaves bags of rubbish in the hall for days. He/She eventually takes them out but there's always a bad smell in the hall as a result.

3 Your friend has long conversations on her mobile when you're out together.

4 A friend often gives you a lift on their motorbike but you think their driving is scary.

B Role-play one of the situations.

C Work with another student and role-play a different situation.

5A Use the prompts to complete the conversation.

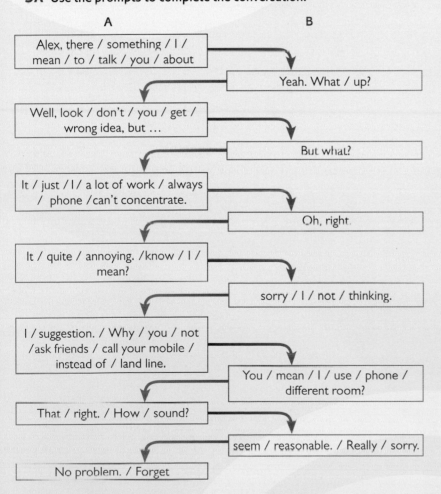

A	B
Alex, there / something / I / mean / to / talk / you / about
	Yeah. What / up?
Well, look / don't / you / get / wrong idea, but …
	But what?
It / just / I / a lot of work / always / phone / can't concentrate.
	Oh, right.
It / quite / annoying. / know / I / mean?
	sorry / I / not / thinking.
I / suggestion. / Why / you / not / ask friends / call your mobile / instead of / land line.
	You / mean / I / use / phone / different room?
That / right. / How / sound?
	seem / reasonable. / Really / sorry.
No problem. / Forget

B Work in pairs and take turns. Role-play the conversation. Use the flowchart to help.

A   B   C

DVD PREVIEW

1A Work in pairs. For each photo A–C discuss the questions.

1   What kind of ritual can you see in each photo?

2   How well do you think the people know each other?

3   Do you do anything similar in your country?

B Read the programme information. Which of the photos could appear in this particular programme?

BBC

The Human Animal

Desmond Morris is widely known for his study of human behaviour, customs and rituals and his writings on the area, such as *The Naked Ape, Manwatching* and *Christmas Watching*. Originally a zoologist, Morris decided to observe and classify human behaviour in much the same way as he would observe animals – in his words 'to do for actions what dictionary makers had done for words.' In this programme in the series, Morris focuses on customs connected with greeting and on the meaning of different gestures.

▶ DVD VIEW

2A Before watching, discuss:

1   How many different ways of shaking hands do you know?

2   How do you express 'You're crazy' with your hands?

B Watch the DVD. Complete each sentence with a number.

Morris talks about:

1 _____ different handshakes.

2 _____ different ways to express 'You're crazy'.

C Watch the DVD again and answer the questions.

1   Why does Morris call himself a 'man watcher'?

2   How long did it take him to complete his classification of human body language?

3   Why do Kurdish farmers in Turkey shake hands for so long? When can they stop?

4   What does Morris say the purpose of handshaking is?

5   What are the different ways of saying 'You're crazy'?

D Work in pairs and discuss. Are there any gestures which would be important for a visitor to your country to know about?

speakout a ritual

3A Read the dictionary extract. Can you think of an example of a personal ritual?

> **ritual** /ˈrɪtʃuəl/ *n* [C] a set of actions that is always done in exactly the same way.

B Work in pairs and discuss the questions.

1 Do you have any customs or rituals that are particular to your family or that are typical in your culture? Think about: holidays, birthdays, particular days of the week, food and drink.

2 Do you know how the ritual developed?

3 How do you feel about it?

C ▶ 8.8 Listen to someone talking about a ritual. What is it and how did it start?

D Listen again and tick the key phrases that you hear.

> ### keyphrases
>
> I don't know how it started
>
> Whenever [we get together/the first grapes are picked/we give a gift]
>
> This involves [giving presents/coming down for breakfast]
>
> All the presents are [laid out... /exchanged...]
>
> It was just something that we invented for [the children/each other]
>
> It's come down from [my side of the family/hundreds of years ago]

4A Prepare to talk about one of the family or cultural rituals that you discussed in 3A. Make notes about:

- what exactly happens
- how it started
- why it's important to your family/culture.

B Present your talk to other students. Listen to other students' presentations and make notes of questions to ask them at the end.

writeback a family ritual

4A Work in pairs and read the forum entry. Did you do anything similar when you were younger?

> ### Tell us about a family ritual
>
> **Stephen:** I'm from South Africa and I spent my childhood in a part of the world where spaces are vast, towns are far apart and we lived fairly harsh lives. One of my best memories was of a kind of family ritual we had where twice a month we would drive forty miles to the next town and meet the family of a colleague of my dad's, Mr. Matthews, on a Sunday afternoon. There were four of us kids and six or seven of them, so when we came together it was a huge rowdy party; kids running around barefoot all over the yard while the adults drank long cool drinks and sat and talked. Then at about five o'clock, as the sun was setting, the Matthews would drive halfway back with us and we'd stop under a huge acacia tree to watch the sun set. We kids would collect wood and make a huge bonfire and we'd all sit talking and telling stories until the fire was ready for a barbecue. And the best part was that Mrs. Matthews would bring out a bowl of sour dough and mix it to make sour dough bread that she would roast on the grill.

B Write about a family ritual you remember from when you were younger. Write 200–250 words.

CONDITIONALS

1A Underline the correct alternative in each sentence ending.

1 If I hadn't started studying English,
   a) I *might study / might have studied* another language.
   b) I *wouldn't go / wouldn't have gone* to university.
   c) I *wouldn't be / wasn't* able to watch films in English.

2 If I had the chance to live in a different country,
   a) I *wouldn't take / would have taken* it.
   b) I *would choose / would have chosen* to live in Spain.
   c) I *would find / would have found* it very difficult to make a decision about where.

3 If computers hadn't been invented,
   a) the world *would be / had been* a less open place.
   b) People would *spend / have spent* more time together now.
   c) my parents would *end up / have ended up* in different jobs.

B For each sentence, circle the ending a), b) or c) that is most true for you.

C Work in pairs and compare your ideas.

COLLOCATIONS

2 Underline the correct alternative in each sentence.

1 I had no time to *analyse/stick to* the situation and had to act quickly – if I had *postponed/come to* the decision any longer, more people would have died.

2 We would like to take more time to *arrive at/weigh up* the pros and cons before we *come to/follow* a final decision.

3 You should *examine/compare* the situation carefully and not be afraid of *doing/putting off* the decision.

4 I always try to *betray/stick to* my principles and never *go against/arrive at* them.

FEELINGS

3A Add the letters to complete the questions about feelings.

1 How do you feel when you wake up in the morning: gro_ _ _, ale_ _ or in-between?

2 How much time passes between the moment you wake up and the moment you feel wid_ awa_ _?

3 What makes you cri_ _ _ more: saying something stupid in front of a group or your best friend doing the same?

4 In which season do you feel at your sha_ _ _ _ _ and when are you at your low_ _ _ eb_?

5 Are there any types of people who you des_ _ _ _ with a pas_ _ _ _?

B Work in pairs and ask and answer the questions.

-ING FORM AND INFINITIVE

4A Complete the sentences with the correct form of the words in brackets.

1 The most difficult thing about my day is _____ to and from work. (travel)

2 I've always been able _____ new words just by _____ them. (learn, hear)

3 It's not very good for a person _____ alone when they're depressed. (be)

4 I never have time _____ the things I really want to do. (do)

5 _____ a bike is one of my favourite ways of relaxing. (ride)

6 I study English an hour a day but I keep _____ the same mistakes! (make)

7 I enjoy _____ films in English. (can watch)

8 _____ a uniform is the worst part of my job. (must wear)

B Tick any sentences you agree with. Make the others true for you.

C Work in pairs and take turns. Student A: read one of your sentences. Student B: ask follow-up questions.
A: The worst part of my job is …
B: Oh, why is that?

AWKWARD SITUATIONS

5A Correct the mistake and add the missing word in each sentence.

1 Excuse me, Wendy. Do have a *moment* ~~monument~~? *(you)*

2 There's nothing I've meaning to talk to you about.

3 Look, I want you to get the right idea, but …

4 It that just I've noticed that …

5 I feel brighter if …

6 How you fill about that?

B Work in pairs. Choose one of the situations below and practise the conversation. Student A: use all of the sentences from Exercise 5A in order. Then choose another situation and exchange roles with Student B.

- telling a colleague that their clothing isn't appropriate for the workplace
- telling a friend that they always forget your birthday and it bothers you
- telling a student that they didn't pass an important exam

BBC VIDEO PODCAST

Download the podcast to view people talking about the question:

What kind of behaviour gets on your nerves?

Authentic BBC interviews

www.pearsonlongman.com/speakout

UNIT
9

trouble

READING

1 Work in pairs and discuss the questions.

1 Would you say you've got a good memory?

2 What tricks do you know for remembering PIN numbers, passwords or people's names?

2A Read the article and find three examples of false memories.

B Read the article again. Are statements 1–8 true (T) or false (F)? Underline any words/phrases that help you decide.

1 In court, evidence from a witness is not important if there are other kinds of proof.

2 Forty percent of people in one study were able to give a very full description of the film of the bus.

3 Ost's study shows that our memories are unreliable.

4 A poor memory doesn't usually matter in day-to-day life, according to the article.

5 In 1998, in the USA, almost all major criminal cases depended mainly on witness evidence.

6 The rumour about the white van was started by one witness.

7 One in five witnesses makes a mistake in ID parades.

8 After an accident, a person often has no memory of the incident.

C Look at the article again. What do the eight words in bold refer to? Draw an arrow backwards or forwards to the word/phrase.

Most of us have some (recollection) of the 2005 terrorist attacks in London. (It) could well be a mental image of …

3 Work in pairs and discuss. Have you ever been a witness? Do you think you would make a good witness?

⟩⟩⟩ page 156 **VOCABULARY**BANK

Memories on trial

Even in these days of DNA tests and other forensic techniques, witness testimony still plays an important part in court cases. But how reliable are our memories? BBC *Focus* magazine's Andy Ridgway finds we know less than we think …

Most of us have some recollection of the 2005 terrorist attacks in London. **It** could well be a mental image of a red double-decker bus in Tavistock Square with **its** roof ripped off by the force of the explosion. That's not surprising given the number of photographs of the damaged bus that were carried in newspapers in the days after the attack.

But what about CCTV footage? Do you remember seeing a video of **the** bus exploding? What can you see in **that** video?

Well, the truth is, you shouldn't be able to see anything in your mind's eye because **such** CCTV footage simply doesn't exist. But don't worry. If it only took a suggestion that you may have seen a video of the explosion to create an image in your mind, you're not alone. In fact, in a study carried out by Dr James Ost at the University of Portsmouth, forty percent of people claimed to have seen this nonexistent footage. Some even went on to describe what happened in vivid detail.

Many of us think we have a good memory. After all, **it**'s got us through the occasional exam. But what Ost's study clearly demonstrates is just how easily influenced our memories are. 'Facts' from the past can become confused in our minds. And it can simply be the fact that we've been asked about something, such as a nonexistent video clip, that can alter our memory.

> Many people believe they have seen video footage of the moment Princess Diana's car crashed – but no such footage actually exists.

In many cases, an unreliable memory is not a problem. **It** just means we forget to send a birthday card on time or a story we tell at a party is not one hundred percent accurate. But sometimes the contents of our memories can have huge consequences – putting people behind bars or even, in the USA, on Death Row.

In ID parades, forty percent of witnesses identified the police's suspect. In forty percent of cases no identification was made. In twenty percent of cases they pointed to a volunteer.

In 1998, an American study calculated that in ninety-five percent of felony cases – the more serious crimes – witness evidence (in other words, people's memories) was the <u>only</u> evidence heard in court. In the UK, despite DNA and other forensic evidence being used more regularly, witness memories are still a vital part of court proceedings.

Even before a case gets to court, a few false memories can get an investigation off to a bad start. In the sniper* attacks that took place in the Washington DC area in 2002, witnesses reported seeing a white van or truck fleeing several of the crime scenes. A white vehicle may have been seen near one of the first shootings and the media began repeating this. When **they** were caught, the sniper suspects were actually driving a blue car. It seems many witness memories had been altered by the media reports.

Immediately after a traumatic event, our memories may be poor and are usually fragmented. A good example is how in car crashes a person might have a vivid memory of the texture of the material on the inside of the car door because he or she looked away at the moment of the crash.

*sniper – someone who shoots at someone from a hidden place and from a distance

GRAMMAR -ing form and infinitive

4A Underline the correct alternative in sentences 1–3. Then check in the article.

1 Do you remember *to see/seeing* a video of the bus exploding?

2 Some people even went on *to describe/describing* what happened in vivid detail.

3 It just means we forget *to send/sending* a birthday card on time.

B Work in pairs and check what you know. What is the difference in meaning between the pairs of phrases in bold?

1 a) I **remembered to set** the alarm before I left the building.
  b) I **remember thinking** the building seemed very quiet.

2 a) I **forgot to phone** for tickets for the Coldplay concert.
  b) I'll never **forget seeing** Coldplay in concert for the first time.

3 a) Henri **stopped to drink** some coffee.
  b) Then he **stopped driving** because he still felt tired.

4 a) After three years' training, Billy **went on to become** a famous dancer.
  b) Billy **went on practising** five hours a day even when he was famous.

5 a) He **tried to recall** her name, but couldn't.
  b) Then he **tried going** through the alphabet and remembered it was Valerie.

C Match rules 1–10 below with meanings a)–j). Use the examples in Exercise 4B to help.

Rules:	
1 *remember* + *-ing* form	a) do something that is one's responsibility
2 *remember* + infinitive with *to*	b) not do something that is one's responsibility
3 *forget* + *-ing*	c) have a memory of an event or a feeling
4 *forget* + infinitive with *to*	d) not have a memory of an event or a feeling
5 *stop* + *-ing* form	e) finish an action
6 *stop* + infinitive with *to*	f) continue an action
7 *go on* + *-ing* form	g) finish an action in order to do something else
8 *go on* + infinitive with *to*	h) do something after finishing something else
9 *try* + *-ing* form	i) experiment with an activity
10 *try* + infinitive with *to*	j) make an effort to do something difficult

5A Look at the phrases in bold in 1a)–3b) in Exercise 4B. Cross out the letters which are silent when they are said at a natural speed.

I <u>remembered to set</u> the alarm before I left the building.

B ▶ 9.1 Listen and check. Then listen again and repeat.

▶ page 144 **LANGUAGEBANK**

PRACTICE

6A Complete the questions with the correct form of the verbs in the box.

> ~~get~~   study   buy   write   hide   take   help   become   witness   think

1 If someone stole your wallet, would you run after them and try *to get* it back?

2 Have you ever forgotten _____ a ticket for a train ride, then got caught?

3 If you were in a hurry and you saw an accident but there were lots of people around, would you stop _____?

4 Is there an event in your country you'll never forget _____, because it was so significant?

5 Do you ever stay awake at night because you can't stop _____ about a problem?

6 Do you always remember _____ breaks when you're studying hard?

7 Has anyone you knew when you were younger gone on _____ famous?

8 Have you ever tried _____ on your hand as a way of reminding yourself to do something?

9 How long do you think you'll go on _____ English?

10 Do you sometimes remember _____ something 'in a safe place' but find you've forgotten where you put it?

B Work in pairs and take turns. Ask follow-up questions to find out more information.

VOCABULARY crime

7 Work in pairs and complete the newspaper extracts with the crimes in the box.

> pickpocketing   kidnapping   hacking   stalking   tax evasion   vandalism
> identity theft   counterfeiting   mugging   arson   shoplifting   bribery

1 A teenager has been accused of _____ after he set fire to an empty factory.

2 There have been a number of cases of _____, mostly of foreign journalists. In the latest case, a demand was made for $500,000.

3 The statue was damaged in an act of _____.

4 A man has been found guilty of _____ film star Uma Thurman for the last two years. He became obsessed with the actress and followed her everywhere.

5 _____ is an ongoing problem, with high-level officials accepting money from companies which want to do business in the country.

6 He was jailed for five years for _____ into government computer systems.

7 The increase in CCTV cameras has cut cases of late night _____ in town centres.

8 Police arrested three people for _____ American dollars. The three people were carrying more than a million dollars in fake $50 bills.

9 Banks revealed that cases of _____ have doubled. Customers are warned to keep their PIN numbers and personal details more secure.

10 Tourists should be particularly careful on public transport, where _____ is a major problem. It is best to use money belts under your clothes.

11 There has been a reduction in cases of _____ in major stores after the introduction of more security guards.

12 Carl was concealing half of his income and was found guilty of _____.

8A Complete the table. Use your dictionary to help if necessary.

Crime	Person	Verb/verb phrase
arson	*arsonist*	*to commit arson*
kidnapping		

B Work in pairs and discuss. Which ones do you think are the most serious crimes and which are more minor offences?

SPEAKING

9A Work alone. Read situations 1–4 and make notes on what you would do. Use questions a)–c) to help you.

1 You witness your neighbour's teenage children committing an act of vandalism, e.g. spraying graffiti on the wall of their school.

2 **You see a friend shoplifting in a department store.**

3 You notice a colleague stealing office supplies from your place of work.

4 You witness a mugging and the mugger threatens to hurt you if you identify him to the police.

a) Would you intervene or try to stop the person?

b) Would you report the person to the appropriate authorities?

c) If you were questioned by the authorities, would you tell the truth?

B Work in groups and compare your ideas.

▶ **GRAMMAR** | past deduction ▶ **VOCABULARY** | synonyms / prepositions ▶ **HOW TO** | speculate about the past

VOCABULARY synonyms

1A Read the dictionary extract. Think of an example of a scam.

> **scam** /skæm/ n [C] *informal* a clever but dishonest way to get money

B Work in pairs. Read the TV programme information and answer the questions.

1 What are your answers to the first three questions in the text?

2 What do you think happens in the five popular scams mentioned?

THE REAL HUSTLE 9.30, BBC 3

If someone came to your door and **pretended to be** a police officer, in uniform and with a badge, would they **fool** you? Would a fight or a loud noise in a public place **distract** you so much that someone could easily **snatch** your wallet or your mobile or **swap** it for an identical one? How easily do you think you could **be taken in** by a professional con artist? *The Real Hustle* aims to show how such scams work so that the viewer doesn't **fall for** them.

The Real Hustle is a factual entertainment programme about scams and cons and how easy it is to **deceive** people in everyday life. It features a team of con artists, Alexis, Paul and Jess, as they are filmed by hidden cameras. Their scams depend on similar techniques, for example they often **divert someone's attention** and **grab** their belongings while they're not looking; or they **switch** a genuine item with a counterfeit one; or **pose as** police officers or other officials to win the victim's trust. Popular scams from the series include: the Jewellery Shop Scam, Free Gift Wrapping, the Bag and PIN* Snatch, the Fake Hire Car Scam and the Counterfeit Money Con.

*personal identification number

C Match meanings 1–6 with two of the verbs or verb phrases in bold in the programme information.

1 act as if you're someone else   *pretend to be,*

2 trick someone

3 cause somebody to <u>not</u> notice something

4 take something quickly

5 believe a trick

6 exchange one thing for another

LISTENING

2A ▶ 9.2 Listen to the conversations. Which two scams from *The Real Hustle* programme happened to the people?

B Listen again and answer the questions.

1 Why did Lise lose her bag?

2 Who did Lise talk to on the man's phone?

3 What did Lise do when she was on the phone?

4 What was the customer in the jewellery shop accused of?

5 What did the man take away?

6 Why did Dan leave his job?

3 Work in pairs and discuss the questions.

1 What should/shouldn't the people have done in each situation?

2 Have you or has anyone you know ever been 'scammed'? What happened?

3 Have you read or heard about any other scams (over the phone, internet or face-to-face)?

GRAMMAR past modals of deduction

4A Match sentences 1–6 with meanings a)–c).

1 He must have taken my bag when I wasn't looking.
2 It can't have been the young couple because I was looking at them all the time.
3 He could have hidden it in his case or he might have given it to another member of the gang.
4 Well, it must have been stolen when I wasn't looking.
5 The woman must have been working with the guy.
6 She couldn't have been a real customer.

a) I'm almost certain this happened.
b) I feel it's possible this happened.
c) I'm almost certain this didn't happen.

B Complete the rules. Use the sentences in Exercise 4A to help.

> Rules:
> 1 To speculate or make a deduction about something that happened in the past, use the modals:
> *must* / _____ / _____ / _____ / _____ + *have* + _____.
> 2 To emphasise that an activity was in progress, use modal + *have* + _____ + _____.
> 3 In the passive, use modal + *have* + _____ + _____

5A ▶ 9.3 Listen to the pronunciation of the past modals in connected speech. Then listen again and repeat.

must have	could have	might have	can't have	couldn't have
/mʌstəv/	/kʊdəv/	/maɪtəv/	/kɑːntəv/	/kʊdəntəv/

B ▶ 9.4 Listen to the sentences in Exercise 4A and repeat.

⫸ page 144 **LANGUAGEBANK**

PRACTICE

6 Complete the accounts of two scams. Use modals of deduction and the verbs in brackets.

I was taking out money at an ATM. Just as my card came out, a guy behind me said I'd dropped some money. Sure enough, there was a twenty-euro note on the floor. I bent down, picked it up and my card was gone … and so was the man! He ¹_____ (drop) the twenty-euro note and pretended it was mine, or the note ²_____ (fall) out of my wallet and he simply took advantage of the situation. He ³_____ (pull) my card out of the ATM when I bent down.

An estate agent was showing me a flat when she got a phone call from another customer who wanted to put down a deposit on that same flat. So I gave the agent my deposit, signed the contract, and was given the key. When I went back later to move in, the key didn't work … and the agent didn't answer her phone number! The woman ⁴_____ (be) an estate agent. She ⁵_____ (be) an imposter and the other customer ⁶_____ (work) with her.

SPEAKING

7A Work in pairs. Read about other scams from *The Real Hustle*. Student A: turn to page 159. Student B: turn to page 161.

B Tell each other your experiences and try to work out how the scam was done. Then turn to page 162 to see if your ideas were right.

VOCABULARY *PLUS*
dependent prepositions

8A Work in pairs. Complete the headlines with a preposition and the correct form of the verbs in brackets.

1

> **Fake police officer charged _____ £600 necklace (steal)**

2

> **Woman accuses con artist _____ bag and PIN (take)**

3

> **Gang arrested _____ one car nine times (sell)**

B Write the headlines in full. Which are active and which passive?

1 A fake police officer has been charged with stealing a £600 necklace. Passive

C Complete the headlines using a dependent preposition and the correct form of the verbs in brackets. Then check with a partner or in a dictionary.

1 Hacker suspected _____ government computers (access)
2 Student apologises _____ in exam (cheat)
3 President blames 'greedy' banks _____ crisis (cause)
4 Local girl dreams _____ top talent (become)
5 Agency criticised _____ size zero models (employ)
6 Train company bans teenager _____ for one year (travel)
7 Mother thanks toddler _____ her life (save)
8 Animal rights activists rescue lobster _____ (be eat)
9 Jury clears actress _____ husband number three (murder)
10 Dolphin saves swimmer _____ (drown)

9A Work in pairs. Choose two of the headlines above and write a news article in three sentences.

B Work in groups and take turns. Student A: read out your article. The other students: guess which headline the article is about.

⫸ page 156 **VOCABULARYBANK**

WRITING a 'how to' leaflet

10A Work in pairs. What advice would you give a visitor to a city about how to avoid getting into trouble?

B Read the extract from a 'how to' leaflet for tourists. Which ideas are different from the ones you discussed?

C Complete the guidelines for writing a 'how to' leaflet with the words in the box.

> bullet-points   title   fonts   sections
> contracted   subheading   underlining

1 Give the leaflet an overall _____.

2 Divide the leaflet into different _____, each with its own short _____.

3 Use different _____ or _____ so that it is easier for the reader to see the main points before they start reading.

4 Use _____ when you are writing a list.

5 To make your leaflet more direct and informal, use 'you' and _____ forms.

LEARN TO avoid repetition

11A Look at the verbs in bold in the leaflet and:

1 put a box around two adverbs used before the verbs.

2 underline five verb phrases used before the verbs

3 circle the remaining four imperatives.

B Complete the rules and examples with words from the leaflet.

To avoid repetition or simply giving a list of advice:

1 use the adverbs *always* and _____.

2 use a range of synonyms (words/phrases) in the imperative:

   a) Make _____ you

   b) Be _____ to

   c) Be particularly _____ to

   d) Try _____

   e) Take _____ to

12 Write a 'how to' leaflet (200–250 words) on one of the following topics. Use a variety of ways to give advice and avoid repetition.

- advice for people travelling solo
- advice for internet banking
- advice for passing exams

How to avoid trouble on holiday

Taxis

Be careful when taking taxis, especially at the airport. As an unsuspecting tourist, you may find yourself charged up to three times the normal fare or in a taxi with a driver who claims to have no change.

- Never **take** a taxi without a company name on its side.
- Always **ask** the approximate fare before entering.
- **Phone** for a taxi ahead of time rather than catching one in the street.
- Make sure you **carry** plenty of change with you.

Money

Be careful around any major tourist sites. Pickpockets often work in gangs and will come up behind you while you're walking and unzip your backpack or may 'accidentally' bump into you and steal your money or mobile before passing these on immediately to a partner. Also, take care when using an ATM. A tiny hidden camera may have been installed to steal your card number and PIN.

- **Keep** your credit cards and larger sums of money in a money belt under your clothes.
- Be sure to **keep** any money that you think you'll use that day loose in your pocket, so that you don't need to pull out large notes.
- Be particularly careful to **cover** the keypad when you enter your PIN into an ATM machine.
- **Use** ATMs inside a bank where they are less likely to have been interfered with.

Tours

If someone offers a 'budget' tour, you may find that the price is cheap but you'll spend more time at shopping places not on your itinerary than the places you intended to visit. This is because your 'guide' is being paid by the shopkeepers for taking you there.

- **Book** tours only with reputable companies.
- Try to **check** with other visitors or with your hotel before booking a tour.
- Take time to **look** on the internet for reviews and recommendations.

> ▶ **FUNCTION** | reporting an incident   ▶ **VOCABULARY** | incidents   ▶ **LEARN TO** | rephrase

READING

1A Look at the photos. What is happening? Would you phone the police if you witnessed these situations?

B Read the article and answer the questions.

1 Which reason do you think is the most ridiculous?
2 List six situations in which you think you should phone the emergency services.

Police are becoming concerned because a significant percentage of calls to the emergency services involve no crime or danger. These calls tend to be about everyday inconveniences and problems or are simply ridiculous. Some of the silliest appeals include:

- My pizza has arrived with the wrong topping.
- There's a spider in my bath.
- Can you tell me the date?
- My back trouble doesn't seem to be improving.
- My girlfriend has left me.
- My fork seems to be bent.
- Can you tell me what my mobile number is?
- There's no toilet paper in this public lavatory.
- I need you to give me a wake-up call tomorrow.
- I can't find my TV remote control.

FUNCTION   reporting an incident

2A ▶ 9.5 Listen to the phone conversation. What happened to the man?

B Listen again and complete the report form.

Incident Report 2047561A

Name: _____

Date and time of incident: _____

Location of incident:_____
_____

Description of incident (what exactly happened?):
_____
_____
_____

Description of stolen or damaged property (serial number, bank card type, value of property, colour, make, model of car, etc.): _____
_____

Description of suspect or offender (age, sex, ethnicity, build, clothing, distinguishing marks or features, etc.):
_____
_____

Witnesses:_____

Contact details:_____

3A ▶ 9.6 Complete the phrases. Then listen and check.

1 _____ I realised what _____ happened, he had run on.
2 It was _____ about thirty seconds _____ _____ I realised my wallet had gone.
3 But did it cross your _____ that it wasn't just an accident?
4 It never _____ to me that he'd done it on purpose.
5 My mind just went _____.
6 He looked _____ if he was just out jogging.
7 It all _____ so quickly.
8 He just _____ like a normal guy.
9 He _____ me a bit _____ that actor.
10 I didn't _____ what he said. It was too quick.

B Work in pairs. Which phrases above:
- describe impressions of a person?
- refer to time?

C Underline a maximum of three main stressed words in sentences 1–10 in Exercise 3A. Listen and check. Then listen and repeat.

▸ page 144 **LANGUAGEBANK**

4A Use the prompts to complete the conversation.

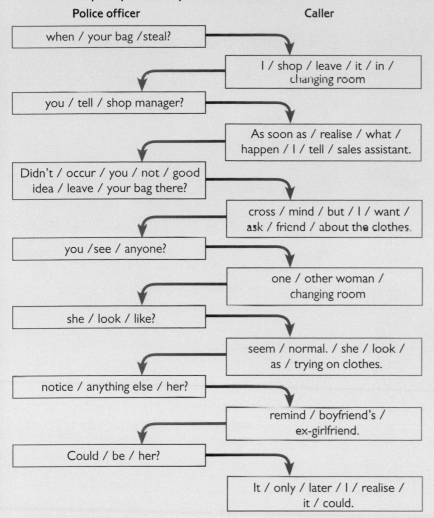

Police officer | Caller

when / your bag /steal?

I / shop / leave / it / in / changing room

you / tell / shop manager?

As soon as / realise / what / happen / I / tell / sales assistant.

Didn't / occur / you / not / good idea / leave / your bag there?

cross / mind / but / I / want / ask / friend / about the clothes.

you /see / anyone?

one / other woman / changing room

she / look / like?

seem / normal. / she / look / as / trying on clothes.

notice / anything else / her?

remind / boyfriend's / ex-girlfriend.

Could / be / her?

It / only / later / I / realise / it / could.

B Work in pairs and take turns. Role-play the conversation. Use the flowchart to help.

VOCABULARY incidents

5A Complete sentences 1–8 with the correct form of a verb phrase in the box.

| fall off   get stuck   knock over   break down   lock out   run over |
| get knocked out   be on fire |

1 My card has _____ in the machine.
2 The house _____ – there's smoke coming from the windows.
3 We crashed into a lamp post and _____ it _____ .
4 My car has _____ on the motorway.
5 A workman was working on my roof and he's _____ the ladder.
6 I've _____ myself _____ of my house.
7 I fell down but I don't remember anything after that. I think I _____ .
8 Someone's just _____ my cat and I think they've killed it.

B Work in pairs and look at the sentences above. Who might the people be speaking to?
1 *They might be speaking to the security department in a bank.*

C Work with other students. Have any of these situations or similar ones ever happened to you?
⫸ page 156 **VOCABULARYBANK**

LEARN TO rephrase

6A Look at the extract. Underline two places where the police officer (A) rephrases something to help the caller (B) understand.

A: Could you tell me exactly when the incident happened?
B: Just now. About an hour ago.
A: Could you be more precise?
B: Excuse me?
A: Could you give me the exact time?
B: I think at 2.50 or 2.55.
A: And where did it happen?
B: Park Avenue.
A: Can you pinpoint the exact location?
B: Pinpoint?
A: Tell me exactly where.

B Match the meaning of the words in bold in 1–5 with phrases a)–e) below.
1 I'll need to **take a statement**.
2 And he **hit into me hard** like this.
3 a sweater, grey colour, with a – you know – something you put over your head.
4 And some sort of dark **trousers, for running or for the gym**.
5 And were there any other people **in the vicinity**?

a) in the surrounding area – nearby
b) tracksuit bottoms
c) a hood … a hoodie?
d) to write down some details
e) collided with

C 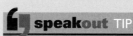 9.7 Listen and check your answers.

speakout TIP

Using familiar words to explain unfamiliar words and complex meanings not only helps communication but is also an opportunity to learn more sophisticated vocabulary.

SPEAKING

7A Work in pairs. There was a burglary in your house last night. Student A: turn to page 161. Student B: turn to page 162.

B Work in pairs. Student B: ask Student A how the burglar got into and out of the house. Draw a line showing his route. Help Student A with difficult vocabulary.
A: *The burglar first climbed the … thing for rainwater … going down …*
B: *The drainpipe? Which one?*
A: *The … drainpipe … on the left/right.*

DVD PREVIEW

1A Work in pairs and discuss. Imagine you are on board a sinking ship. Which three things from the list would be the worst that could happen?

- no one is in charge
- the power goes off
- the ship's hull is damaged
- everyone gives up hope of being rescued
- someone falls into the water
- the crew jump ship, leaving the passengers behind
- an airlift harness breaks
- there are gale-force winds
- there aren't enough lifeboats

B Read the programme information. Who organised the rescue on the *Oceanos*? Why, do you think?

BBC 999

In this series, Michael Buerk presents sensational stories of ordinary people caught up in extraordinary life-or-death situations. Tonight's programme features a remarkable account of the cruise liner *Oceanos* that sank near South Africa in 1991, as told by Moss Hills, one of the 581 people on board the ship. Despite being on the ship simply as entertainers, Hills, his wife and other members of the entertainment team found themselves coordinating the evacuation of hundreds of passengers in a race against time before the vessel disappeared beneath the waves.

▶ DVD VIEW

2A Work in pairs and number the events in the order you think they happened.

a) The storm hit. *1*

b) Helicopters arrived.

c) The helicopters ran out of fuel.

d) The power on the ship went off.

e) The captain and crew got off the ship.

f) 350 people successfully got into lifeboats.

B Watch the DVD and check the order.

C Work in pairs. Complete the extracts. Then listen and check.

1 There was a great _____ when we set sail. It's kind of typical, there's always people partying, there's a whole sail-away _____, it's one of the highlights of a cruise.

2 So I followed them and saw crew members _____ their bags, and everyone was in a real state of _____.

3 By 4a.m., 350 people including the crew had got off, leaving the entertainers in _____ _____ the frightened passengers.

4 Water continued to _____ through the hull, but the gravity of the situation was kept from the passengers to _____ panic.

5 Swinging uncontrollably in gale force _____, two Navy divers were dropped on board the ship to _____ with the rescue.

6 We had twelve passengers left, myself, Tracy, and we had Robin on the bridge, so it was fifteen people left on _____, and they disappeared to go and drop those passengers off.

D Work in pairs and discuss. How do you think the following people felt during and after the rescue?

- the captain of the *Oceanos*
- the passengers
- Moss Hills

speakout items for a life raft

3A ▶ 9.8 Listen to people deciding on six things to take on a life raft. Which items below do they talk about? Why do they decide to take/reject each one?

- blankets
- tinned food
- torch (with generator)
- lighter
- dried fruit
- plastic raincoat
- first aid kit
- hand mirror
- fishing kit (line, hook)
- sun cream
- survival manual
- drinking cup

B Look at the key phrases. Listen again and tick the phrases you hear.

> **keyphrases**
>
> It depends on [what/whether] we …, doesn't it?
>
> It's important to … isn't it?
>
> It's (not) top priority to be able to …
>
> I can't see the point of (taking) …
>
> What would we do with a … ?
>
> I'd say that … are [essential/vital/crucial].
>
> … to keep you [warm/dry/alive],
>
> … to [prevent/keep] you from [dehydrating/ getting …]
>
> [It/That] hadn't occurred to me.
>
> We need to prioritise them.

C Work alone and choose six items from the list in Exercise 3A. Make notes on why they are important and why other items are not as important.

D Work in groups and take turns. Try to persuade the other students that your choices are important then decide on six items as a group.

writeback a lucky escape

4A A website has asked readers to write a story about a lucky escape using the string of words. Work in pairs and discuss. What story can you imagine for the first word string below?

| spring countryside lost dark fence garden dog sandwich run jump escape |

| August camping forest dry tent sleep smoke fire trapped soup rain escape |

| sea cool friends swim snorkel hours tired cold stiff drowning save escape |

B Read the story. What happened and how did the man get out of the situation without being hurt?

It was early spring, and I was taking a walk in the countryside with my girlfriend. We were mostly walking along country roads, but sometimes cutting across fields and gardens. Late in the day, as it started to get dark, we realised we were lost. We had a map with us, but it didn't help because we didn't really know where we were.

There was a fence running along the road next to us, and I decided that we should go over the fence and cross that property to get to the next road. So we climbed the fence, and started crossing the grass. It was in fact someone's private garden, and there was a very big house on it. There was also a very big dog, and it was running towards us, barking. I'm terrified of dogs, but my girlfriend kept a cool head, took a sandwich out of her bag, and threw it to one side.

Amazingly, the dog went for the sandwich, and we had enough time to run to the next fence and jump over. It was a very lucky escape.

C Choose another word string. Write your story (200–300 words) using three paragraphs.

D Read other students' stories. Which one do you think was the most unusual escape?

-ING FORM AND INFINITIVE (2)

1A Underline the correct alternative in the article.

OK, you've just been mugged. Your first impulse may be to go on ¹*doing/ to do* whatever you were doing, but don't. First, stop ²*checking/ to check* that you're fine. Some victims forget about ³*being/ to be* hit or ⁴*falling/ to fall* and only discover injuries later. Try ⁵*finding/ to find* a safe place, maybe a café with people (you may need to borrow a phone). You're probably in shock – give yourself time to stop ⁶*shaking/ to shake* and take slow, deep breaths to calm yourself. If this doesn't work, try ⁷*drinking/ to drink* some cool water – avoid coffee. Remember ⁸*phoning/ to phone* someone you know and tell them where you are and what happened. If you remember ⁹*seeing/ to see* what the mugger looked like, write down the details. If you forget ¹⁰*doing/ to do* this you may find that you can't recall much detail later, when you talk to the police.

B Work in pairs and discuss. Which ideas do you agree with?

CRIME

2A Make a list of as many crimes as you can remember.

B Work in pairs and think of:

1 two crimes that involve damage to property

2 four crimes that involve people and can happen on the street

3 three crimes that involve technical expertise on computers or other machines

4 two crimes involving money that could be committed by a company

5 one crime that involves theft but not usually in a street

C Work in pairs and discuss. Which crimes are most often in the news in your town/city/country?

SYNONYMS

3A Rewrite the sentences with a synonym for the words/phrases in bold.

1 Does listening to music when you study **divert your attention**?

2 Can you **snatch** fifteen minutes' sleep in the middle of the day?

3 Would you find it easier **to pretend to be** someone older or younger?

4 If you exaggerate your internet profile, are you **fooling** people unacceptably?

5 Have you ever **been taken in by** a lie someone told you?

B Work in pairs and take turns. Ask and answer the questions.

MODALS OF DEDUCTION

4A Work in pairs and read the situations. For each one, rewrite the options using a modal of deduction.

1 A man checked his post box every day but it was always empty. Meanwhile his friends sent him dozens of letters a week.

   a) I'm sure the man moved recently. *The man must have moved recently.*

   b) Maybe his friends sent mail to the old address.

   c) I'm certain the postmen didn't deliver the letters.

2 A pianist performed a concert in a concert hall. She played perfectly but at the end no one clapped.

   a) She was probably practising in an empty concert hall.

   b) I'm certain she was deaf.

   c) They definitely didn't like the music.

B Look at the extra information below and make a final guess to explain each situation. Then turn to page 161 and check your ideas.

1 The friends wrote the correct address on the letters./The postman always put the letters in the post box./There wasn't a hole in the bottom of the post box.

2 The concert hall was full./No one had hearing problems – everyone heard the performance and liked it.

DESCRIBING AN INCIDENT

5A Complete the sentences with the correct form of a word in the box. One of the words is not used.

~~occur~~ if go catch remind become like cross realise happen (x2)

1 It _occurred_ to me that he/she shouldn't have …

2 He/She _____ me of …

3 It was only later that I _____ …

4 My mind _____ blank.

5 Before I realised what had _____, she/he'd …

6 I _____ (not) the number plate.

7 It all _____ so fast.

8 It _____ my mind that …

9 He/She looked as _____ …

10 He/She seemed _____ …

B Work in pairs. Choose one of the following incidents to report to the police and decide which sentences from Exercise 5A you could use.

• someone shoplifting in a department store

• someone looking at confidential information on someone else's computer

• someone hanging around an ATM with two friends sitting in a car nearby

C Work in pairs and take turns. Role-play the phone call. Student A: you are the police officer. Student B: you have seen the incident.

BBC VIDEO PODCAST

Download the podcast to view people discussing the question:

Do you have any phobias?

Authentic BBC interviews

www.pearsonlongman.com/speakout

UNIT **10**

culture

VOCABULARY adjectives

1A Work in pairs and discuss. Do you like the types of films shown in the photos? Why? Why not?

B Work in pairs and complete the table with the words in the box. Check any words you don't know in a dictionary.

> ~~gripping~~   predictable   touching   weak
> awesome   chilling   horrific   moving
> unforgettable   dull   creepy   brilliant
> fast-paced   electrifying   poignant

full of action/ suspense	*gripping*
frightening	
emotional/ often sad	
not good	
very good	

C Work in pairs. Tick five ungradable/extreme adjectives (ones which can't be used with *very*).

2A Work in groups. List the names of five films you all know.

B Take turns. Student A: describe one of the films using at least three of the adjectives from Exercise 1B. The other students: ask a question each and then guess the film.

A: It's fast-paced and the special effects are brilliant but some of it is predictable.

B: Is it a thriller?

A: Yes.

C: Does it star …?

LISTENING

3 Read the information about a radio programme. Why do you think people listen to this programme? Would you listen to it?

The Edith Bowman Show

Join Edith Bowman's daily afternoon show on BBC Radio 1, with its mix of music and chat. Studio guests this week include singer Calvin Harris, guitarist Serge from Kasabian and, from the world of film, Emma Watson and Elijah Wood. Also, latest reports from the festival circuit. James King appears in his regular slots: on Wednesday he answers listeners' movie questions and on Fridays he chats to Edith about the latest films.

4A ▶ 10.1 Listen to James King's review of the film *Let the Right One In* and underline the correct alternative.

1 He *loved/ quite liked/ hated* the film.

2 He says the film is *fast-paced/ slow-paced/ has too much blood.*

3 He doesn't talk about *the plot/ the setting/ the director/ the acting.*

B Listen again and complete the extracts from the review.

1 I certainly am. _____, _____ horror film, this one.

2 It's a _____, _____ film, it really is very, very good …

3 It's sort of slow, and really _____ _____.

4 … because of that, I think really, really _____ …

5 … and the most _____ things are happening on screen …

6 Absolutely. And I think a really _____ film.

7 You can have something that's really _____ and …

8 The two kids in this are, well, just _____.

C Work in pairs and discuss. Have you seen or heard of this film? If not, would you watch it based on this review? Why/Why not?

GRAMMAR relative clauses

5A Check what you know. Complete the extract from an online review with *who*, *which*, *whose*, *where* or *when*.

I've never liked films [1]_____ are designed to frighten me, but *Let the Right One In* is a horror film [2]_____ goes beyond the usual moments of terror [3]_____ any good horror film delivers.

The story centres on the relationship of two young adolescents: twelve-year-old Oskar, [4]_____ is bullied by other kids, and Eli, a young girl [5]_____ he makes friends with. However, Eli is a vampire and she needs blood, [6]_____ gives Oskar a real possibility of striking back against the bullies.

I saw the film as being less about vampires and more about the insecurities and horrors of growing up, [7]_____ we can all identify with. Some of my favourite scenes in the film are the most poignant such as the moment [8]_____ Oskar asks Eli, 'Will you be my girlfriend?' and Eli says, 'Oskar, I'm not a girl', by [9]_____ she means of course that she's a vampire.

Oskar is played by Kare Hedebrant, [10]_____ is appealing in his portrayal of pain and innocence. Eli is played by Lina Leandersson, [11]_____ sad eyes and gentleness are an ironic contrast to her violent needs. The film was mostly shot in northern Sweden, [12]_____ the snow that was needed to create the bleak, empty atmosphere was guaranteed.

B Work in pairs and answer the questions about the review above.

1 Which relative clauses are defining (give essential information) and which are non-defining (add extra information). Write D or ND.

2 Which type of clause, D or ND, always has a comma before it, and a comma or full stop after it?

3 What does *which* in examples 6 and 7 refer to?

4 In which five relative clauses can you use *that* instead of *who*, *which* or *when*?

5 In which three relative clauses can you omit the relative pronouns *who*, *which* and *when*?

6 Look at examples 5, 7 and 9. Where is the preposition in the relative clauses?

6 Look at the extract from the review. Underline the non-defining relative clauses.

The story centres on the relationship of two young adolescents: twelve-year-old Oskar, who is bullied by other kids, and Eli, a young girl who he makes friends with. However, Eli is a vampire and she needs blood, which gives Oskar a real possibility of striking back against the bullies.

7A ▶ 10.2 Listen to the intonation in the non-defining clauses. Are they spoken in a higher or lower voice than the rest?

B Listen again and say the recording at the same time. Try to copy the intonation.

▸ page 146 **LANGUAGEBANK**

PRACTICE

8A Join the sentences using a relative clause.

1 In *The Curious Case of Benjamin Button*, Brad Pitt plays a man. He lives his life backwards.
   In The Curious Case of Benjamin Button, Brad Pitt plays a man who lives his life backwards.

2 Megastar Zac Efron gives an emotional and mature performance in his latest film. He shot to fame in *High School Musical*.

3 *Invictus* is a story about leadership and forgiveness at a critical period. Nelson Mandela had just become president of South Africa.

4 The film *Star Trek* was based on a popular TV series. The series has been watched around the world.

5 The film is Daniel Craig's second outing as James Bond. It is directed by Marc Forster.

6 Adrian Brody plays a Jewish refugee in *The Pianist*. He is a famous Polish piano player.

7 *Lost in Translation* is a film about two Americans in a Tokyo hotel. They meet and form an unusual bond there.

8 *The Hurt Locker* is a gripping story about the insanity and foolishness of war. It was made in Jordan.

B Work in pairs. Write three sentences about films. Use a relative clause in each sentence.

C Work with another pair. Read out your sentences but replace the film with *this/these film(s)*. The other pair guess the film or film star.

A: These films, which were filmed mainly in New Zealand, were some of the most successful ever.

B: The Lord of the Rings?

SPEAKING

9A Complete the sentences below so that they

> I loathe films where …

> My favourite male actor is …, who …

> I like the work of the director …, whose …

> The film which … is …

> My favourite actress is …, who …

> I like it in films when …

are true for you.

B Work in pairs and take turns. Talk about your ideas and ask follow-up questions.

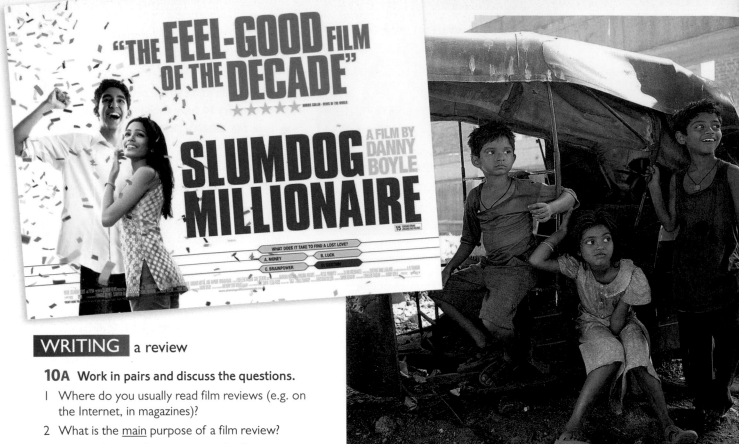

WRITING a review

10A Work in pairs and discuss the questions.

1 Where do you usually read film reviews (e.g. on the Internet, in magazines)?

2 What is the <u>main</u> purpose of a film review?
- to make people want to see the film
- to help people decide if they want to see a film
- to give factual information about the film

3 Which of the items in the box do you usually find in a film review?

> plot summary   description of the film's ending   actors' names
> recommendation   ticket prices   setting of the film
> reviewer's opinion of different elements

B Read the film review and write the topic of each paragraph.

FILM REVIEW

1   *Slumdog Millionaire* is set in Mumbai and stars Dev Patel as Jamal, an illiterate call-centre worker from the city slums, and Rubina Ali as Latika, his childhood friend and lost love.

2   As the film opens, Jamal is about to answer the last vital question to win the jackpot in the Indian version of the quiz show *Who Wants to be a Millionaire*? However, the show's host is suspicious because of Jamal's run of correct answers, and when the programme has to break overnight, he calls in the police. Convinced he is a cheat, the police take Jamal away and torture him. Through a series of flashbacks, we see a number of horrific incidents experienced by Jamal and his brother Salim as orphans in the slums of Mumbai. Remarkably, each answer from the show relates to one of these situations.

3   Skilfully directed by Danny Boyle, the film cuts between the glitter of the TV studio and the poverty, companionship and cruelty of the Mumbai slums. The script is alternately gripping, shocking and hilarious and the camerawork is sensational. As Jamal, Dev Patel is electrifying although, for me it is the character of young Jamal, poignantly acted by Ayush Khedar, who is the most moving of all.

4   With its breathless intensity, *Slumdog Millionaire* is a hard-hitting, emotionally-draining film which I'd thoroughly recommend.

rate this review ✓ ✗

LEARN TO write descriptively

11A Underline two adverb + past participle combinations in paragraph 3 of the review.

B Write three adverbs from the box next to each participle to complete the phrases. Some can be used more than once.

> convincingly   harshly   skilfully
> widely   sensitively   overwhelmingly
> highly   poignantly   heavily

1 _____ / _____ / _____ directed by …
2 _____ / _____ / _____ acted by …
3 _____ / _____ / _____ praised by …
4 _____ / _____ / _____ criticised by …

12A Make notes about a film you have seen recently. Use the topic areas from Exercise 10B.

B Write a first draft of your review (120–180 words). Use adjectives and at least two adverb + past participle combinations.

C Exchange with another student and read each other's review. Is it interesting and clear? Suggest two or three improvements.

D Write a final version of the review.

► **GRAMMAR** | participle clauses   ► **VOCABULARY** | two-part phrases   ► **HOW TO** | talk about popular culture

READING

1A Work in pairs and look at the photos. What do you think is the most difficult part of each performer's job?

B Work in pairs. Student A: read the text on this page. Student B: read the text on page 163. Read each question and predict the answer. Then read the answer and check your ideas.

C Work in pairs and take turns to tell your partner about the answers.

Popular culture Q&A

Want to know the best-kept secrets of popular culture? Read our Top 10 Questions & Answers to find out.

Q: How do actors cry on demand?
A: There are certain ways of making it look like you're crying, such as putting glycerine in your eyes, sniffing a freshly cut onion or, on stage, concentrating on a bright point of light. Most actors use more internal techniques that exploit emotional memory. By recalling a time when they were sad or upset, an actor can often get the tears flowing. Or sometimes they'll build an association between an object – a prop they'll be handling during the scene – and that emotion, so that, when they touch the prop, they feel inclined to cry. Interestingly, most actors say it's easier to cry convincingly than to laugh convincingly.

Q: How do singers keep their voices steady when they're dancing?
A: Singers such as Beyoncé, whose stage show involves her dancing all over the stage, can't always deliver high-quality vocals live as it's physically extremely difficult to control the voice while jumping around. Because of this, many performers rely on a backing track to provide vocals during some songs, and whilst they may be singing live, the audience can't actually hear their voice. Some stationary performers use a backing track when they're concerned about difficult parts of the performance, for example hitting a very high note or even remembering the words to a song.

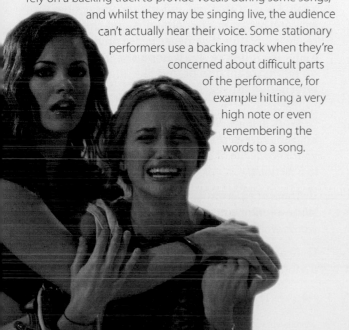

Q: Who decides whether something is 'art' or not?
A: This is an age-old question, and you need to be flexible in your outlook. Art is about crossing boundaries, and the range of works and styles of painting regarded as art by different people is astounding – from cave paintings to Rembrandt to Jackson Pollock. One argument goes that a painting is art if the painter says it is, and gives sound reasons to support their position. Many artists would reject that idea as they don't care who regards their work as art. We'll probably never agree on who the most beautiful woman or best-looking man is, so we'll just have to enjoy exploring and sharing our notions of art and beauty without a definitive answer.

Q: What's the secret to making an audience laugh?
A: Every stand-up comedian knows that making people laugh with prepared material, on stage, is very different from making your friends or colleagues laugh in an informal setting. You need to focus on technique, such as which words to stress, when to pause, how to use facial expressions and body movements, as well as sensing how to work each individual audience. Ironically, shows with paying audiences are better than freebies. Having paid to be entertained, people are often more ready and willing to laugh.

Q: Why do great photographers need to change their photos on a computer?
A: In this digital age, the average person sitting at his or her home computer is able to manipulate photographs easily. People talk about digital photography destroying the purism of traditional photography. But what they aren't aware of is that photographers who printed photographs on paper were able to manipulate colour, contrast, framing and content as much as someone working with a computer nowadays. It's just that, in the past, very few people were involved in the printing process, with most people paying for someone else to develop their photos.

GRAMMAR participle clauses

2A Read the article below. Why do celebrities use fake names?

B Work in pairs and look at the participle clauses in bold in the article. Then complete the rules.

Do stars use their real names when travelling?

In short, no. In fact, stars [1]**registered at hotels under their real name** are a rarity – their day can be ruined by paparazzi [2]**trying to take their pictures** and members of the public [3]**seeking autographs**. So if you're going to change your name, why not have fun doing it? Names [4]**involving wordplay** are common: Britney Spears uses Ms Alotta Warmheart among other names, and Brad Pitt and Jennifer Aniston, [5]**married in 2000 but divorced five years later**, used to call themselves Mr and Mrs Ross Vegas. And the fun doesn't end there – George Clooney travelled [6]**using the name Arnold Schwarzenegger**. 'It was funny, the hotel staff had to call me Mr Schwarzenegger, [7]**knowing, of course, I wasn't him**,' said Clooney.

Rules:
1. A participle clause begins with either a _____ or a _____.
2. Some types of participle clause can replace a relative clause. There are five examples in the text: numbers _____.
3. A participle clause beginning with a _____ is active in meaning and a clause beginning with a _____ is passive.

C Compare each pair of sentences below and underline the correct alternative to complete the rules.

1 a) Names which involve wordplay are common.
  b) Names involving wordplay are common.

2 a) When George Clooney travelled, he used the name Arnold Schwarzenegger.
  b) George Clooney travelled using the name Arnold Schwarzenegger.

Rules:
1. When a relative clause has a verb in the present simple, the participle clause uses *a present participle / the present simple*.
2. When two actions happen at the same time and have *the same / a different* subject, they can be joined by using a participle clause.

🎤 speakout TIP

Using participle clauses can improve the level of your writing and speaking. Try to improve this sentence by using a participle clause: *I stayed at home and I read the paper and watched the sport on TV.* Recognising participle clauses can also help you understand complex sentences when reading, e.g. *The people stopped at the border were all Americans.*

➡ page 146 **LANGUAGEBANK**

PRACTICE

3A Rewrite the sentences using a participle clause.

1 People who take photos should ask their subjects' permission first.
2 Films that are based on books are usually disappointing.
3 It's great to see rock stars in their sixties who still play concerts.
4 Architecture which was designed in the 1960s is generally quite ugly and ought to be pulled down.
5 Photos of people who are posing for the camera don't work as well as spontaneous pictures.
6 Film and TV stars who appear in the theatre attract huge audiences.
7 Jokes which involve racial stereotypes are not funny.
8 Photos which have been altered to make celebrities look thinner should be banned.

B Work in pairs and discuss. Do you agree with the statements in Exercise 3A? Give examples where possible.

VOCABULARY the arts

4A Which of the forum comments are generally positive (✓), negative (✗) and mixed (−)?

> I'd read a lot about this new singer in the music press. She's certainly **creating a stir** with her **ground-breaking** mix of rap and folk. Ever since she got those **rave reviews** in the press, each performance has been a **sell-out** and it's impossible to get tickets. Everyone says it's the **must-see** performance of the year. Is she really that good?

> Well after all the **hype** surrounding her concerts, I went to see her on Friday, expecting something really sensational … but the concert was a real **letdown**! It was a complete **flop** because we couldn't hear her properly.

> Yeah, I was at that gig and the technical side was pretty bad but her album is amazing, really innovative. I've never heard anything quite like it before. I just hope she doesn't go **mainstream** and boring like all the other **alternative** artists.

B Work in pairs. What do you think the words in bold above mean? Use the context, grammar and your knowledge of similar words to help. Then check in a dictionary.

C Think of a performance you have seen or heard. Write a forum entry about it using at least four of the words which are new to you.

D Read other students' forum entries. Find a performance you would like to see or hear.

➡ page 157 **VOCABULARYBANK**

SPEAKING

5A Choose three of the questions below to answer. Write the name of the thing/person and two or three words to explain why you liked it/him/her.

1 What's the best gig/concert or dance performance you've ever been to?

2 What's the best music album ever made?

3 Who's the funniest comedian you know?

4 What's the most moving, scary or exciting film you've ever seen?

5 What's the most memorable exhibition you've ever been to?

6 What's the best photo you've ever taken?

7 Who's the painter or other type of artist you most like? What's your favourite work of his/hers?

8 What's the most unforgettable show or play you've ever seen?

B Work in pairs and take turns. Talk about your experiences and feelings.

C Work in groups and take turns. Recommend something you've recently been to/seen/heard.

VOCABULARY *PLUS* two-part phrases

6A Work in pairs and look at the two-part phrases in sentences 1 and 2. What do you think they mean?

1 There are some basic **dos and don'ts** when taking a good photo.

2 I've worked in the film business **off and on** for most of my life.

B Check your ideas with the dictionary entries.

> **dos and don'ts** things that you should and should not do: *the dos and don'ts of having a pet*

> **off and on/on and off** for short periods of time but not regularly: *I worked as a secretary off and on for three years.*

7A Match a word from A with one from B to make a two-part phrase.

A   B

peace   ready   tired (of)
leaps   pros   quiet   then
on   rough   now   and   bounds   through
   sick   ups   cons   take
  through   give   on   downs

B ▶ 10.3 Listen and check. Then listen and repeat, paying attention to the linking, the weak form of *and* and the dropping of /d/ in connected speech.

peace and quiet
    /ən/

8A Work in pairs. Student A: turn to page 163. Student B: turn to page 160. Read the definitions and then complete five of the sentences below.

1 I hate having music on in the background. I prefer some _____ and _____.

2 I used to go to rock concerts a lot but nowadays I only go _____ and _____.

3 I'm a reggae fan _____ and _____.

4 I'm _____ and _____ of having to listen to people's favourite music on the train. I wish they'd turn their MP3 players down.

5 Any skill such as playing the piano improves in _____ and _____ if you practise enough.

6 Every relationship has its _____ and _____ so it's not surprising that most bands break up after a few years.

7 I don't like jazz. Some of the pieces go _____ and _____ for far too long.

8 It's OK for my neighbours to play music I don't like. You have to have a bit of _____ and _____. I'm sure they don't like my music!

9 There are _____ and _____ to buying a live recording as opposed to a studio album.

10 Some of the music videos made by ordinary people on YouTube are a bit _____ and _____ but that's OK.

B Work in pairs and take turns. Help your partner to complete the sentences and understand the two-part phrases.

C Discuss. Which of the ideas in Exercise 8B do you agree with?

➡ page 157 **VOCABULARYBANK**

A   B   C

SPEAKING

1 Work in pairs and discuss the questions.

1 When was the last tour you took? How was it?

2 Look at the photos and answer the questions.

a) Which photos are of Greenwich Village in New York, USA and which are of Oxford in the UK?

b) What do you know about each place?

c) Which place would you most like to visit? Why?

FUNCTION giving a tour

2A ▶ 10.4 **Listen to two people showing friends around Greenwich Village and Oxford. Number the photos in the order you hear them.**

B Listen again and write one fact you hear about each place.

1   The Blue Note Jazz Club

2   The Café Reggio

3   Greenwich Village in general

4   Washington Square Park

5   The Bodleian Library

6   The Oxford colleges

7   The Bridge of Sighs

8   New College

9   The 'Schools'

10 Christ Church College

3A Work in pairs and complete the phrases. Sometimes there is more than one possible answer.

Leading the way

Let's ¹_____ over to Washington Square Park and then ²_____ back.

Why don't we ³_____ our steps and go back to the Café Reggio?

Giving facts

It was ⁴_____ on the Arc de Triomphe.

It was built to ⁵_____ the hundredth anniversary of the inauguration of George Washington as president.

In front of us is the Bodleian, ⁶_____ after the ⁷_____ – Thomas Bodley.

Commenting on facts

⁸_____ I'm sure you _____, Greenwich Village has always been a centre of artistic life – very bohemian.

⁹_____, the oldest college was actually only founded a hundred or so years earlier!

¹⁰_____, the biggest room can seat somewhere in the region of 500 students although I haven't seen it myself.

We can actually go inside if we're quick. It's well ¹¹_____ a visit.

B Compare your answers with the audio script on page 174.

C ▶ 10.5 **Listen to the intonation in the phrases. Then listen again and repeat.**

Interestingly, the statue disappeared at the time of his death.

The story goes, he threw it in the lake.

Apparently, it was made of gold.

Surprisingly, no one has ever tried to find it.

▌▶ page 146 **LANGUAGE**BANK

LEARN TO express estimates

6A Look at the extracts and underline five phrases for expressing estimates (when we don't know the exact number).

1 A: How many colleges are there?

B: Just under forty. Well, thirty-eight to be exact.

2 A: How 'new' is new?

B: Roughly 1370.

A: You're kidding!

B: No, really! Interestingly, the oldest college was actually only founded a hundred or so years earlier!

3 Apparently the biggest room can seat somewhere in the region of five hundred students

4 A: How many students are there at the university in total?

B: To be honest, it depends. In term time, you'd probably get upwards of twenty thousand.

B Which phrases in Exercise 6A could be replaced by 1) *fewer than*, 2) *more than* or 3) *about/around/ approximately?*

C ▶ 10.6 Listen and tick the exact number.

1 a) 1,400   b) 1,518

2 a) 30   b) 38

3 a) 1,180   b) 1,220

4 a) 712   b) 746

5 a) 2.13   b) 1.10

6 a) 318   b) 371

D Work in pairs and take turns to estimate:

- the number of students in your school/employees in your workplace.
- the age of the building you're in.
- the population of your town/city.
- the distance from your home to where you are now.
- the cost of dinner in a good restaurant in your town/city.
- the number of contacts on your mobile phone.
- the number of English words you know.

4A Complete A's part in the extracts from a tour of Paris.

A: ¹Let's / head / over / the cathedral, Notre Dame.

B: On the island? Do we have time to go inside?

A: ²It / well worth / visit / but we / not have / time / to look inside today.

B: ... So that's the Arc de Triomphe?

A: ³Yes, / model / a famous Roman arch.

B: And why was it built?

A: ⁴celebrate / one / Napoleon's great victories.

A: ⁵... So here we are / the Eiffel Tower / named / its designer, Gustave Eiffel.

B: Wow! It's impressive.

A: ⁶Yeah / apparently / can sway six to seven centimetres in the wind!

B Work in pairs and take turns. Practise the conversations using the prompts above.

VOCABULARY dimensions

5 Complete the tourist's questions with the noun or verb form of the adjectives in brackets.

1 What is the _____ of the tower? (high)

2 Does this road go the _____ of the town? (long)

3 When did they _____ the entrance? (wide)

4 What is the _____ of the wall here? (thick)

5 The road _____ here. Why's that? (narrow)

6 What's the _____ of the river and _____ of the water here? (broad, deep)

7 Why don't they _____ the map? It's so small. (large)

8 It's nine o'clock and it's still light. When do the days _____ here? (short)

SPEAKING

7A Work in pairs. Design a one-hour walking or cycling tour of your town/city for a visiting friend. Make notes on:

- four or five places to see.
- a fact or personal opinion about each place.
- some approximate numbers associated with the place (how many people visit it; how much it costs; how old/long/high etc. it is).

B Work with a new partner and take turns. Role-play the tour. Student A: lead the way. Student B: ask questions.

DVD PREVIEW

1A Work in pairs. Look at the picture above and the background photo. Which of the words/phrases in the box would you use to talk about graffiti?

> eye-catching   has artistic merit   positive
> defaces buildings   striking   stimulating
> offensive   provocative   conveys a message
> ugly   hideous   pleasing to the eye   messy

B Read the programme information and answer the questions.

1 Who is Banksy?
2 Why do you think he keeps his identity a secret?
3 Why did Bristol host a Banksy show?

BBC The One Show

The mysterious graffiti artist Banksy, whose pioneering work has brought graffiti into mainstream art and whose pictures fetch hundreds of thousands of pounds, is rumoured to be from the city of Bristol. While no one knows for certain if this is true as his identity is a closely guarded secret, the city recently hosted an exhibition of Banksy's work. So what do local people think of Banksy and graffiti in general? Cerrie Burnell, a reporter from BBC 1's topical magazine programme went along to find out.

▶ DVD VIEW

2A Watch the DVD. Do these people think graffiti is art (A) or vandalism (V)?

Spud Murphy   _____
Woman 1   _____
Man 1   _____
Man 2   _____
Woman 2   _____
Woman 3   _____
Man 3   _____
Man 4   _____

B Watch the DVD again and complete the sentences.

1 We've been astounded by the number of people coming through the door and _____ down the street.
2 The spray painting work is onto canvas, so it's actually _____ his work in a different way.
3 ... you can't have _____ for one and not for the other.
4 Has graffiti really become a credible and _____ art form or is it seen by most as just vandalism?
5 Very, very artistic, very _____ to the eye, and sometimes it has a very _____ message...

3 Work in pairs and discuss whether you agree/disagree with the statements.

1 Holding an exhibition of graffiti is irresponsible because it encourages people to think spray-painting graffiti on public buildings is acceptable.
2 There's a difference between artistic graffiti and simple vandalism. There should be separate laws for graffiti artists like Banksy and for kids who just deface property.

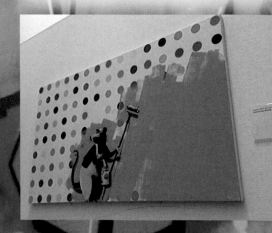

speakout a town project

4A ▶ 10.7 Listen to three people discussing a new artistic project for their town. Which project does each person, Tim, Nigel and Sarah, like from the list below? Why?

- an outdoor sculpture (modern or traditional)
- a concert space
- a theatre workshop space for young people
- a state-of-the-art multiplex cinema
- a botanical garden
- a skateboarding park

B Listen again and tick the key phrases you hear.

keyphrases

I'm really in favour of [the state-of-the-art multiplex cinema/the fountain]

I think that it would be [useful and beneficial for the community/popular].

I'd rather have something that would [appeal to all ages/make a statement]

We have to consider [costs/maintenance]

Can you see the [older/younger] generation [using/liking] it?

5A Work in pairs. You are responsible for choosing an artistic project for your town/city. Choose two items from the list in Exercise 4A. The items must:
- have artistic and/or architectural merit.
- represent the town/city in some way.
- convey a positive image.

B Work with other students. Discuss your ideas and decide on one project.

C Present your decision to the class.

writeback a work of art

6A Work in pairs. Read about the competition and tell your partner what you would choose and why.

We want you to write about a favourite work of art or building. It could be a statue or sculpture, a fountain or bridge, a painting or even a favourite room. Send us your description in 150–250 words, and we'll put the five best entries on our website.

B Read the description and tick (✓) the things in the box that the writer mentions.

| setting | when it was made | material | colour |
| size | who made it | why he/she likes it |

My favourite building is Bilbao's Guggenheim Museum. It's an awe-inspiring structure, more like a sculpture than a building. Sometimes it reminds me of a collection of building blocks, and at other times it makes me think of a ship reflected in the nearby river.

Its architect, Canadian Frank O Gehry, designed it with flowing curves and covered it with shiny titanium panels that look like the scales of a fish. The museum's colour alters with the light, from silver in the sunlight to gold in the evening.

This twentieth century masterpiece is absolutely breathtaking inside and out. It is without doubt my favourite building in the world and a sight no one should miss if they are visiting this part of Spain.

C Write your competition entry.

ADJECTIVES

1A Work in pairs. Make a list of as many adjectives for describing films as you can remember.

B Complete comments 1–4 with a suitable adjective.

1 It touches all of your emotions in ninety minutes! Very _____!

2 I knew how it was going to end after the first five minutes. Totally _____!

3 It kept my attention for two hours. Utterly _____!

4 I could hardly stay awake. Extremely _____!

C Work in pairs. Write four reviews similar to the ones above. Use a suitable adjective for describing films in each review.

RELATIVE CLAUSES

2A Underline the correct alternative.

I'd like to find …

1 a person *who/for whom/whose* main interests include **doing sports**.

2 a place *that/which/where* I can **speak English with native speakers**.

3 someone *that/whose/whom* knows **a famous person**.

4 a shop *where/which/that* I can buy **reasonably-priced clothes**.

5 a person for *whose/that/whom* **money** is not important.

6 three **interesting places in this town/city** *which/ to which/where* I've never been to.

B Change the words in bold in four of the sentences above so that they are about things/people you'd like to find.

C Ask other students questions about your sentences in Exercise 2B.

A: Do you know anyone whose main interests include going to the cinema?

B: Yes – me.

A: Right. Who's your favourite actor?

B: At the moment, Robert Pattinson.

PARTICIPLE CLAUSES

3A Complete the quiz with the present or past participles of the verbs in brackets.

TRIVIA QUIZ

1 It's an arts building _____ (stand) in Sydney Harbour and _____ (make) of white tiles to look like sails.

2 It's a company _____ (start) by Steve Jobs, Steve Wozniak and Ronald Wayne, best _____ (know) for its iPod and iPhone products.

3 It's a game _____ (play) by two players, _____ (involve) a small rubber ball and racquets and _____ (take) place in a four-walled court indoors.

4 He was a great leader, born in Corsica, _____ (crown) Emperor of France in 1804 and _____ (defeat) at Waterloo in 1815.

5 It's a statuette _____ (award) to people in the film world every year by the American Academy of Motion Picture Arts and Sciences.

6 They're a group of people _____ (live) in cold, snowy parts of the USA and Canada, and _____ (use) blocks of ice to build their houses, _____ (call) igloos.

7 It's a Japanese dish _____ (consist) of raw fish and rice _____ (roll) up in seaweed.

8 It's a play _____ (write) by Shakespeare and _____ (feature) a Danish prince.

B Work in pairs and do the quiz.

C Check your answers on page 161.

THE ARTS

4 The words in bold are in the wrong sentences. Put them in the correct sentences.

1 The musical was a complete **sell out** and had to close early.

2 Does the Picasso exhibition really deserve all its **hype** reviews?

3 You can't get tickets for the show. It's a complete **rave**.

4 I thought the new album was a real **must-see**, very poor. I expected better. What do other people think?

5 That new comedian is certainly creating a lot of **flop** at the festival. Everyone's talking about him.

6 This Virtual Worlds Exhibition is a **let-down** event. Don't miss it!

GIVING A TOUR

5A Complete descriptions 1–4 below with the words in the box. Where are the places?

~~was~~	story	worth	it	honour
named	rebuilt	you		

1 It *was* built in the 17th century by the ruler Shah Jahan in of his dead wife. As may know, it's made of white marble and is well a visit.

2 It was after its designer and was built in 1889. The goes that many Parisians hated it because it was too modern.

3 Parts of it were many times. Believe or not, more than two million Chinese may have died in its construction.

B Write two sentences about a tourist site you know.

C Read out your sentences. The other students guess the place.

BBC VIDEO PODCAST

Download the podcast to view people answering the question:

What areas of the Arts do you enjoy?

Authentic BBC interviews

www.pearsonlongman.com/speakout

IRREGULAR VERBS

VERB	PAST SIMPLE	PAST PARTICIPLE
be	was	been
beat	beat	beaten
become	became	become
begin	began	begun
bend	bent	bent
bet	bet	bet
bite	bit	bitten
bleed	bled	bled
blow	blew	blown
break	broke	broken
bring	brought	brought
broadcast	broadcast	broadcast
build	built	built
burn	burned/burnt	burned/burnt
burst	burst	burst
buy	bought	bought
catch	caught	caught
choose	chose	chosen
come	came	come
cost	cost	cost
cut	cut	cut
deal	dealt	dealt
dig	dug	dug
do	did	done
draw	drew	drawn
dream	dreamed/dreamt	dreamed/dreamt
drink	drank	drunk
drive	drove	driven
eat	ate	eaten
fall	fell	fallen
feel	felt	felt
feed	fed	fed
fight	fought	fought
find	found	found
fly	flew	flown
forbid	forbade	forbidden
forget	forgot	forgotten
forgive	forgave	forgiven
freeze	froze	frozen
get	got	got
give	gave	given
go	went	been/gone
grow	grew	grown
hang	hung	hung
have	had	had
hear	heard	heard
hide	hid	hidden
hit	hit	hit
hold	held	held
hurt	hurt	hurt
keep	kept	kept
know	knew	known
lay	laid	laid
lead	led	led
leap	leapt	leapt
lean	leaned/lent	leaned/lent
learn	learned/learnt	learned/learnt

VERB	PAST SIMPLE	PAST PARTICIPLE
leave	left	left
lend	lent	lent
let	let	let
lie	lay	lain
light	lit	lit
lose	lost	lost
make	made	made
mean	meant	meant
meet	met	met
mistake	mistook	mistaken
pay	paid	paid
put	put	put
read /riːd/	read /red/	read /red/
ride	rode	ridden
ring	rang	rung
rise	rose	risen
run	ran	run
say	said	said
see	saw	seen
sell	sold	sold
send	sent	sent
set	set	set
shake	shook	shaken
shine	shone	shone
shoot	shot	shot
show	showed	shown
shrink	shrank	shrunk
shut	shut	shut
sing	sang	sung
sink	sank	sunk
sit	sat	sat
sleep	slept	slept
slide	slid	slid
smell	smelled/smelt	smelled/smelt
speak	spoke	spoken
spell	spelt	spelt
spend	spent	spent
spill	spilled/spilt	spilled/spilt
split	split	split
spread	spread	spread
stand	stood	stood
steal	stole	stolen
stick	stuck	stuck
sting	stung	stung
swim	swam	swum
take	took	taken
teach	taught	taught
tear	tore	torn
tell	told	told
think	thought	thought
throw	threw	thrown
understand	understood	understood
wake	woke	woken
wear	wore	worn
win	won	won
write	wrote	written

GRAMMAR

1.1 questions

direct questions

Word order for most questions is: (question word) + auxiliary verb + subject + main verb.

What does 'strategy' mean? Have you finished yet?

Subject questions: When the question word is the subject of the sentence, use the affirmative form of the verb.

What happened then? NOT ~~What did happen then?~~

Prepositions in questions usually come at the end.

Who did you go with?

In *very* formal English, prepositions can come at the beginning.

With whom did you correspond?

Use *Wh-* + *be* + subject + *like* to ask for a description of a thing or person.

What's your new boss like?

indirect questions

Use indirect questions to ask for information in a more polite way or to ask personal questions. After the introductory phrase, use the affirmative form, not the question form.

Do you know **what time the class starts?**

In *yes/no* questions use *if* or *whether* + the affirmative form.

I'd be interested to know **whether** *Mike's married.*

The following phrases are often used to introduce indirect questions: *Do you know … ? Can I ask (you) … ? Could you tell me … ? I was wondering … ? I wonder … I'd be interested to know … Do you mind me asking … ? Have you any idea … ? I'd like to know … What/Why etc. + do you think … ? Would you mind telling me… ?*

Only use a question mark if the introductory phrase is a question.

I wonder where Derek is. How do you think he did that?

spoken grammar

Two or three word questions are common in conversation:

A: *I'm going out tonight.*   **A:** *I didn't go to the party.*
B: *Where to? / Who with?*   **B:** *How come? / Why not?*
A: *I hate spicy food.*
B: *Why's that? / Such as?*

In conversation we sometimes use the affirmative form with a rising intonation.

You're living in Saudi Arabia now?

In informal conversation we sometimes leave out the auxiliary.

You been here long? Anyone seen my bag?

1.2 present perfect/past simple

present perfect

Use the present perfect to talk about:

• **time up to now**: an event that happened at some point in the past e.g. *in my life, this year, today*. The exact time it happened is not mentioned.

I've met four US presidents. (In my life up to now)

• **recent events** which are in some way relevant to the present. The exact time it happened is not mentioned.

No coffee for me, thanks. I've already had one.

• **ongoing situations** or repeated events that started in the past and continue up to now.

Julia has swum on the national team since she was fifteen.

Note: The present perfect continuous can often also be used for this meaning. See unit 2.1

past simple

Use the past simple to talk about:

• **a completed event** where an exact time is given or is obvious.

The plane crashed in the Pacific last week.

• **a situation** or repeated events that started and finished in the past.

We lived in China for four years before moving here.

As a child, I practised the violin for at least an hour every night.

time phrases to talk about the past

past simple	last month, yesterday, ago, this time last week, on date/day, last week/month/year
present perfect	just, already, yet, ever, lately, since, so far
both	never, always, for, recently, before, in the summer, today, this morning/afternoon

today, this morning/ afternoon can be used with both verb forms, depending on whether the period is finished or not.

1.3 polite enquiries

opening phrases	
I'd like to I'm calling/phoning to	ask/find out about … enquire about … talk to someone about …

Polite enquiries	
I was wondering/I wonder I'd be grateful/I'd appreciate it	if you could see if there's a place available.
Can/Could you tell me Do you mind me asking	when the manager will be back?
Would there be any chance of Would you mind	giving me a refund?

PRACTICE

1.1

A Write A's questions in full.

A: [1]Do you mind / me / ask / where you've been?

B: At a meeting.

A: [2]I'd be interested / know / where / the meeting / was!

B: It was in town.

A: [3]What / meeting / like?

B: Oh, you know. Long.

A: [4]you / know / what time / be / now?

B: Um … is it late?.

A: [5]Why / you / not / phone?

B: My mobile was dead.

A: [6]you / lie / to me?

B Put the words in the correct order to make indirect questions.

1 if / you / here / credit / they / know / Do / cards / accept?

2 me / you / model / mind / how / a / you / asking / became / Do?

3 you / coffee / got / any / at / idea / this / where / time / I / can / get / Have / a?

4 you / me / computer / Would / telling / the / available / mind / when / is?

5 get / if / married / you're / Can / planning / I / to / ask?

6 was / I / briefcase / that / bought / you / where / wondering.

C Complete the two-word questions.

A: I can't meet you tonight.

B: No? How (1)*come*?

A: Because I'm going out.

B: Where (2)_____?

A: To the theatre.

B: Who (3)_____?

A: Nobody you know. The tickets were very expensive.

B: How (4)_____?

A: I'm not telling. I'll get home late.

B: What (5)_____?

A: After midnight. You know, you shouldn't ask so many questions.

B: Why (6)_____?

1.2

A Complete the email with the past simple or present perfect of the verbs in brackets.

To:	m.smith24@gmailbox.com

Dear Mum and Dad,

Sorry I [1]_____ (not write) in a while, but things are crazy here. I can't believe it [2]_____ (be) 6 months ago that I left and that we [3]_____ (not see) each other for that long.

This trip [4]_____ (be) fantastic so far, at least until a few days ago, when things [5]_____ (take) a turn for the worse. We [6]_____ (arrive) in Istanbul and [7]_____ (check) into the first hotel we [8]_____ (see). Now, you know I [9]_____ (stay) in a lot of one-star hotels in my life, but this one [10]_____ (be) really bad, so we [11]_____ (go) straight out to see the city.

Unfortunately, we [12]_____ (forget) to lock our room, and when we [13]_____ (get) back, our luggage and most of our money was gone. We [14]_____ (call) the police right away, and I [15]_____ (go) back to the police station several times since then, but no one [16]_____ (hand) in any of our things.

Anyway, could you send me €1,000 please?

Thanks and love,

Joanna

B Underline the correct time phrase.

1 I've never played squash *before moving here/ before.*

2 No wonder I've got a headache! It's two o'clock and I didn't have a coffee *this morning/this afternoon.*

3 *Up to now/Until I took this course,* I always believed that English was easy.

4 I've known Maria *for/since* ten years now.

5 *So far/In the first week of term* I haven't missed any classes.

6 I had trouble concentrating at work *since/until* I got new glasses.

7 I've never ridden a scooter again *after/since* the accident.

8 I haven't worked *this month/last month* so money is tight.

9 I haven't downloaded it *already/yet.*

10 We came back from holiday *this time last week/ lately.*

1.3

A Complete the conversation by adding one word from the box to each line.

help	be	ago	will	when	check	about	out
at	afraid	with	there	chance	is		

A: Yourpick.net. My name's Dave. How can I *help* you?

B: Hi, I'm phoning to find about a DVD I ordered. The reference number 3714.

A: OK. Is a problem?

B: Yes, it hasn't arrived yet and I ordered it a month. Could you tell me I can expect it?

A: Bear me a moment. I'm afraid we have no information the arrival date.

B: And you don't know when it be in?

A: It's coming from the US so I'm not. Do you want to cancel?

B: No, but I'd grateful if you could look into it.

A: No problem all.

B: And would there be any of phoning me when it arrives?

A: Sure … let me just if we have your phone number …

GRAMMAR

2.1 present perfect simple or continuous?

Use both tenses to talk about situations or repeated actions which started in the past and continue into the present.

• Often there is no important difference, particularly with verbs such as *work, live, study*.

Ella's worked / 's been working for the company for a year now.

• The present perfect continuous is often used for verbs of longer duration (*wait, stay, run, play, sit, stand,* etc.).

I've been staying with friends for the last six months.

• The present perfect simple is used for state verbs (*know, have, understand, be*) and verbs of short duration (*drop, start, finish, leave, break, lose,* etc.)

I've known Stella all my life. NOT ~~I've been knowing Stella all my life.~~

Oh no! I've left my ticket at home. NOT ~~I've been leaving my ticket at home.~~

Use the present perfect continuous to emphasise a continuous or repeated activity and the present perfect simple to emphasise a completed action.

I've been answering emails all morning.

I've answered all my emails.

• The present perfect simple often emphasises a completed result and answers questions such as: *How many? How much? How far?*

She's run 500 kilometres and she's raised 5,000.

NOT ~~She's been running … She's been raising …~~

• The present perfect continuous is used when there is present evidence of a recent activity.

You look hot. Yes, I've been running.

NOT ~~Yes, I've run.~~

Sorry about the smell. I've been cooking fish.

NOT ~~Yes, I've cooked fish.~~

2.2 the passive

Form the passive with *be* + past participle. In a passive sentence, the *agent* may or may not be mentioned.

	active	passive
present simple	The press **follows** him everywhere.	He**'s followed** everywhere by the press.
present continuous	The police **are monitoring** his emails.	His emails **are being monitored** by the police.
past simple	Fire **destroyed** the building.	The building **was destroyed** by fire.
present perfect	Someone**'s eaten** my sandwich.	My sandwich **has been eaten.**
will	Someone **will tell** you.	You**'ll be told.**
modals	We **can't do** it this week.	It **can't be done** this week.
-ing form	I don't like people **criticising** me.	I don't like **being criticised.**
infinitive with *to*	The organisers want people **to give** feedback.	The organisers want **to be given** feedback.

Use the passive:

• when the object of the verb rather than the subject (the agent) is the focus of the sentence.

The president was honoured by his staff at a special banquet.

• when the agent is obvious, not important or unknown

A man's been arrested on suspicion of murder.

I hate being watched when I'm practising Tai Chi.

I'm being sent all sorts of spam about weight loss.

• to create a distance between the agent and the action, for example to avoid responsibility.

Your ideas will be considered and the good ones put into effect.

All complaints will be taken seriously.

• in more formal texts (e.g. academic writing, business reports) and certain text types (e.g. newspaper articles, radio/TV news).

No survivors have been found in the disaster.

spoken grammar

To avoid using passive in spoken English, we can use pronouns (e.g. *they/someone*) with an active voice.

They say no one survived the crash.

2.3 giving and responding to opinions

Use these expressions to express your opinion:

I'm (very much) in favour of / (really) against …

I think / feel / believe that …

It seems to me that …

The way I see it …

agreeing	partially agreeing	disagreeing
That's right. I agree (with you). Exactly/Absolutely/ Definitely I suppose so	You've got a point there, but … I agree to some extent, but … I take/see your point, but … Fair enough, but … I know what you mean, but …	I (totally) disagree. I don't agree (with you). I'm not so sure. I'm (still) not convinced.

PRACTICE

2.1

A Complete the answers with the present perfect simple or continuous form of the verbs in brackets.

1 Why are you looking so pleased with yourself?

Because I _____ for some clothes and I've found something I like. (look)

Because I _____ a new pair of jeans. (just buy)

2 You look hot.

Yes, I _____ 15 km. (do)

Yes, I _____. (run)

3 What's the matter?

We _____ to decide where to go on holiday this year. (try)

We _____ we can't afford a holiday this year. (decide)

4 What's up with Jake?

He _____ his knee (hurt)

He _____ with Serge again! (fight)

5 I feel sick.

That's because you _____ a whole packet of biscuits. (eat)

That's because you _____ ice-cream all afternoon. (eat)

B Write a question about each sentence. Use the underlined verb in the present perfect simple or continuous form. If both are possible, use the continuous form.

1 I <u>teach</u> biology at the high school.

How long _____

2 I <u>collect</u> antique books.

a) How long _____

b) How many _____

3 I <u>think</u> Dan's a bit of an idiot.

How long _____

4 I'm <u>saving</u> up money for university.

a) How long _____

b) How much _____

5 I <u>have</u> a house on a Greek island.

How long _____

6 I <u>know</u> Maria well.

How long _____

2.2

A Put the words in the correct order to make sentences.

1 cat's / operated / this / My / being / on / afternoon

2 be / He'll / later / or / sooner / caught

3 badly / in / fire / was / burnt / the / Kim

4 of / middle / the / in / up / woken / being / mind / don't / They / night / the

5 hurt / you / care / Someone / get / if / could / take / don't

6 the / asked / whole / I've / give / been / to / speech / to / school / a

7 at / by / She's / be / desk / day / to / her / 9a.m. / expected / every

8 monitored / sometimes / emails / supervisor / by / their / are / Employees'

B Complete the article with the correct active or passive form of the verbs in brackets.

Google street view helps find missing child

Google Street View [1]<u>has been used</u> (use) to help find a kidnapped child in rural Georgia. Ten year old Maria Nadal, from Atlanta, Georgia, [2]_____ (find) safely at a motel on Tuesday. She [3]_____ (discover) by Police Officer Ned Beales and Deputy Fire Chief Louis Thomas. They [4]_____ (put) the coordinates from Maria's mobile phone into Google Street View and were able to identify one of the buildings as a motel.

A woman [5]_____ (arrest). She [6]_____ (believe) to be Maria's grandmother, and family friends said that the woman had complained about [7]_____ (separate) from the little girl. Legal experts say she [8]_____ (might/give) a warning and a fine rather than go to prison because she is a family member.

2.3

A Complete the conversation with the words in the box.

~~in~~ it still what to the enough point sure

A: I'm /favour of the idea of compulsory school uniforms.

B: Are you? I'm really against.

A: Well, way I see it, with uniforms everyone's the same, rich or poor.

B: I take your, but they can be very expensive – especially as children get bigger.

A: I know you mean, but kids' clothes are expensive anyway.

B: Fair, but having uniforms deprives children of individual expression.

A: I agree some extent, but uniforms provide a sense of belonging.

B: I'm not so. Lonely kids don't feel any less lonely just because they have a uniform on.

A: Maybe not, but I'm not convinced.

GRAMMAR

3.1 used to, would, be/get used to

used to, would

Use *used to* + infinitive for past habits, repeated actions and states which have changed. We can also use the past simple.

Jon **used to smoke** but he gave up a few years ago.

We always **had/used to have** a pet when I was young.

We can avoid repeating *used to* when telling stories by using *would* instead. We can use *would* + infinitive for past habits and repeated actions (but not states) which have changed. With *would*, we often use a past time reference.

We'**d** often **meet up** on a Friday evening after work.

be/get used to

Use *be used to* + noun or *-ing* form to talk about a situation which you are familiar with. Use the negative form for a situation which is new and strange for you.

I'**m used to eating** with a knife and fork.

I'**m not used to eating** with chopsticks.

Use *get used to* + noun or *-ing* form to talk about a situation which is becoming more familiar to you.

We'**re getting used to** the cold winters.

I **can't get used to** sleeping during the day.

3.2 future forms

plans, intentions and decisions

Use *be going to* + infinitive to talk about general plans, arrangements and intentions about the future. Use *might/could* + infinitive when a plan or intention is not definite.

I'**m going to look** for a job after arriving in Kuala Lumpur.

We **might go** away for the weekend, we're not sure yet.

Use the present continuous to talk about definite arrangements or plans, often involving other people.

What **are** you **doing** today? I'**m having** lunch with Mitsuko.

The following phrases can also be used for intentions and plans: *planning to/hoping to* + infinitive, *thinking of* + *-ing*

Pete's **hoping to go** to university next year.

Are you **thinking of leaving** the company?

Use *will* ('*ll* in spoken English) to talk about new decisions made at the moment of speaking. This is often used with *I think*.

I'm tired. I think I'**ll go** to bed now.

future facts

Use the present simple to talk about facts in schedules, timetables and itineraries.

The course **starts** in September.

We **arrive** at 6a.m. at Milan airport.

predictions

Use *will/might/could/won't* + infinitive to make predictions based on opinion. Use with verbs such as *think, hope, expect, know, reckon, guess, be sure*, or adverbs such as *maybe, perhaps*.

I expect Sara **will be** late as usual.

When the prediction is based on present evidence or something that has already started, use *be going to*.

Look at those clouds. It'**s going to rain**. (I can see dark clouds)

Lisa'**s going to have** a baby. (the pregnancy has started)

Use *will* + *definitely/certainly/possibly/probably* to say how certain you are. Note the word order with *won't*.

Jodie and Al **will probably get divorced** soon.

You **definitely won't get** a ticket now. They'll be sold out.

The following phrases also express strong possibility: *be likely (to/that), may well, there's a good chance that*.

I'**m likely to be** / It'**s likely that I'll be** tired after the journey.

The internet **may well** mean the end of printed newspapers.

There'**s a good chance** that Brazil will win the Cup.

after conjunctions of time

To talk about the future, use present simple (or present perfect) after conjunctions of time such as *before, when* etc.

Let's get together **as soon as** you **arrive**. NOT ~~as soon as you'll arrive~~

3.3 describing procedures

the aim of an activity
The aim/goal/object/point is (for + subject) to …

emphasise an important point
The main/key/most important thing is to …

different procedures or steps
The way it works is that the first player…
What happens (next) is that you …
The first/next/last thing they/you do is you …
After they've/you've finished/done that, you …
First,/Next,/After that,/Then,/Finally, you …

PRACTICE

3.1

A Complete the exchanges with the correct form of *used to, would, be used to* or *get used to*. Sometimes there is more than one possibility.

1 A: Did you know John before?

B: Yes, we _____ be at school together.

2 A: How are you finding your new flat?

B: It's OK but I'm finding it difficult _____ the long journey to work.

3 A: How often did you see your grandmother when you were young?

B: We _____ see her most weekends.

4 A: Everyone here speaks English so fast. I can't understand a word.

B: Don't worry, you _____ it after a while.

5 A: How's your new flat?

B: It's great but I _____ having so many rooms!

6 A: Is this a photo of you on holiday when you were young?

B: Yes, we _____ go to Portugal every year.

7 A: Are you enjoying working from home?

B: Yes, but I miss the people. I _____ working alone with no one around.

8 A: How can you get any sleep with all that noise outside?

B: I don't even notice. I suppose I _____ it.

B Complete the second sentence so that it means the same as the first. Use *used to, be used to* or *get used to* and the verbs in brackets.

1 I lived alone before, but now I have a roommate and it's strange.

I _____ (live) alone, so I _____ (have) a roommate.

2 He feels it's normal for him to stay out late because he always did it before we got married.

He _____ (stay) out late because he always _____ (do) it before we got married.

3 She never had so much free time. Now she does and it's unfamiliar, but less and less so.

She _____ (have) so much free time but now she _____ (have) it.

4 I don't feel comfortable travelling by public transport. Until last year I drove to work.

I _____ (take) public transport. I _____ (drive) to work until last year.

5 I've never had a dog before. I'm sure I'll find it normal soon.

I _____ (have) a dog. I expect I _____ (have) one soon.

3.2

A Cross out the incorrect option in the conversation.

A: Hey Mike, [1]*are you coming / are you going to come / will you come* on the ski trip this weekend?

B: Of course. I haven't signed up yet, but [2]*I'm likely to do / I'm going to do / I'll do* that now. Where [3]*does the bus leave / is the bus leaving / is the bus planning to leave* from?

A: It [4]*leaves / might leave / 'll leave* from the front of the office unless it [5]*will rain / 's raining / rains*.

B. Great! What are the snow conditions [6]*likely to / going to / hoping to* be like?

A: It's already snowing there now so [7]*it's being / it's going to be / it'll be* perfect conditions.

B: Great. [8]*I'll probably see / I'm seeing / I might see* you before then, but if not, see you on the bus!

B Complete the sentences with an appropriate future form. Sometimes there is more than one possibility.

1 I suppose I _____ (stay) at home this evening, but I haven't decided yet. Maybe I _____ (watch) a DVD or something.

2 _____ Sandra _____ (be) there tomorrow? Then I _____ (definitely/go)!

3 The first metro _____ (go) at 5a.m.

4 Rick _____ (think of/move) abroad. I expect he _____ (be) happier there.

5 The deadline _____ (be) midnight tonight, so you _____ (probably/not finish) the application in time.

6 I _____ (see) her before she _____ (leave) but it's not certain.

3.3

A Complete the rules to the game *Cyclops* by putting the underlined words in the correct order.

[1] it works is that The way you have two players and just one dice. [2] thing The is they first do roll to see who goes first. Then the first player rolls the dice, and adds up the numbers that they roll. [3] object is The to get a hundred points.

[4] point the , Basically is to be lucky enough not to roll a one, because if you get a one, you lose all your points for that turn. [5] that is happens What a player gets greedy, thinks he can make a run to a hundred, but then gets a one and loses it all. That's the best part – it's really funny. [6] to is thing key The work in little steps, end your turn after a few rolls and don't get greedy!

GRAMMAR

4.1 narrative tenses

Use the **past simple** for completed actions in the past which tell the main events in a story.

She **picked up** the phone and **ordered** a taxi.

Use the **past continuous**:

- to set the general scene of a story

The music **was playing** softly, and the **guests were** arriving one by one.

- to talk about actions in progress at or around a particular point in a story, often interrupted by another (shorter) action or event (usually in the past simple).

He **was talking** loudly when the waiter brought his food.

Use the **past perfect simple** to talk about actions or situations that were completed before another action in the story. The actions are often mentioned out of time sequence, and the past perfect makes the order clear.

When I **got** to the restaurant, all my friends **had eaten** and some of them **had left**.

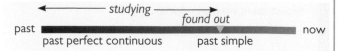

Use the **past perfect continuous** to talk about longer actions or situations which started before and continued up to a point in the story.

She **had been studying** for hours when she found out the exam was cancelled.

4.2 *I wish, If only, should have*

expressing regret about the present

Use *wish* + past tense to express regret about the present.

I wish I **wasn't** sitting here right now. (I am sitting here)

I wish I **had** more time. (I don't have enough time)

I wish I **could** run faster. (I can't run very fast)

Using *were* instead of *was* is considered more correct but can sound quite formal.

I wish I **weren't** sitting here right now.

If only can often be used instead of *wish*.

If only I had more time. **If only** I could run faster.

Use *would* + infinitive after *if only/ I wish* to talk about other people's habits that you want to change.

*I wish Sam **wouldn't** spend so much time on the computer.*

expressing regret about the past

Use *wish* + past perfect to express regret about the past.

I wish I**'d stayed** at home. (I didn't stay and I regret it)

We can also use *should* + *have* + past participle.

I **should have stayed** at home.

spoken grammar

In spoken English, we usually say *should've* instead of the full form *should have*.

I **should've** stayed at home.

4.3 expressing likes and dislikes

expressing likes	expressing dislikes
I'm a big fan of ...	I'm not a big fan of/not that keen on...
I'm very/really/quite keen on...	I'm not really into .../I'm really not into... (stronger)
I'm really into ...	I can't/couldn't stand/get into ...
What I like(d)/love(d) about it is/was ...	What I don't like/hate about it is ...
The thing I like about it most is that ...	The thing I don't like/hate (most) about it is

Some of these expressions use special structures to put extra emphasis on the main point:

What I + verb (*about it*) + *be that* + key information

What I don't like (*about it*) **is that** some of the dialogue is not very natural.

(compare: *I don't like the unnaturalness of some of the dialogue.*)

The thing I + verb (*about it*) + *be that* + key information

The thing I liked (*most*)(*about it*) **was that** the characters seem so real.

(compare: *I liked the reality of the characters most.*)

PRACTICE

4.1

A Complete the sentences using the correct narrative tense.

Last night I saw Jean at the top of a ladder, climbing into the upstairs window of a house. She was using a ladder to get through the upstairs window because ...

1 she _____ (forget) her key.

2 she _____ (rob) the house.

3 all of the downstairs floors _____ (just/paint) and she didn't want to walk on the fresh paint.

4 she _____ (use) the door all her life and she wanted a change.

B Complete the news story by putting the verbs in brackets in the correct narrative tense.

Missing child found safe and sound

A search for a missing child in East Paterson [1]_____ (end) happily last week after five-year-old Ricky Ross was found asleep in his own room. Last Monday, Julie Ross, the boy's mother, [2]_____ (work) in the front garden when she [3]_____ (hear) her son cry out.

He [4]_____ (play) in the living room but when she [5]_____ (ran) to the house, she [6]_____ (see) that the back door was open and there was no sign of her son.

Neighbours [7]_____ (join) in the search and as they [8]_____ (search) in the forest behind the house, they [9]_____ (find) a few pieces of children's clothing. There was initial panic but it was soon clear that the clothing [10]_____ (be) there for years and didn't belong to the boy. Ricky was eventually found by another child who [11]_____ (go) into the boy's room while the search [12]_____ (go) on because she [13]_____ (hear) a noise from the toy chest. When she [14]_____ (open) it, there was Ricky safe and sound – he [15]_____ (sleep) in the toy chest the whole time, unaware of the panic he had caused.

4.2

A Underline the correct alternative in the sentences.

1 It was a mistake to tell him the truth. You should *lie/have lied* to him.

2 It's difficult to work with Harry, because we don't really like each other. I wish we *liked/had liked* each other a bit more.

3 I have to take buses everywhere. If only I *knew/had known* how to drive.

4 Guys don't ask her out because she's too good-looking. If only she *were/had been* less good-looking.

5 We moved to a new flat last year, and I don't like it. I wish we *didn't live/hadn't lived* in this flat.

6 I never knew him. I wish I *met/'d met* him.

7 I forgot my umbrella and it's raining. I shouldn't *leave/have left* my umbrella at home.

8 I love to sing but I have a terrible voice. If only I *had/had had* a good voice.

B Complete the sentences using the information and the correct form of the verbs in brackets.

1 We live in the city and I hate it.
   If only we _____ (live) in the country.

2 You party far too much. You came home so late last night.
   If only you _____ (party) so much. You should _____ (come) home so late last night.

3 You forgot my birthday again.
   I wish you _____ (always forget) my birthday. You should _____ (remember) this time.

4 The neighbours were playing loud music last night.
   I wish they _____ (play) their music so loudly. If only I _____ (sleep) better, I wouldn't feel so tired now.

5 I'm just not strong enough to lift anything heavy.
   If only _____ (be) stronger. I wish I _____ (be) so weak.

6 You bite your nails. It annoys me more than any bad habit.
   I wish you _____ (bite) your nails. If only you _____ (have) some other bad habit instead.

4.3

A Correct the mistake in each sentence.

1 I'm not that keen of opera.

2 I can't stand on depressing books like that one.

3 The thing I liked about it most it was the surprise ending.

4 I'm not really going into sci-fi books or films.

5 Who I love about Lee's films is that there's always a message.

6 I'm a big fan for historical novels.

7 What I like her acting is that she brings something special to every role.

8 I don't get into classical music.

GRAMMAR

5.1 articles

indefinite article (a/an)

when it's not clear (or important) which one is being talked about.	We got an email from Carla. She's renting a room in a flat in Berlin.
when it is the first time something is mentioned.	Can you help me? I've got a problem with my homework.
in phrases of quantity or frequency	2 euros a kilo, 5 days a week, 70 km an hour

no article

to talk about things in general.	People need about seven hours sleep every night.
for most continents, countries, towns, roads, stations, individual mountains and lakes	Asia, North-east Spain, Moscow, Kings Cross Station, Mount Everest, Lake Garda

definite article (the)

when it's clear what is being talked about.	Sonya brought the children with her (we understand 'her children')
when something is unique.	Neil Armstrong was the first man on the moon.
when something has been mentioned before.	I've got a problem. The problem is that I didn't understand the homework.
+ adjective or singular countable noun to talk about things in general	The city is divided between the rich and the poor. The tiger could soon be extinct.
for oceans, rivers, groups of islands/ regions, deserts, mountain ranges, decades	The Pacific, the Danube, the USA, the Netherlands, the Seychelles, the Alps, the Sahara, the 1990s

5.2 zero, first and second conditionals

	if clause	main clause
Zero conditional	if + present simple	present simple
First conditional	if + present simple	will/can/could/ may/might/should + infinitive
Second conditional	if + past simple	would/could/might/ should + infinitive

'real' conditionals

Use the zero conditional to talk about a real situation that is always true with a result that always happens.

*If you **pay** by debit card, there's a 5% discount.*

Use the first conditional to talk about a real possibility in the present or future. In the main clause, use *may/might/can/could* instead of *will* for an uncertain result, and use *should* for advice.

*If you **put in** the wrong pin number three times, the machine **will take** your card.*

*If your card **gets stuck**, you **should** ring the number on the machine.*

hypothetical or 'unreal' conditionals

Use the second conditional to talk about a hypothetical situation in the present or future. In the main clause, use *might/could* for an uncertain result.

*If Valerie **practised** more, she **could be** really good.*

Use *If + were to* + infinitive to talk about a situation which is more hypothetical or in a more formal situation.

*If I **were to** sign the contract, when could I expect payment?*

alternatives to if

Use *providing/provided (that)*, *on condition that* and, less formally, *as long as*, to mean *if* and *only if*.

*Children may take part, **providing** they are over ten.*

Use *unless* to mean *if ... not*

*I'll be there at 10a.m. **unless** the train is late.*

spoken grammar

In spoken English, we often use *suppose/supposing* and *imagine* instead of *if* to emphasise the 'imagining.'

***Suppose** you won the lottery, **what would you do**?*

5.3 brainstorming

proposing/suggesting ideas	
How do you feel about What (do you think) about Would you consider	this idea? trying something completely different?
Could we go for	something radical?
How does	this idea strike you?
I was thinking of	using a celebrity.
It'd be great if we could get	a celebrity spokesperson.

reacting to or commenting on ideas	
+	That's a great/fantastic/ idea. Let's go with/I'd go for X.
unsure	I can't make up my mind. I'm torn between X and Y.
−	I think it's too obscure/predictable. That's not original/ funny enough. It doesn't grab me. (informal) I think we're on the wrong track here.

PRACTICE

5.1

A Complete the text with *a/an*, *the* or no article (–).

The Thomas Edisons of food

When people think of [1]_____ inventors, they might think of Thomas Edison and [2]_____ light bulb or Gutenburg and [3]_____ printing press, but do you know who invented some of the food you eat?

- George Crum was [4]_____ head chef at [5]_____ resort in Saratoga Springs, New York. One day [6]_____ customer complained that the French fries were too thick, so Crum sliced [7]_____ potato paper-thin and fried it, just to make [8]_____ customer happy. And so, [9]_____ crisps were born.

- Sausages of all sorts have been common in Europe for centuries, but [10]_____ hot dogs were first sold as sausages in buns by German immigrants on the streets of [11]_____ New York City in [12]_____ mid-19th century.

- Mayonnaise was probably invented by [13]_____ French chef in [14]_____ mid-18th century and was first sold in glass bottles in [15]_____ US in 1912.

- Popcorn was invented by Native American Indians, but it's not clear by which group or where [16]_____ snack food first appeared. Early American settlers ate [17]_____ popcorn with milk for [18]_____ breakfast! So the next time you're sitting in [19]_____ cinema, munching on popcorn and crisps, remember [20]_____ people who first discovered these treats. Now, who were they again … ?

5.2

A Complete the sentences with the appropriate form of the verbs in brackets. Add an auxiliary verb where necessary.

1 If you give me your phone number, I _____ him to call you back. (ask)

2 Would you be interested if we _____ you a free sample? (send)

3 If I were _____ another chance, I'd do it differently next time. (have)

4 If I got there a day early, it _____ me the chance to look around. (give)

5 I'm going to be really angry if you _____ me. (not call)

6 If it _____ you should wear a waterproof jacket. (rain)

7 I may go home early if Anna _____ there. (not be)

8 If you were _____ to the plan, we could put it into action immediately. (agree)

B Underline the correct alternative in the sentences.

1 I'll tell you *provided/supposing* you promise to keep it a secret.

2 We won't go *imagine/unless* they pay our expenses.

3 *Supposing/Provided* that you lost your job tomorrow, what would you do then?

4 *If/Providing* that we have enough time, I intend to visit all of my relatives.

5 I'm going to leave *unless/if* you stop being aggressive with me.

6 *Unless/Imagine* we met them in the street; how might you react?

C Complete the sentences so that they mean the same as 1–6 above.

1 I won't tell you unless _____.

2 We won't go if_____.

3 What would you do if you were _____?

4 I intend to visit all of my relatives unless _____ .

5 I'm going to leave if _____.

6 How might you react if we were_____?

5.3

A Complete the conversation by adding the missing words from the box.

~~think~~ between   brilliant   consider   feel   go   grab
obscure   original   sound   track

         think
A: What do you̸about naming our language school *Tongues4U!*

B: That's an awful idea!

C: How do you about *Talk2Me?*

A: It doesn't me.

B: I think it's not enough.

C: Would you *English246?*

B: I think we're on the wrong here. All these numbers.

A: How does *Language Lab?*

B: Hmmm… Not bad.

C: I'm torn *Language Lab* and *Lingo Lab.*

A: Lingo is a bit.

B: Let's with *Language Lab* then.

C: That's a idea.

GRAMMAR

6.1 modal verbs and phrases

	present	past
obligation (strong)	have to/have got to must need to am obliged to am required to	had to/had got to – needed to was obliged to was required to
obligation (mild)	should ought to am supposed to	should have ought to have was supposed to
lack of obligation	don't have to don't need to needn't am not obliged to am not required to	didn't have to didn't need to needn't have wasn't obliged to wasn't required to
prohibition	mustn't can't oughtn't shouldn't am not supposed to am not allowed to	– couldn't oughtn't to have shouldn't have wasn't supposed to wasn't allowed to
permission	can am allowed to may	could was allowed to might
ability	can am able to manage to	could was able to managed to

obligation

To express that someone causes another person to do something, use *make someone do something*.

My mum **makes me study** for two hours every night.

Must can express that the obligation is internal, not (only) because of a rule.

I **must finish** this report – I don't want to annoy the boss.

lack of obligation / prohibition

Note the difference between *don't have to* and *mustn't*:

You **don't have to** arrive before 5pm. (it's not necessary, but you can)

You **mustn't** arrive before 5pm. (you're not allowed to)

permission

Use *let + someone*, or *allow someone to* to say that someone gave permission to someone.

Do you think she'll let me take a day off?

My company allows us to work from home one day a week.

ability

For ability on a single occasion in the past, use *was/were able to* or *managed to* (not *could*).

He was able to find his way out of the forest and get help. NOT He could find his way ...

Use *manage to* for something that is/was difficult to do.

It was his first marathon and he managed to run it in under three hours.

6.2 future perfect/future continuous

future perfect

Use *will + have +* past participle to talk about something that will finish before a specific time in the future.

I'll **have finished** this report by the end of the week.

Future perfect is often used in conjunction with the time expression *by ...*, meaning 'at the latest'.

future continuous

Use *will + be + -ing* form to talk about:

• something that will be in progress at or around a specific time in the future.

I'll **be driving home** when you call, so just leave a message.

• things that will happen in the future, when you don't want to express the idea that the action is part of a particular plan or intention, but will happen in the normal course of events.

I expect I'll **be talking to** Ian tomorrow, so I could ask him then.

Will you **be phoning** Mum this weekend?

spoken grammar

In spoken English, we often add an adverb and the modal verbs *might, could, may* to express degree of likelihood.

By tomorrow morning he'll **probably have realised** that it was a big mistake to leave her.

I **definitely won't have spoken** to him by then.

By then I **might have passed** my driving test, so we **could drive** there.

6.3 persuading

Use the following phrases to persuade someone by giving a strong opinion:

Surely Clearly Anyone can see that	parents need to take more responsibility for their kids' education.

Use negative questions when you want to persuade someone by inviting them to agree with you.

Don't you agree that Don't you think Isn't it true that Don't you see that Isn't it obvious that	the internet is destroying human relationships?
Shouldn't people Don't parents need to	spend more time with their families?

PRACTICE

6.1

A Underline the correct alternatives in the blog.

TRAVELLER'S JOURNAL – CHANGING TIMES

... it was the 1980s and travel there was very restricted back then. Of course you ¹*should / had to* get a visa to enter the country, but you also ²*needed to / must* get a permit to travel to most cities. Or at least you ³*were supposed to / needed to* get a permit; I didn't always get one, and still I ⁴*could / managed to* go to many places that foreigners technically ⁵*couldn't / needn't* go to. In one remote town, the police called me in for questioning; I spoke the language a little so I was ⁶*able to / obliged to* communicate with them. Once they were convinced that I wasn't a spy, they ⁷*allowed / let* me go and I was ⁸*allowed to / obliged to* stay there as long as I wanted.

Of course, it's changed so much now. You still ⁹*must / have to* get a visa to enter, but you're not ¹⁰*supposed to / obliged to* get a permit to go anywhere within the country. As was always the case, if you ¹¹*could / can* speak the language, it's a really enriching experience, and I think everyone ¹²*should / is supposed to* try to spend at least a few weeks travelling there.

B Rewrite the sentences. Use the word in brackets so that the meaning stays the same.

1 I fell asleep. It was difficult. (manage)

I _____

2 We stayed for dinner. It was our obligation. (oblige)

We _____

3 It's OK to listen to your MP3 player here. I give you permission. (allow)

You _____

4 It was too dark to see anything. (not able)

He _____

5 It's a good idea for her to leave before dark. (ought)

She _____

6 The rule was to pay before going in. We didn't pay at all. (suppose)

We _____

7 The maximum age to enter this disco is eighteen. (not allow)

Adults _____

8 A passport was necessary. (have to)

We _____

6.2

A Complete the sentences with the future perfect or the future continuous form of the verb in brackets.

1 Her plane lands at 11.45p.m.

At 11.50 tonight she _____ the plane. (probably/get off)

By the time we wake up tomorrow, she _____ home. (arrive)

2 The film starts at eight, and it's about two hours long.

At nine, I _____ the film. (watch)

By eleven, the film _____ (finish).

3 The world hotdog-eating champion can eat more than six hotdogs a minute.

In ten minutes from now, he _____ over sixty hotdogs. (eat)

Tonight in his sleep, he _____ about hotdogs! (dream)

4 Give me a day to think about it.

By this time tomorrow, I _____ (decide).

This time next week, I _____ my decision. (definitely/not regret)

B Find and correct the mistakes in A's part of the conversations.

Conversation 1

A: ¹Will you seeing Frank today?

B: Yes, do you want me to give him a message?

A: ²Yes, could you tell him I won't probably have finished the report until tomorrow.

Conversation 2

A: ³Just think – this time tomorrow you'll finish all your exams.

B: I know. That's what keeps me going.

A: ⁴And you be celebrating with your friends.

Conversation 3

A: ⁵Will you use your computer at lunchtime today? I've got a problem with mine.

B: No, I'm going out and I won't be back till four if you want to use it till then.

A: ⁶I might still using it when you get back. The technicians might not have fixed mine by then.

6.3

A Write the underlined phrases in full.

A: ¹Don't / agree / people / should / able / start a family when they're teenagers?

Don't you agree that people should be able to start

B: What, even at 16 or 17?

A: Yes. ²Clear / they at the peak of their physical health.

B: ³Is / obvious / most / 17-year-olds aren't even mature enough to be responsible for themselves?

A: Yeah, ⁴but does / depend / the individual? Some 18 year-olds might make good parents.

B: ⁵But / sure / they / need / time to sort out their own lives first.

A: ⁶But / is / it / fact / that in some cultures 18 is a normal age to have a family?

B: Yes, ⁷but / anyone / see / that what works in one culture won't necessarily work in every culture.

A: Hmm. Maybe you're right.

GRAMMAR

7.1 quantifiers

	100%	a large amount	a small amount	0%
uncountable or plural nouns	all, any	a lot of, lots of, plenty of, most	some, hardly any	no, not any
uncountable nouns		much, a large amount of, a great deal of	a little, little	
plural nouns	both (= all of two)	many, a large number of, quite a few	several, a small number of, a few, few	
singular nouns	each, every			no, not any, neither (= none of two)

a few / a little = some or a small amount
There's still a little butter left.

few / little = not many/much or not as many/much as wanted or expected
Very few people came to the meeting.

any = It doesn't matter which/who
I like any brand of chocolate.

spoken grammar

With *a ____ number of* + a plural noun, a singular verb is more correct but a plural verb is often used in spoken English.

*A large number of books **were** destroyed in the fire. A small number **were** saved.*

7.2 reported speech

In reported speech, the original verb form often goes back further into the past. Pronouns, time references etc. also change.

direct speech	reported speech
present simple/continuous 'I want to be a pilot.' 'We're working.'	past simple/continuous He told us he wanted to be a pilot. She said they were working.
past simple/present perfect 'Ben phoned me last week.' 'I've read your book.'	past perfect She told me Ben had phoned her the week before. She said she'd read my book.
will/would/can/could/should 'We'll help you tomorrow.' 'You can stay with me.'	would/could/should He said they'd help me the next day. She said I could stay with her.

It is not necessary to change the verb form into the past when:
• reporting something that is still true now, or which was said very recently.
• using the present form of a reporting verb.
'I think it's going to snow.' Jake says he thinks it's going to snow.

reported questions

Use normal statement word order. Don't use *do/does/did* or a question mark. *'What does Ian think?'*
She asked me what Ian thought.
NOT *She asked me what did Ian think.*

With *yes/no* questions, use *if* or *whether*.
'Are you going to the party?'
*He asked me **if** I was going to the party.*

Use *asked, wanted to know, enquired* and *wondered*.
*They **wanted to know** what time the train left.*

reported requests

Use verb + pronoun/noun + infinitive with *to*.
'Could you open the window?'
She asked me to open the window.

time phrases and place references

Time phrases and place references usually change.

now → then/at that time,
yesterday → the day before/previous day
tomorrow → the following/next day
a week ago → the week before
here → there

7.3 adding emphasis

auxiliary verbs	
add or stress auxiliaries	I **do** hate it when people smoke indoors. It **is** annoying.

intensifiers	
really, totally, so + any adjective	It's **so** worrying.
absolutely, completely + extreme adjectives	It's **completely** ridiculous.
such (a/an) + (adjective) + noun	It'll be **such an** amazing experience. It was **such** terrible weather.

emphasising phrases	
pronoun/noun + be + the one who	You're the one who wanted to guess.
the + adjective + thing is	The amazing thing is the colours.

informal phrases	
There's no way (that) ...	There's no way Tom stole the money.
What/Who/Where/ Why/How on earth ...?	Why on earth didn't you say so?

PRACTICE

7.1

A Underline the correct alternative.

What does your ring tone say about you?

Almost everyone now has a mobile phone and ¹*a great deal/a large number/the most* of us have our own ring tone. Is it only so that we can distinguish our own phone from others or is it because ²*each/a large number of/both* time our phone rings we want to be able to say, 'Listen to that. That's me!'? Maybe ³*either/both/each* reasons are true. Here is a quick guide to ⁴*some/few/a little* typical ring tones and what they say about their users.

If your ring tone is ⁵*either/both/neither* a hip hop tune or a current hit, then you are young at heart but not particularly original.

⁶*Any/All/Either* classic rock tune means you're probably over thirty but you know you're still cool.

⁷*Not much/A few/Very few* people think annoying animal noises are as funny as the phones' owners obviously do. So ⁸*no/any/neither* points for maturity there.

You download a new one every month? You must be a teenager or you have ⁹*plenty of/ a large number of/hardly any* time and money.

You never change it? Either you're too lazy or you don't know how. ¹⁰*Neither/Both/Any* is an acceptable reason!

B Complete sentences 1–8 with a quantifier from the box.

| quite a few   a few   very few   a little |
| very little   any (x2)   either |

1 Everyone wanted to get home and so there were _____ questions at the end of the lecture.

2 I'm afraid I've spilt _____ wine on the carpet.

3 _____ of the students (four of us to be exact) have signed your petition.

4 I've watched _____ basketball games in my time, probably hundreds, but I've never seen such an exciting match.

5 Carla couldn't afford a taxi because she had _____ money left.

6 You can press _____ 'save' or 'save as' and then give the document a name.

7 Are you having _____ other problems with the photocopier?

8 I like _____ music by Jade. She's my favourite singer.

7.2

A Read the questions then complete the reported speech below.

1 Where have you been all day?

2 What did you watch on TV last night?

3 Have you washed your hands for dinner?

4 Have you got any homework for tomorrow?

5 Are you going to help me with the housework this weekend?

My mother used to ask me questions at the strangest times:

• When I came home from school she wanted to know
  ¹ *where I ...*

• The morning after we'd spent the evening watching TV together, she asked me ² _____

• At 10 in the morning, she used to ask ³ _____

• In the middle of the summer holiday, she asked ⁴ _____

• When she knew I was going on a weekend camping trip with friends, she asked ⁵ _____

B Find and correct ten mistakes with reported speech in the story.

My first (and most embarrassing) job interview

I was eighteen when I went for my first job interview, at a photo laboratory. The personnel manager asked me take a seat and then asked what's my name and I was so nervous that I told him I don't understand the question. Then he wanted to know do I have any plant experience; I said that I did some work in my grandmother's garden. He laughed and said that by 'plant' he had meant 'factory', not trees and flowers. I felt terribly embarrassed and simply told him that I have never worked in a factory. He had my file of photos and he asked that I talked about them. I was so nervous that I dropped them all on the floor! Then he asked me if I have any referees; I thought he meant the kind of referees they have in a football match, so I told him that I didn't play team sports but that I had been doing long-distance running for years. I was sure that I had messed up the interview, but then he enquired when I can start! He wanted me that I start the following Monday!

7.3

A Make the soap opera script more dramatic by using the words in brackets.

1 A:: What's the matter? You look terrible. (on earth)

2 B: I've just seen Marco with Claudia. I'm furious, I can hardly speak. (so)

3 A: That's crazy. I'm sure there's a mistake. Why don't you call him? (totally)

4 B: I'm not going to phone him. (there's no way)

5 A: But Marco's a great guy and you're good together. (such, so)

6 B: Well you can be sure that Claudia's going to regret it. (really)

7 A: I hope you're not going to do anything stupid. (do)

8 B: You told me to fight for him. I'm just following your advice. (the one)

GRAMMAR

8.1 second, third and mixed conditionals

second or 'unreal' conditional

Use *if* + past simple, *would/might* + infinitive to talk about hypothetical situations in the present/future.

If I saw a person in trouble, I would/might help them

third or 'past unreal' conditional

Use *if* + past perfect, *would/might/could* + *have* + past participle to talk about hypothetical situations in the past.

If he'd known the woman, he might have helped her.

For a longer action, use the past perfect continuous.

If I hadn't been sitting there, we wouldn't have met.

mixed conditionals

We can also use a mix of second and third conditionals:

Use *if* + past perfect, *would/might/could* + infinitive to talk about a hypothetical situation in the past with a result in the present. This is often used with the verbs *be/feel/seem*.

If he hadn't missed his plane, he'd be in Mexico by now.

Use *if* + past simple, *would/might/could* + infinitive to talk about a general hypothetical state with a past result.

If I were taller, I could have become a police officer.

clause order

It is possible to change the order of the clauses. Note the use of the comma.

If you'd checked your emails, you would have known about the meeting.

We wouldn't have believed it if we hadn't seen it with our own eyes.

spoken grammar

In formal English, we use *were* instead of *was* with *I/he/she/it*. In spoken English (apart from in the phrase *If I were you*), we usually use *was*.

*Chris would tell me **if he was** in trouble.*

***If I were you**, I'd go to the doctor's.*

8.2 infinitive and -ing forms

infinitive with to

• Use after the following verbs: *afford, agree, arrange, decide, expect, hope, intend, learn, manage, need, offer, promise, seem, start, tend, want.*

*We hope **to start** the meeting at 9.*

• Use as part of semi-fixed phrases e.g. *be good/lucky/happy, be necessary/prepared to do, have the chance/opportunity/desire/time to do, someone's goal/aim/ambition/aim is to do.*

*We were lucky **to have** the opportunity **to go**.*

• Use to express purpose.

*I'm going to the shops **to buy** some groceries.*

• Use after the following verbs with an object: *ask, advise, expect, help*, invite persuade, remind, require, teach, want.*

*Will wants me **to go** to the party with him.*

infinitive without to

• Use after modal verbs.

*They might **be** late.*

• Use after *had better* and *would rather*.

*You'd better **take** an umbrella – it looks like rain.*

• Use after *let, make, help** with an object.

*Our supervisor let us **go** early today.*

* help can be used either with or without *to*, e.g.

*He helped me **do/to do** the homework.*

-ing form

• Use after the following verbs: *avoid, come, consider, discuss, despise, enjoy, finish, go, hate, Involve, keep, like, loathe, love, mind, miss, practise, suggest.*

*I keep **getting** bad headaches.*

*Dave's gone **fishing** with his father.*

• Use as a subject or object, i.e. as a noun.

***Going** for a walk is much better than **sleeping**.*

• Use after certain phrases, e.g. *not mind, be keen on, can't bear/stand, it's not worth, it's no use.*

*I can't stand **listening** to his voice all day long.*

• Use after prepositions (often part of a fixed phrase), e.g. *look forward to, be used to, be keen on, instead of.*

*I'm keen on **sailing**.*

8.3 handling an awkward situation

preparing the ground

There's something I've been meaning to talk to you about.
There's something I'd like to talk to you about.

giving the message

I hope you don't take this the wrong way, but …
I don't want you to get the wrong idea, but …
It's just that, (you know you borrowed/you said you'd … etc.)

suggesting a solution

I have a suggestion/an idea.
It would put my mind at ease if …
I'd feel better if …

getting the other person's point of view

Do you see where I'm coming from?
How does that sound?
How would you feel about that?
Do you know what I mean?

PRACTICE

8.1

A Choose the correct sentence ending. In one case, both endings are possible.

1 If the builders had begun the job two weeks ago,
   a) they might have finished it by now.
   b) they might finish it by now.

2 If you found money in the street
   a) what would you have done?
   b) what would you do?

3 If Chun had started the race better,
   a) she could win the gold medal.
   b) she could have won the gold medal.

4 We wouldn't be lost
   a) if you hadn't given me the wrong directions.
   b) if you gave me the wrong directions.

5 If Marco hadn't ignored my advice,
   a) he wouldn't be in this mess now.
   b) he wouldn't have been in this mess now.

B Join the sentences using a past or mixed conditional form and the words in brackets. In some cases both forms are possible.

1 Beth didn't study. She didn't pass the exam. (could)
   If Beth had studied, she could have passed the exam.

2 You didn't invite me to the party. That's why I didn't come. (would)

3 Ludmila lost all her money on the stock exchange. That's why she's not rich now. (would)

4 Greg wasn't travelling fast. That's probably why he didn't hit the motorcyclist. (might)

5 They stopped the fire. That's probably why it didn't destroy most of the building. (could)

6 The plant died because you didn't water it. (would)

7 Mei-li was able to afford a new car because she had just won some money. (could not)

8 We were working together in Tokyo and now we're married. (would not)

8.2

A Find and correct the mistakes in the sentences. Do not change the underlined phrase.

1 <u>It's no use</u> to explain – you never listen anyway.
   It's no use explaining – you never listen anyway.

2 <u>There's no point in</u> go to bed now – we have to get up in an hour.

3 <u>Do you expect</u> that I know all the answers?

4 Listen <u>to your MP3 player</u> during class is rude.

5 My parents never <u>let me</u> to stay out past 8 o'clock.

6 We all <u>look forward to</u> see you in person.

7 <u>You'd better</u> to get ready – the taxi's arriving in ten minutes.

8 The trip was <u>a good opportunity</u> practising speaking English.

9 <u>They're used to</u> speak English with each other even though they're both Japanese.

10 <u>I phoned the station</u> for asking about departure times.

B Use the correct form of the verbs in the box to rewrite the sentences so that they mean the same.

avoid   consider   expect   keep   manage   remind   teach

1 Why don't you become a doctor?
   Have _____.

2 I've passed my driving test – after three tries!
   I've _____.

3 I can type without looking. I learnt that from my mother.
   My mother _____.

4 We didn't talk to each other all through the party.
   We _____.

5 Jorge thinks that he'll finish the painting by the end of the week.
   Jorge _____.

6 My computer freezes whenever I hit the delete button.
   My computer _____.

7 Don't let me forget to lock the door, Jan.
   Could you _____?

8.3

A Complete the conversation with phrases a)–f). There is one phrase you do not need.

a) How does that sound
b) It's just that
c) There's something I've been meaning to talk to you about
d) I'm sure we can sort it out
e) Do you see where I'm coming from
f) I don't want you to get the wrong idea, but

A: Max, ¹_____.
B: Sure, go ahead.
A: Look, ²_____
B: That sounds bad …
A: ³_____ you know how you always open the window when you come into the office? Well, it's often too cold for me.
B: Oh, right. I find it too stuffy.
A: It's a bit annoying because you don't ever ask us. ⁴_____?
B: Fair enough. Look, I'll make sure I check first. ⁵_____?
A: Good. I'd really appreciate that.

GRAMMAR

9.1 -ing form or infinitive

-ing form or infinitive with *to* (difference in meaning)

Some verbs can be followed by the -ing form or the infinitive with *to* with different meanings.

	+ infinitive with *to*	+ -ing form
remember forget	for things you plan or want to do or it is your responsibility to do He **remembered to buy** the tickets.	have a memory of an earlier action I'll **never forget going** to Canada when I was ten.
try	make an effort or attempt to do something which is difficult Angus **tried to change** his ticket but it was impossible.	experiment to see if something will work Why don't you **try clicking** on 'OK' on the dialogue box?
stop	stop one action in order to do another (infinitive of purpose) We **stopped to have** some lunch	finish an action or activity My father **stopped driving** after his eightieth birthday.
go on	for a change of activity The doctor started with a general introduction about obesity and **went on to talk** about its causes.	continue Debra **went on working** there even though she hated her job.

-ing form or infinitive with *to* (no difference in meaning)

Some verbs can be followed by the -ing form or infinitive with *to* with no difference in meaning: *like, love, hate, prefer, can't stand, can't bear.*

I **hate writing/to write** by hand. I much **prefer using/to use** a computer.

In American English, the infinitive with *to* is often preferred. In British English, the infinitive with *to* is mainly used to talk about choices and habits.

I **like to go** to the dentist twice a year.

I **hate to** interrupt, but we have to go.

If the verb after *prefer* is in the negative, use the infinitive with *to*.

I **prefer not to write** by hand.

When we use the verbs *begin, continue* and *start* in continuous forms we usually use the infinitive with *to*.

They're **beginning to annoy** me.
NOT ~~They're beginning annoying me.~~

9.2 past modals of deduction

Use modal verb + *have* + past participle (perfect infinitive) to make deductions or guesses about past actions or states.

You **could have left** it in the café.

Use modal verb + *have* + been + -ing form to make deductions about continuous actions or states.

She must have been feeling ill.

Use modal verb + *have* + been + past participle for deductions using the passive.

It could have been stolen from your bag.

must have	you are almost certain that something is true, based on the evidence.	I **must have deleted** the email. I can't find it anywhere.
might/could/ may have	you think it is possible that something is true, based on the evidence.	The plane **could have been delayed** by the weather. There's a bad storm at sea.
couldn't/ can't have	you are almost certain something is not true or is impossible, based on the evidence.	It **can't have been** the waitress. She wasn't in the room when the bag was stolen.

9.3 reporting an incident

referring to time	
Before/As soon as/When	I realised what had happened/ was happening ...
It was only (a minute/much later)	(that) I realised/remembered ...
It all happened	so quickly/fast/slowly.

describing impressions of a person or thing	
He reminded me of	Tom Cruise.
He looked/seemed	as if he was a student. like a student. about 30/very strong.

other phrases for reporting	
It never occurred to me It didn't cross my mind	(that) he was a thief.
My mind / I	went blank.
I didn't catch	the car number plate. what he said.

PRACTICE

9.1

A Match the sentence halves.

1	I tried drinking the medicine	a)	but I couldn't – it was too disgusting.
2	I tried to drink the medicine	b)	but it didn't help.
3	He stopped to smoke	c)	a cigarette before continuing.
4	He stopped smoking	d)	because he wanted to get fitter.
5	Julia remembers to text me	e)	whenever she needs a lift from the station.
6	Julia remembers texting me	f)	but I didn't get any messages from her.
7	Xavier went on to perform	g)	even though audiences became smaller and smaller.
8	Xavier went on performing	h)	at all of the best opera houses in the world.

B Underline the correct alternative. Sometimes both are possible.

Most people prefer not ¹*getting/to get* involved in a crime investigation, according to Detective Jaime Lopez. 'I'll give you an example,' said Lopez. 'Last week we were just starting ²*investigating/to investigate* a car theft that had happened in broad daylight in the city centre, and we realized that our biggest challenge might be to find someone who remembered ³*seeing/to see* anything at all. We estimate that twenty or thirty people witnessed the crime but no one tried ⁴*intervening/to intervene* and most people went on ⁵*doing/to do* what they were doing. Interestingly, one tourist stopped ⁶*taking/to take* pictures of the theft in process but then continued sightseeing. He only came forward three days after the incident. 'Sorry, I forgot ⁷*telling/to tell* you that I have some pictures of the crime,' he said. We tried ⁸*identifying/to identify* the thief from the tourist's photograph but it wasn't clear enough.' We asked Lopez how he can bear ⁹*doing/to do* such a frustrating job. 'I like ¹⁰*helping / to help* people. I love this city.'

9.2

A Rewrite the underlined sentence with *must/might/may/could/can't/couldn't have*.

1 <u>Perhaps Jenna phoned while we were out.</u> Let me check on the answerphone.

Jenna might have phoned while we were out.

2 Knock louder. You know he's a bit deaf. <u>I'm sure he didn't hear you.</u>

3 I locked the door. I'm certain. <u>Maybe the thieves got in through the window.</u>

4 I lost all my work yesterday. <u>I realised it was impossible that I saved the document.</u>

5 Ooh, that was a bad knock to your head. <u>I'm certain it hurt a lot.</u>

6 I don't know why Wanda was late for the meeting. <u>Maybe her plane was delayed.</u>

7 <u>I'm sure I've made a mistake.</u> The looks date wrong.

8 Paola should have won the race. <u>It's impossible that she was trying hard enough.</u>

B Complete the conversations with the correct form of a verb from the box and a modal of deduction.

look	tell	think	cost	work	switch off

1 **A:** Look at her necklace. Are those real diamonds?

   B: Yes. It _____ a fortune!

2 **A:** I tried phoning Mike four times but he didn't answer.

   B: Don't worry. He _____ his phone or maybe he didn't have it with him.

3 **A:** Why was Danielle in the office at midnight?

   B: She _____ late. I know she had an important meeting the next day.

4 **A:** I'm sure Len told me you were a doctor.

   B: He _____ of my sister, Rachel, or maybe he confused me with someone else.

5 **A:** I've lost my boarding card. It's not in my bag!

   B: You _____ properly. I saw you put there just now.

6 **A:** Do you think Yves knows he didn't get the promotion?

   B: I suppose he _____ by the boss but I really doubt it.

9.3

A Correct each of B's sentences by adding a word from the box.

looked	realised	crossed	occurred	if	strange

A: Why didn't you phone us when you first saw the man behaving strangely?

B: ¹It never my mind until I saw the picture on *Crimebeat* on TV.

A: And when you saw *Crimebeat* ...?

B: ²It to me then that I should contact you.

A: We appreciate that, sir. Could you tell me about the incident?

B: ³Yes. I saw him near the factory. He looked as he was taking photos of the building.

A: Do you remember anything else?

B: ⁴When he saw me, he went away very quickly and he guilty.

A: Why didn't you call someone right away?

B: ⁵It was only later that I that there was something strange about how he left.

A: Maybe he'd finished?

B: ⁶I don't know. It just seemed quite but then I didn't think any more about it till I saw the programme.

GRAMMAR

10.1 relative clauses

types of relative clauses

Use defining relative clauses to give essential information about which person, thing, place or time is being talked about. Do not use a comma before the relative pronoun.

*This is the room **where I usually work**.*

Use non-defining relative clauses to give additional, non-essential information. Use commas to separate this clause from the rest of the sentence.

*This room, **where I usually work**, is in the quietest part of the house.*

relative pronouns

Use *who* for people, *which* for things, *when* for time, *where* or *which ... in* for places and *whose* for possession.

*This is the room **which** I usually work **in**.*

In defining relative clauses:

• we can use *that* instead of *who, which where* and *when*.

*I just ran into a woman **who/that** I went to university with.*

• we can omit the pronouns *who, which, that, when* or *where* if they are the object of the relative clause.

*Gwen's the woman **(who)** I'm going to marry.* (The subject of the relative clause is *I*. *Who* is the object, so we can omit *who*.)

*Mike gave me a ring **which** belonged to his mother.* (The subject of the relative clause is *which*, so we cannot omit it.)

In non-defining relative clauses:

• we cannot use *that*.

*She's staying with her ex-husband, **who/~~that~~** lives in the south of France.*

• we cannot omit the pronoun.

Gwen, who I'm going to see later, is my fiancé. NOT ~~Gwen, I'm going to see later, is ...~~

• we can use *which* to refer to the whole of a previous clause or sentence.

*The plane was delayed by bad weather, **which** meant we had a four-hour wait.*

When two sentences are joined with a relative clause, we omit words which have been replaced by the relative pronoun (e.g. *here, there, then, him, her, it*).

She's a woman. I know her well.

She's a woman who I know ~~her~~ well.

spoken grammar

In very formal English, use prepositions at the beginning of the relative clause. In this case always use *whom*, not *who*.

*He was someone **to whom** she regularly wrote.*

In spoken (and informal written) English, we use prepositions at the end of the relative clause.

*He was someone **(who)** she regularly wrote **to**.*

10.2 participle clauses

Use participle clauses (clauses that start with a present or past participle) to vary your style or to include more information in a single sentence.

The present participle (-*ing* form) has an active meaning

***Seeing** her across the room, he went to speak to her.*
= he saw her (active)

The past participle has a passive meaning.

*The film, **directed** by Miyakazi, won an award for animation.*
= which was directed (passive)

Use participle clauses:

• as an alternative to relative clauses. Omit the relative pronoun and any auxiliary verbs. Use the present participle to replace simple *and* continuous verbs.

*The children **caught in the rainstorm** came home soaked.*
= The children who were caught ...

*Do you know that man **standing in the corner**?*
= that man who is standing ...

*Anyone **taking a photograph** will be arrested.*
= anyone who takes ...

• to create longer, more complex sentences. This is used particularly in writing when two actions happen at the same time and have the same subject.

*He sat at the lakeside, **surrounded by trees, writing a letter** and **thinking of his childhood**.*

• to give a reason for something.

***Knowing how unsafe the area was**, he decided to stay indoors.*
= because he knew how unsafe ...

10.3 giving a tour

commenting on facts
As you may know,/As I'm sure you know, …
The story goes that …
Apparently,/Supposedly, Interestingly, …
Surprisingly,/Strangely, …
Believe it or not, …
It's well worth (going/seeing/a visit)

leading the way		
Let's/ We could	head over to	the park.
Shall we Why don't we	head back to retrace our steps to	the café?

giving facts		
It was	built	to celebrate … to commemorate … in honour of …
	founded by named after	(Thomas Bodley).
	modelled on modelled after	(the Arc de Triomphe).
	burnt down destroyed rebuilt restored	in the 15th Century. in the 1990s.

PRACTICE

10.1

A Complete the review with who, which, whose, where or when.

I normally don't go for films ¹_____ make me cry, but everyone ²_____ sees *Marley and Me* should be warned to take tissues – it's a real tear-jerker. Marley is a dog, and the 'Me' in the title is newspaper columnist John Grogan, ³_____ book by the same title inspired the film. Grogan is played by Owen Wilson, ⁴_____ manages to play the role with surprising sensitivity. Jennifer Aniston, ⁵_____ plays Grogan's wife Jenny, also a journalist, gives a solid performance.

At the start of the movie, John and Jenny move to Florida, ⁶_____ they find positions with competing local newspapers and acquire a dog ⁷_____ they call Marley. The film alternates between hilarious moments ⁸_____ Marley makes a complete mess of things, and scenes ⁹_____ focus on the human dimension of John and Jenny's relationship. Throughout the ups and downs of their married life, the realistic attitude ¹⁰_____ they take helps their marriage survive.

While *Marley & Me* is not a movie ¹¹_____ you would see again and again, it's an entertaining family film ¹²_____ strikes a good balance between humour and drama.

B Which relative pronouns in the review can be replaced by that? Which can be omitted?

C Combine the sentences using a relative clause. Omit the relative pronoun where possible. Sometimes there is more than one answer.

1 The man is marrying Suzanne. He's very lucky.
The man _____.

2 The house burnt down yesterday. I used to live in it.
The house _____.

3 Pablo Picasso spent his early childhood in Malaga. His father was also an artist.
Pablo Picasso _____.

4 That was the most important moment of my life. I realised I wanted to be an actor.
The moment _____.

5 The holiday was in Canada. I enjoyed it most.
The holiday _____.

6 Usain Bolt is a famous Jamaican runner. He won three gold medals at the Beijing Olympics.
Usain Bolt, _____.

7 I lived with a guy while I was a student. His name was Jon.
Jon is _____.

8 You should make a speech. This is that sort of occasion.
This is _____ _____.

10.2

A Complete the verbs in the present or past participle form.

1 Walk*ing* into the room, he was stunned to see Julia wait_____ at the table.

2 The guests stood around, chat_____ loudly, not notic_____ the strange noises outside.

3 Hid_____ by the branches of a tree, the boy was able to spy on his friends without them noticing.

4 The large number of people wait_____ outside meant the doctor would be working late that night.

5 I knew two people injur_____ in the fire.

6 Disgust_____ with his team's defeat, he spent the next week watch_____ the video of the match over and over again.

B Combine the sentences using a participle clause.

1 The taxi almost drove over a man. He was lying in the street.

2 I don't know those people. They live next door to me.

3 Some factories were forced to close during the recession. They still haven't reopened.

4 The army was led by Napoleon. They advanced towards the hill.

5 Those apartments overlook Central Park. They are the most expensive.

6 Hundreds of young people camped along the river illegally. They were chased away by the police.

7 She closed her eyes. She listened to the sound of the building site. She wished she wasn't there.

8 The wedding will be taking place tomorrow. It's the Mayor's son's wedding.

10.3

A Correct eight mistakes in A's part of the conversations.

1 A: So here we are at Margit Island, named from a nun whose father was once king.
B: Wow! It's beautiful.
A: Yeah, interesting at one time it was three islands and only used by people who had land here.

2 A: Supposingly these caves run for miles.
B: What were they for?
A: The story tells that when there was an invasion, the local people hid in these tunnels.

3 A: That's the Vajdahunyad Castle. It was modelled from a castle in Transylvania.
B: And why was it built?
A: It was built for the city's millennium exhibition in 1896, to memorise the one thousand year anniversary of the founding of the state.

4 A: Let's retrace our feet to Castle Hill.
B: Great. We hardly spent any time there this morning.
A: Exactly, and the museum is well worse a visit.

VOCABULARY BANK

PERSONALITY ADJECTIVES

1A Match the adjectives in the box with descriptions 1–10.

> cautious   eccentric   flexible   genuine   mean   moody
> naive   sympathetic   trustworthy   witty

1 My friend always has time for me when I've got a problem. She seems to understand and wants to help.

2 Cheung always takes a long time to make up his mind and he's careful to avoid problems or danger.

3 Joe thought his first job would be easy and people would be nice. He soon learnt differently!

4 I really like your fiancé – he seems honest and sincere.

5 Lucia makes me laugh a lot. She's very quick-thinking and clever with words.

6 My last teacher wasn't very kind. She often laughed at students when they made mistakes.

7 Noriko is a great addition to the team. She adapts quickly to new situations and doesn't mind change.

8 Karl acts a bit strange sometimes and wears the oddest clothes, but he's a good guy.

9 You can tell Marta a secret and you know she'll never tell anyone else.

10 Sam's a typical teenager. He always seems to be unhappy or else he suddenly gets angry for no reason.

B What type of personality do you think the people in photos A–C have?

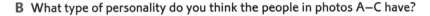

WORD FORMATION

2A Complete the table with the adjective form of the nouns.

noun	adjective
abs**ence**, pres**ence**	absent *present*
viol**ence**, pati**ence**	*violent patient*
independence silence	*independent silent*
parmanence intelligence	*parmanent intelligent*
secr**ecy**, accur**acy**	secret *accurate*
democra**cy**, decen**cy**	*democratic decent*
urgency fluency	*urgent fluent*
privacy	*private*

B Complete the table with the adjectives below and add the noun forms. Use a dictionary to help.

> **independent**
> **urgent**
> **silent**
> fluent
> **permanent**
> **private**
> intelligent

C Complete the questions with the noun or adjective form of one of the words in the table.

1 What do you think is the best way to gain _____ in a language?

2 How _____ is your spelling in your language and in English?

3 Are you good with young children or do you lose _____ very easily?

4 Is it better to have a boring but _____ job for life or a number of short-term jobs that you love?

5 Some people aren't academically brilliant, but have high emotional _____. Which is more important?

6 Would it be possible for people in your town to give up their _____ cars and use only public transport?

7 How often are you _____ from English lessons or from work due to bad health?

8 Do you think there is too much _____ on television nowadays?

D Ask and answer the questions.

ISSUES

1 Match the natural disasters to the photos.

1 flood
2 earthquake
3 drought
4 forest fire
5 landslide
6 tornado
7 tsunami
8 volcanic eruption

2A Complete the collocations with *issue/ question/problem* using an adjective from the box.

political	economic	ethical	global
industrial	domestic	rural	urban

1 This problem has nothing to do with any other country. It's a purely _domestic_ issue.

2 You can't decide on the basis of finance or politics. It's a/an _ethical_ question – a matter of right or wrong.

3 People in cities don't understand. It's a/an _rural_ problem.

4 The decision on the election date is a/an _political_ question and will depend on the government's popularity.

5 The country has serious _economic_ problems, which mean that taxes will probably have to double next year.

6 The typhoid epidemic started as a/an _urban_ problem but has rapidly spread to the countryside.

7 The situation can't be decided by one or two countries acting alone. It's a/an _global_ issue.

8 These are typical _industrial_ problems and affect most kinds of factories, from food production to car manufacture.

B Write the equivalent noun for each adjective in Exercise 2A. Keep the same context.

political – politics

urban – city

A   flood

B   tornado

C   landslide

D   drought

E   tsunami

F   earthquake

G   forest fire

H   volcanic eruption

VERBS/NOUNS WITH THE SAME FORM

3A Underline a word in each question which has the same noun/verb form.

1 What's the worst <u>delay</u> you've ever experienced on a flight?

2 Do you have an exam at the end of the course or does your teacher test your English every week?

3 Do you ever shout when you're angry or do you take a deep breath and count to ten?

4 Would you ever queue overnight for a product you've seen in a sale?

5 When you're cooking, do you weigh everything exactly or do you just make a guess?

6 Is the best cure for a headache to take a pill or just to relax?

7 Do you think people should get a fine for driving too fast or should they lose their licence?

8 In a restaurant, do you complain if the service is bad? Do you always tip the waiter if it's good?

9 Would you ever lie or do you always tell the truth?

10 When you compare yourself to other people, are you quite calm or are you often in a hurry?

B Work in pairs and discuss the questions.

VOCABULARY BANK

1A Cross out the collocation which is not possible.

1 beat / win / tackle / defeat / lose to   + an opponent.

2 win / lose / play / beat / draw   + a match

3 throw / bowl / score / pass / bounce   + a ball

4 get / shoot / score / miss / let in   + a goal

5 do +   weight-training / judo / chess / yoga

6 play + athletics / baseball / snooker / football

B Write the correct collocation under the photos A–F

C Which of these sports, games and activities have you tried? Which would you like to try?

2A Look at the common phrases and idioms in bold which come from some of the sports above. Match each phrase 1–6 with its meaning a)–f).

1 I've told you what I want to do, now **the ball is in your court.**

2 Shall we **kick off** today's lesson by looking at our latest blog entries?

3 I think that 70,000 euro is probably **in the ballpark** for that house.

4 I was very impressed by Jamal. He's really **on the ball**.

5 We need to discuss how to **tackle** the problem quickly.

6 It's **a whole new ballgame** for me, I've never directed a video before.

a) a completely new situation

b) to deal with a problem in a determined way

c) to start something happening

d) a reasonably accurate estimate

e) the next move is yours.

f) able to think or understand or react to something very quickly

B Do you have similar expressions in your language?

A

B

C

D

E

F

3A Complete the groups of things with a collective noun from the box.

| batch | bunch | crowd | flock | gang | herd |
| pack | series | set | swarm | | |

1 A _____ of bananas, flowers, grapes, keys, idiots, amateurs

2 A _____ of thieves, robbers, youths

3 A _____ of events, lectures, accidents, mistakes, disasters

4 A _____ of sheep, birds, geese

5 A _____ of cakes, bread, exam papers, test results

6 A _____ of bees, locusts, protestors, journalists

7 A _____ of football supporters, fans, spectators, commuters

8 A _____ of cows, deer, dairy cattle, protestors

9 A _____ of dogs, wolves, lies, football hooligans

10 A _____ of instructions, beliefs, ideas, keys, books, friends

B Which of the collective nouns have a negative meaning when used to talk about people?

VERBS USED IN STORIES

1A Match the verbs of movement with the pictures.

1	stagger	4	crawl	7	wander
2	wade	5	tiptoe	8	limp
3	march	6	slide	9	creep

B The verbs in Exercise 1A are often used metaphorically. Underline the best alternatives.

1 Our bus *slid/crawled/staggered* along at 10 kph in the traffic jam

2 I've got to *creep/stride/wade* through a hundred-page report before tomorrow.

3 Sorry, my mind was *wandering/tiptoeing/limping*. Could you say that again?

4 Old age *crawls/slides/creeps* up on you before you notice it.

5 The badly damaged plane *limped/waded/wandered* back to the airport.

6 Stop *wading/crawling/tiptoeing* around the subject. Just ask me directly.

7 The economy will *slide/wander/limp* into a serious recession next year.

8 He was absolutely *staggered/marched/waded* when he heard her question. He never would have guessed!

9 Time *marches/wades/staggers* on and we must finish at this point.

A

B

C

D

E

F

G

H

I

MULTI-WORD VERBS (1)

2A Look at the sentences and answer the questions.

1 We brought up Simon to be polite.

2 We brought Simon up to be polite.

3 We brought him up to be polite.

a) Where can you put a noun object?

b) Where must you put a pronoun object?

B Replace the noun in each sentence with the pronoun in brackets.

1 Kieron wanted the job but they turned ~~down Kieron~~ *him* down. (him)

2 The shop had some great clothes but the loud music put off Lena. (her)

3 Fifty people wanted to be extras in the film and the director took on all fifty people. (them all)

4 Señor Almeida isn't here at the moment. Can you ring Señor Almeida back? (him)

5 I finished the essay last night and gave in the essay this morning. (it)

6 If I don't know new words, I just look up the words in my electronic dictionary. (them)

7 The sound of the doorbell at 2a.m. woke up everyone. (us)

8 Is that a new coat? Anyway, take off the coat and hang up the coat here. (it, it)

VOCABULARY BANK

ADVERTISING AND BUSINESS

1A Complete the collocations with nouns from the box.

a product a business a market a meeting a price

B Add the verbs from the box to the collocation word webs.

| cancel demonstrate expand increase manage |
| postpone promote reduce re-enter see a gap in |

1
advertise — manufacture — launch
a product

2
arrange — open — close
2 _____

3
raise — lower — set
3 _____

4
set up — run — take over
4 _____

5
break into — enter — leave
5 _____

COMPOUND ADJECTIVES

2A Match the beginnings and endings to make compound adjectives for products.

1 long-	a) proof watch
2 high-	b) efficient lightbulb
3 pocket-	c) life batteries
4 water-	d) activated dictaphone
5 voice-	e) in dishwasher
6 built-	f) powered torch
7 hand-	g) held GPS system
8 solar-	h) friendly detergent
9 eco-	i) definition TV
10 energy-	j) sized camcorder

B Which items can you see in the photos?

A

B

C

D

E

F

HEALTH AND AGEING

1A Match the symptoms to the pictures.

1 It's very **swollen**.

2 I feel quite **dizzy** and thirsty.

3 I've been **sneezing** non-stop.

4 I can't sleep and I'm **irritable** all the time.

5 When I drive, everything looks **blurry.**

6 I can't stop **shivering** and I've got no energy.

7 The left-hand side of my face feels **paralysed**.

8 I think I ate some bad fish or something. I want to **vomit**.

9 The joints in my fingers are very painful and **stiff**.

B Match diagnoses a)–i) to symptoms 1–9 above.

a) You must be **allergic to** something.

b) It sounds like **food poisoning**.

c) So you're suffering from **insomnia**.

d) It could be **arthritis**.

e) You've probably **sprained** it.

f) You may have had a minor **stroke**.

g) You've got a **bug** that's going round.

h) You're probably **dehydrated**.

i) You must be **nearsighted**.

WORD FORMATION

2A Complete the table with the verb form of the nouns.

noun	verb
contribut**ion** explos**ion** intent**ion**	*contribute*
argu**ment** develop**ment** govern**ment**	
def**ence** off**ence** occurr**ence**	
revers**al** remov**al** dispos**al**	
clos**ure** signat**ure** expos**ure**	
employ**ee*** pay**ee** address**ee**	

*-ee: the person who is employed, paid, etc.

B Put the verbs below in the correct place in the table and add the noun forms. Use a dictionary to help you.

VOCABULARY BANK

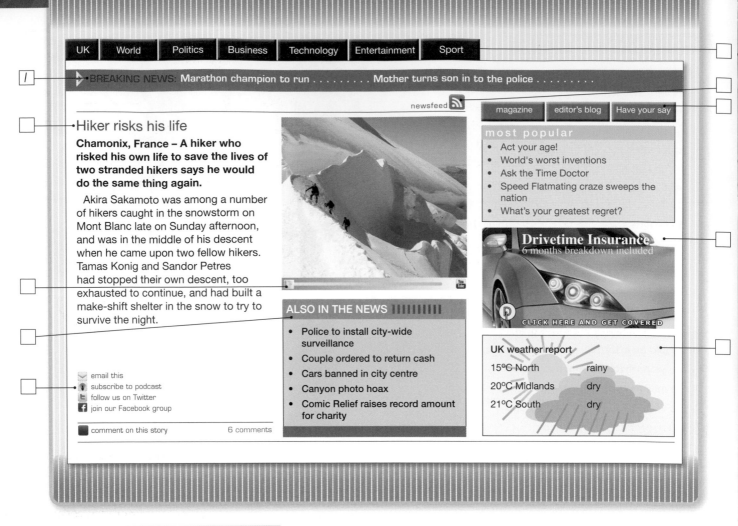

PARTS OF A NEWS WEBSITE

1A Match the parts of the news website to the picture.

1 breaking news	5 forum	9 navigation buttons
2 lead story	6 weather forecast	10 banner ad
3 headlines	7 video link	
4 news feed	8 podcast	

MULTI-WORD VERBS (2)

2A Look at the sentence pairs. How are the meanings of the multi-word verbs in bold different?

1 a) Did your parents **bring** you **up** as a Buddhist?

   b) Oh, here's Edith now. Just don't **bring up** anything about her divorce.

2 a) Anna keeps **putting off** the meeting. I don't think we'll ever get a chance to discuss things.

   b) Stop talking about your illnesses. You're **putting** me **off** my food!

3 a) Why did they **turn** Neil **down** for the job?

   b) Could you **turn** the cooker **down** – the sauce in the pan is going to burn.

4 a) If we **go by** her work so far, I don't think she has the skills for the new position.

   b) Time can **go by** slowly when you're a child.

5 a) The company **took on** ten school-leavers last month.

   b) After Brazil won the semi-finals, they **took on** the favourites, Spain.

B Complete the table with the multi-word verbs from Exercise 2A.

a		hire compete against
b		say no lower the level
c		pass judge from
d		make sb dislike sth postpone
e		raise start to talk about

FEELINGS

1A Write the feelings in the correct groups

apprehensive	disorientated	mystified
cheerful	furious	petrified
cross	glad	puzzled
delighted	livid	terrified
depressed	miserable	upset

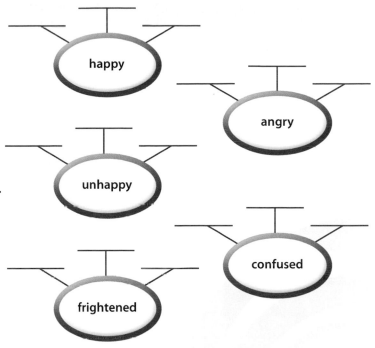

B Replace the word in bold with one of the words above.

1 Sam's always very **happy** first thing in the morning, while I'm usually in a bad mood until I have my first coffee.

2 Sometimes I get very **angry** with the children.

3 Richard was a little **frightened** before he went into the meeting.

4 Neera is **unhappy** because she's just hurt her hand.

5 It's common to feel **confused**, at first, in this building until you work out where everything is.

IDIOMS

2A Match the phrases and idioms in bold with pictures A–H.

1 The boss completely **lost his head** and started shouting at the client. <u>A f)</u>

2 Could you **catch** the waiter's **eye**? I'd like to ask for the bill. __ __

3 The job hunting isn't going well, but if I can **get my foot in the door** things will be fine. __ __

4 I can't afford this mobile – it **costs an arm and a leg**. __ __

5 I don't really mind paying taxes, but filling out these forms **is a pain in the neck**. __ __

6 He's **got a big mouth** – he told everyone in the office about my problems at home. __ __

7 Sorry, we just don't **see eye to eye** on this, and I don't think we'll ever agree. __ __

8 The teacher **turned a blind eye to** cheating in the exam, so almost all the students did it. __ __

B Match meanings a)–h) to the phrases and idioms.

a) have the same opinion

b) get someone's attention

c) be very annoying

d) get a chance to start

e) be very expensive

f) be unable to think clearly under pressure

g) ignore a bad thing

h) be someone who tells secrets

VOCABULARY BANK

CARS AND ACCIDENTS

1 Match the car parts 1–12 to A–L in the picture.

1	boot	*J*	7	tail light
2	bonnet		8	windscreen
3	number plate		9	tyre
4	indicator		10	windscreen wiper
5	wing		11	sun roof
6	wing mirror		12	steering wheel

2 Write the verb phrases in bold in the correct sentences.

skidded
1 The car ~~overtook~~ on the ice.

2 She **collided with** to avoid hitting the dog.

3 She increased her speed and **skidded** the car in front.

4 He **pulled out** – the police said he was going at 100 kph.

5 She **drove in the wrong lane** the side of the car by parking too near a wall.

6 He was driving too fast in a narrow street and **swerved** another car.

7 A car suddenly **exceeded the speed limit** in front of him and he almost went into the back of it.

8 She **scratched** along the motorway.

DEPENDENT PREPOSITIONS

3 Complete the headlines with a dependent preposition.

1 Innocent man mistaken _____ gang leader

2 Woman jailed for hiding robbers _____ police

3 Couple punished _____ balloon hoax

4 Mugger caught after boasting _____ crimes in local bar

5 Jailed criminal prohibited _____ selling his story

6 Politician condemned _____ involvement in banking scandal

7 Murderess given strong sentence for joking _____ crime

8 Local teacher fired for participating _____ protest march

9 College president conceals finanical woes _____ board of trustees

10 Mother fined _____ leaving baby unattended in car

MUSIC

1A Match the instruments 1–12 with the photos.

1. acoustic guitar
2. drums
3. bass guitar
4. violin / fiddle (informal)
5. cello
6. grand piano
7. trumpet
8. trombone
9. flute
10. clarinet
11. saxophone
12. harp

B Can you play any of the instruments above? Which instrument would you most like to learn?

2 Match the phrases and idioms in bold with meanings a)–h).

1. There goes Jim again, saying how great he is, **blowing his own trumpet**.
2. Clara began **fiddling with** her necklace. I could see that she was worried.
3. We need to **drum up** some new business or we'll have to close down.
4. I'm tired of **playing second fiddle**.
5. Interesting how Larry **changed his tune** after he found out it was his own assistant who stole the money.
6. I know, it looks like an expensive car but I got it **for a song**.
7. The boss wants to see me about my mistakes on the contract. It's time for me to go in and **face the music**.
8. Her name **rings a bell** – maybe I've met her before.

a) take a less important role
b) remind sb of sth, sound familiar
c) talk positively about oneself
d) touch or play with something in a restless or nervous way
e) get (support or attention) through making a lot of effort
f) accept responsibility for mistakes
g) suddenly take a different perspective
h) very cheaply

TWO-PART PHRASES

3A Complete the sentences with the words in the box.

| take | death | leave | later | swim | another | miss | nothing |

1. It's only a question of time, and **sooner or** _____ you'll find a new job.
2. That's the highest salary we can pay you. We can't go higher, so **take it or** _____ it.
3. You've finished the training, and now you have to go out and do the job. It's **sink or** _____.
4. The shop is about twenty kilometres from here, **give or** _____ a kilometre.
5. It was **all or** _____ – she either had to get in the car with him or lose him forever.
6. This is the biggest choice of my life – it's a **life or** _____ decision.
7. Mark took a **hit or** _____ approach to finding a girlfriend. He simply asked every girl he saw out on a date.
8. I know, we're lost, but **one way or** _____ we'll find our way back.

B Match meanings a)–h) with the two-part phrases in Exercise 3A.

a) the offer won't change
b) risking everything
c) to within (a small amount)
d) unplanned
e) eventually
f) somehow
g) fail or succeed
h) extremely important

1.3

6A Student B: look at Situation 1 and follow the instructions.

> **Situation 1 (Service person)**
>
> You work for the customer service department at an airline. Complete the information:
>
> Name of airline _____
>
> Cost of rebooking _____
>
> A customer calls to change the date of a booking.
>
> - When he/she gives the new date, say that the morning flight on that date is booked.
> - After he/she reacts, say there is a place on the evening flight.
> - Tell him/her there is a charge for the rebooking (you decide how much).

6B Student B: Look at Situation 2 and follow the instructions.

> **Situation 2 (Customer)**
>
> Your friends are visiting and you booked a room at a hotel for them online. Complete the information:
>
> Name of your friends _____
>
> Most you will pay for room upgrade _____
>
> You call the hotel to:
>
> - confirm that the booking exists.
> - find out how much a nicer room costs.
> - change the booking to the nicer room if it's not too expensive (you decide).
>
> To prepare, make notes on two or three enquiries you will make and on what the customer service person might say.

7.3

8A

The top five countries with the tallest people

1 Netherlands
2 Sweden
3 Denmark
4 Norway
5 Estonia

2.1

10A Student B: look at the quiz. Underline the stress in the words in bold.

> 1 How old was Michael Jackson when he **recorded** his first hit *I want you back*? Seven, nine or eleven?
>
> 2 Which two of these products are among Italy's top **exports**: chemicals, pasta, wine?
>
> 3 How many grams of honey does a worker bee **produce** in its lifetime? 2 grams, 250 grams, or 1,000 grams (one kilogram)?
>
> 4 In Sweden, what percent of crime **suspects** are men? 50%, 80% or 95%?
>
> 5 How long did the shortest war on **record** last? 38 minutes, 38 hours or 38 days?

8.2

9C Student B: look at the dictionary entries and check your choice of key words. Then make notes on the meaning and write your own example.

> **cut** /kʌt/ *v* **cut sth short** to stop doing something earlier than you had planned: *The band had to cut short its concert tour*

> **bide** /baɪd/ *v* **bide your time** to wait until the right time to do something

> **time** /taɪm/ *n* **time after time** *again and again*

> **drag** /dræg/ *v* **drag your feet/heels** to delay doing something: *The government were dragging their feet over reforms*

4.1

1C

> **Starfish (ending)**
>
> Smiling, the young man bent down to toss another starfish out over the water. 'It's just made a big difference to that one,' he replied.

> **HOSPITAL WINDOW (ending)**
>
> When, at last, Frank had the energy to sit up in the new bed, he looked out. To his astonishment, he saw nothing outside the window except a blank wall. It was then that he realised that Walter had been blind.

3.1

3A Student A: read Sam's story. Circle two words/ phrases in the box that best describe how Sam sees himself. Underline two words/phrases that describe how he sees Jade.

> selfish   patient   talkative   a good parent
> neglected   rude   a good friend

I think I'm a good husband …

SAM'S STORY

When I met Jade I liked her straightaway. She was pretty and she was a good laugh. She used to visit me at my flat and she'd enjoy watching me play *Battle Galaxy 2525*, so she knew what to expect when we got married. *BG2525* is amazing! I've been playing it for years. You start off with a character at level one and you fight monsters and aliens in order to make your character stronger and become a Guild Lord.

I think I'm a good husband. I sometimes cook dinner, and I play with my two-year-old son Joe, and only go onto the computer after that. Jade doesn't seem to understand that it helps me relax. On average I spend about three hours a night on *BG2525*, sometimes till midnight. It's fast-paced and needs concentration so it's annoying when Jade asks me to do something else. I either pretend I don't hear or I tell her to go away – my head's in another space, playing with my friends.

The weekend's great because I have more time to play. I don't know why Jade invites my parents over then, so I just leave her to chat to them. She enjoys that. I'd rather see friends and family outside the home, you know, meet up for a meal or go to their places so I can give them more attention.

Jade says I'm insensitive, but I think she's the insensitive one. For example, once she unplugged the computer when I was at a critical point in the game and some of my fellow players were killed! I was furious with her. I mean, she was just thinking of herself and what she wanted but these people are my mates. I've got friends now from all over the world.

When we had Joe, quite honestly, it didn't make a huge difference. I mean, I always make sure I spend time with him every evening, but I still spend as much time playing. And Joe's used to me sitting at the computer. He's never known anything different. I often sit him on my knee and his little hands reach out and he starts tapping at the keyboard, so he's kind of copying me, which is great. When he's old enough I'm going to teach him how to play.

6.3

7B Student A:
1 You are the DJ. Ask Student B to tell you about their situation. Ask for clarification to check you understand. Then invite Student C to give their opinion. Encourage B and C to exchange their points of view.
2 Now change roles. You are a caller. Give your opinion when the DJ asks you.
3 Now change roles. You are a different caller. Explain your situation to the DJ:

A well-known social networking site has a minimum age of thirteen. Your daughter is thirteen next week and she says some of her friends' parents have allowed their kids to join. You think she's too young.

9.2

7A Student A: imagine the following situation happened to you. Add some details about the place, time, the amount of money and your feelings. Prepare to tell Student B.

> I went round to a house to look at a car. I'd seen the advert earlier. A young mother showed me round the car – it was a fantastic bargain and I wanted to buy it. She couldn't show me the car papers because her husband had just taken them to pay the car tax. She told me that she'd got lots of other interested people coming round later so I gave her a deposit of £250 and she said I could pick up the car at six. At six o'clock, I found eight other people outside the house, no car and no one at home.

B Who was the woman? How did she trick people into thinking she was a mother? Who did the car belong to? Who were the other eight people?

7.3

8A
The top five cities for art lovers
1 Berlin
2 Chicago
3 Florence
4 London
5 New York

10.2

8A Student B

> **through and through** completely: *a typical Englishman through and through*

> **on and on** used to say that someone continues to do something, or that something continues to happen: *He talked on and on about his job.*

> **rough and ready** (= not perfect, but good enough to use)

> **(every) now and then/now and again** sometimes: *He sees her every now and then at college.*

> **ups and downs** *n* [plural] the good and bad things that happen in life, business etc: *Every marriage has its ups and downs.*

5.4

3A Student A:

Self-heating bowl

A metal bowl that heats water or food, has a rechargeable battery in its base and could be used when travelling and for baby food.

Colour-changing ice-cream

Ice-cream that changes colour based on temperature. For example, it's blue while in the freezer; when you take it out and it's at room temperature, it turns purple; when it starts to melt, it turns pink.

Digestible chewing gum

Chewing gum that you can swallow and digest. You don't need to find a place to throw out your gum or worry about it sitting in your stomach for 100 years.

6.2

8A

Key

a) = 4 points, b) = 3 points,
c) = 2 points, d) = 1 point

16–20: You are amazingly optimistic! On the one hand, your positive attitude can make people around you feel good. On the other hand, sometimes people may find your constant cheerfulness slightly irritating.

11–15: You are calm and level-headed and can always see both sides of a situation. This means you don't have great highs and lows but can also mean you miss out on some of the drama of life.

5–10: You're not always easy to be with, usually seeing the negative side of things. However, this can be extremely useful in some situations because you will tend to be more cautious and see what could go wrong with any plans or projects.

6.3

7B Student B:

1 You are a caller. Explain your situation to the DJ:

Your son, who is seventeen, has started going out with a young woman who he says is the love of his life. He wants to get a tattoo linking her name and his. You're strongly against the idea.

2 Now change roles. You are the DJ. Ask Student C to tell you about their situation. Ask for clarification to check you understand. Then invite Student A to give their opinion. Encourage A and C to exchange their points of view.

3 Now change roles. You are a different caller. Give your opinion when the DJ asks you.

5.5

2B

1 a 2 b 3 b 4 c 5 a

7.3

8A
The top five most dangerous animals

1 mosquito
2 Asian cobra
3 Australian box jellyfish
4 great white shark
5 African lion

9.2

7A
Student B: imagine the following situation happened to you. Add some details about the place, time, the amount of money and your feelings. Prepare to tell Student A.

It was [name of a festival] and everyone was buying presents. I was in a shopping mall and I'd bought some games and a camera for people in my family. In the middle of the mall there was a big sign saying 'Free Gift Wrapping', so I left the presents with a woman there and collected them half an hour later. On the morning of [name of festival], the kids opened their presents and inside the boxes there were just oranges and straw.

B Who swapped the presents? How did they trick people into giving them the presents? Why didn't people notice that the presents felt different?

10.5

3C
1 Sydney Opera House
2 Apple Inc.
3 Squash
4 Napoleon Bonaparte
5 Oscar
6 the Inuit
7 sushi (makizushi)
8 Hamlet

8.2

9C
Student A: look at the dictionary entries and check your choice of key words. Then make notes on the meaning and write your own example.

pressed /prest/ *adj* **be pressed for time/money** *informal* to not have enough time or money

nick /nɪk/ *n* [C] **in the nick of time** at the last moment before it is too late to do something: *The doctor arrived in the nick of time*

once /wʌns/ **once in a blue moon** very rarely

make up for sth *phr v* **make up for lost time** to do something quickly because you started late or worked too slowly

9.3

7A Student A

9.5

4B
1 The man always checked the post box before the postman came. His wife took the letters out when they arrived.
2 A record company was making a recording of the performance and had asked the audience not to applaud, so that the recording would be clean.

6.3

7B Student C:

1 You are a caller. Give your opinion when the DJ asks you.

2 Now change roles. You are a different caller. Explain your situation to the DJ:

Your eighteen-year-old son has just passed his driving test. He wants to borrow your car so that he can drive his friends around. He says that his other friends' parents let them borrow their cars. You think he's not ready yet.

3 Now change roles. You are the DJ. Ask Student A to tell you about their situation. Ask for clarification to check you understand. Then invite Student B to give their opinion. Encourage A and B to exchange their points of view.

7.3

8A
The top five friendliest countries

1 Ireland
2 USA
3 Malawi
4 Fiji
5 Thailand

2.1

10C

Answers to quiz 1

1 Kenya
2 black and white
3 banana
4 the Sahara
5 43%

Answers to quiz 2

1 nine
2 chemicals, wine
3 2 grams
4 80%
5 38 minutes (between Britain and Zanzibar in 1896)

9.2

7C Hire car scam

Preparation:

1 The con artist team hires an expensive car, changes the number plates and removes any evidence that it's hired.

2 The team places an advert in a newspaper or online offering the car at a very low price.

3 The team finds an empty house, breaks in and puts some toys around the rooms. This address is given when people answer the advert.

The Scam:

4 An attractive female con artist poses as a young mother and greets customers as they arrive. She explains to the customers why there are no car papers. Some of the customers will offer a cash deposit.

5 At the end of the afternoon, the team clears out of the house, returns the car to the hire agency and disappears.

Free gift wrapping

Preparation:

1 The con artist team goes to a busy shopping mall during the festival season and sets up a tent with a sign saying 'Free gift wrapping'.

2 An attractive, friendly, female con artist stands behind the counter.

3 The other two con artists are inside the tent, out of sight. They have a scale for weighing things, oranges and packing material.

The Scam:

4 When a customer brings an item for wrapping, the woman passes it into the tent.

5 The two con artists there open the package, remove the item and weigh it, then put the same weight in oranges into the box with packing material and wrap it attractively.

6 They pass it back to the female colleague, who gives it to the customer. The package feels like the original and won't be opened till later!

9.3

7A Student B

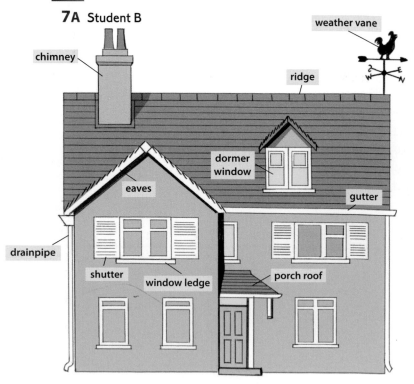

10.2

1B Student B

Q: Do big stars have to audition for film roles?

A: A big star auditioning for a part is almost unheard of. Actors such as Tom Hanks go straight from film to film, so directors and producers have access to a whole portfolio of their work. The closest such actors ever get to anything resembling an audition is when they're invited to chat about the project informally, which gives the director and producer a chance to evaluate the actor without it feeling like a test. The stars don't usually even have to read part of the script. More often, it's actually a matter of the actor choosing whether to work with the director!

Q: Why do works of art get stolen if they can't be sold without attracting attention?

A: Criminals steal paintings only when they already have a buyer. Sometimes, a wealthy private collector actually requests a particular piece to be stolen – essentially orders it – for part of their private collection. The collector knows that it can never be shown publicly but that's not why they want the piece in the first place. Valuable works of art are a favourite commodity for criminal organisations, who will use them in place of cash for making deals with each other. They are also useful for money launderers, as works of art are easier to transport and harder to trace than cash, as well as easily traded on the black market.

Q: Why is rock music played so loud at concerts?

A: Rock music is characterised by a heavy reliance on a strong bass line and hard, driving rhythm and percussion parts, which are greatly enhanced by amplification. At some point in the evolution of rock, audiences became almost addicted to the sensations of the music they loved 'vibrating' inside them at concerts. The listener goes beyond hearing the music and feels it through their whole body, feels its vibrations, provided it is loud enough. Heavy metal played softly sounds stupid and can only be played as it was intended to be: very, very loudly.

Q: How does a comedian deal with hecklers?

A: Every comedian has his or her own strategy for dealing with members of the audience interrupting their performance with rude comments. Strategies range from simply telling the heckler to be quiet ('Shut up!') to humiliating the heckler into silence by insulting them or someone with them such as their girlfriend. Armed with the microphone, the comedian has a great advantage over the heckler. Some comedians, known for their particularly aggressive way of handling hecklers, actually become more famous for this aspect of their act than their scripted sections.

Q: How much luck is involved in taking a great photo?

A: As the photographer Ansel Adams said, 'There are no rules for good photographs, there are only good photographs.' A great photographer can probably take a better photograph with a five-dollar disposable camera than an amateur can with their 3,000-euro Nikon, simply because the photographer has a sensitivity to light, colour, composition and choice of subject. He or she also has a knack for timing, for being in the right place at the right time – and this is how they're able to be 'lucky' more often than the average amateur.

5.4

3A Student B:

Coloured salt

It's available in different colours (for example, red, purple, green), and makes food look more interesting. It also makes it easier to see how much salt you're putting on your food.

Self-closing bag

A bag of snacks, for example crisps/chips or pretzels with magnetic strips along the top so that if you leave it overnight it will close itself and keep the contents fresher for longer.

Two-compartment thermos

The thermos has two sections so that you can have coffee in one and tea or soup in the other.

10.2

8A Student A

give and take *n* [U] If there is give and take between two people, each person agrees to do some of the things that the other person wants: *In any relationship there has to be some give and take.*

be sick of sb/sth to be annoyed and bored with a person or situation: *I'm sick and tired of waiting.*

peace and quiet When everything is quiet and calm: *All I want is some peace and quiet.*

leaps and bounds *He improved in leaps and bounds* (= very much, very quickly).

the pros and cons (of sth) the advantages and disadvantages of something

AUDIOSCRIPT

UNIT 1 Recording 1

P = Presenter M= Matt

Part 1

P: Now you might have heard of speed dating – those events for the young, free and single who are just too busy to find the love of their lives – but what about applying the same principle to finding a lodger for your spare room? Natalie Steed went to experience 'speed flatmating'.

M: My name's Matt Hutchinson and I'm with SpareRoom.co.uk. Basically what we do is we have an evening that introduces people looking for places to live with people who've got a spare room in their house and it's just a chance for people to meet the people that are involved rather than just see the flats. It's a chance to actually see who you'd be living with because it makes such a difference. And everybody that arrives gets a list of who's here so if you're looking for a room for example, you get a list of everybody who's got a room, what their area is, what their budget is. Everybody has a badge to say who they are and whether they've got a room or are looking.

UNIT 1 Recording 2

P = Presenter   M1 = Man 1   M2 = Man 2
W1 = Woman 1   W2 = Woman 2
W3 = Woman 3

Part 2

P: You're wearing a white label. You've got a room to rent.

M1: We both have a room to rent.

P: Oh, I see.

M1: So we're seeking another person to join us.

P: Why are you looking for someone to move in?

M1: Our magnificent German room-mate, who was away every weekend, has moved out. So as a result we're looking for someone equally magnificent who will be there as little as possible.

P: You're looking a little bit lost and you're wearing a pink badge. What does that mean?

M2: That means I'm looking for a room and also I'm willing to buddy up with someone else who's looking.

P: How long have you been looking for a room?

M2: A couple of weeks. I'm sort of new to the game. So I'm just trying to understand what's going on and how it works. You know, it's a bit of a shock and a bit of a steep learning curve for me.

P: Do you think you're pretty good at spotting the kind of person you can get on with?

W1: Yes I think it's easy. You just know straightaway.

P: When you've done it before, when you've done it through an online service, and you've presumably had people come to look at your house, how has that been?

W1: Well I must be a bit choosy I suppose, but the two best lodgers I had, I just knew immediately, as soon as I looked at them, smiled at them, I knew that they were somehow the right sort of people and that we would get along.

P: So, really it's … this kind of event's quite good for you, rather than sitting down with somebody where you know straightaway you don't want to live with them but they're in your house, you feel obliged to show them round,

W1: Yes, because that's so embarrassing, having to show someone round when they're not interested. Sometimes I open the door and because I'm older they look at me and go 'Oh god, I don't want to live with my mother.'

W2: It's two bedrooms. There's one bathroom which is why I always ask people what time they get up in the morning. Because I do have a bad habit that I like to have half an hour bath in the morning.

W3: That's not a bad habit!

W2: Other than that I'm not largely in the house at all. I'm actually a little bit sort of brain dead from all the conversations I've had but it's been so so useful.

P: You seem to have to be quite open straightaway, I mean, I heard you talking about your bathing habits earlier.

W2: I think that's important. I mean they're going to be living with you. They're going to be in really close contact and it's best to [cut] advertise yourself as you are from the outset.

P: And have you had any firm interest yet?

W2: I have met several people that I'd like to follow it up with. Several people that I feel I could live with.

UNIT 1 Recording 5

S1 = Speaker 1 S2 = Speaker 2 S3 = Speaker 3
S4 = Speaker 4 S5 = Speaker 5

S1: I didn't enjoy it much. For a start, I was very anxious and I think animals can sense it when you're nervous and worried. It was OK when we were going at a walk but then we went faster and I found it difficult to stay on. Actually, I was extremely relieved when the lesson finished and I could get off.

S2: It was the first time I'd tried it and it was a kind of competition. So I chose a song I knew well and I really enjoyed doing it. I came second so I was really thrilled. There were about twenty people entered and I was absolutely fascinated to see how different people behaved when they got in front of the microphone.

S3: It took me ages to do and I got really annoyed and frustrated at one point because I couldn't make it straight. Eventually, I put the books on it and it looked great. I felt really satisfied when I'd finished because it was the first one I'd ever put up on my own. Yeah. It was a really satisfying thing to do.

S4: Most people were there for the first time and I was really impressed by how quickly they learnt the steps. But I was useless and I'm sure my partner thought so too. I was very embarrassed because I kept treading on her toes. She was very patient but you could tell she was getting annoyed. So it was a bit of a disaster, quite disappointing.

S5: He should never have started it. I think he wanted to impress me because it was our first date but I found out later that he'd never changed one before. Anyway, after three hours, I suggested calling the repair company. I felt very awkward about it but I thought we'd never get home. I didn't get to bed till two in the morning and I was completely exhausted.

UNIT 1 Recording 7

1 I've thought about it a lot.
2 I thought about it a lot.
3 We tried to phone you.
4 We've tried to phone you.
5 She's had her first lesson today.
6 She had her first lesson today.
7 I've changed my email address.
8 I changed my email address.
9 I think he's left the building.
10 I think he left the building.

UNIT 1 Recording 9

W = Woman M = Man

M: Hello, English Language College. Can I help you?

W: Yes, I'd like to enquire about a course.

M: OK. Have you seen the information on our website?

W: Well, actually the situation is that I booked myself onto a course through your website yesterday, and now I'd like to change.

M: Could you tell me your name?

W: Misa Radnoti.

M: And which course was it?

W: A general English course, pre-advanced.

M: Bear with me a minute. Yes, I've got it. What would you like to change to?

W: I've just noticed this morning that you have an advanced course in business English starting next week.

M: That's right.

W: I was wondering if it would be possible for me to change to that group.

M: OK, let me just check. There are still a few places in that group, but you'll have to do a level test.

W: But I've already done an online test for the other course.

M: I appreciate that, but for this course you need to do a level test in person.

W: Can you tell me why I have to do it in person?

M: It's because it's a specialised course and there's an oral component to the level test.

W: I see. Would there be any chance of doing the level test on the phone?

M: Hold on, let me check … sorry to keep you. No, I'm afraid it has to be in person.

W: I see. Do you mind me asking what it involves?

M: There's a written task that you have to do under timed conditions, and preparation materials for the oral interview.

W: I see. Sorry to be difficult, it's just that I'm really busy this week and can't make it up to the school for the level test.

M: That's going to be a problem. I'm not sure what we can do about that.

W: I'd really appreciate your help.

M: Hmm … You couldn't come in on Thursday evening, could you?

W: No, I'm afraid not. But I tell you what. I could come in on Saturday to do the level test.

M: The problem is, that's leaving it very late and we might have other applicants.

W: I'd be really grateful if you could hold a place for me till Saturday morning.

M: Can you hold on a minute? I'll just see … OK, we can do that. We'll provisionally transfer the course fee over as a deposit.

W: That's great. Oh, I've got one more question, if I'm not keeping you.

M: No, go ahead.

W: If I don't get into this group, do I lose my course fee?

M: I'm afraid we can't refund the deposit, but you could apply it to another course.

W: That's a relief. Would you mind putting that in an email for me?

M: Certainly.

W: And could you tell me when the school opens on Saturday?

W: We're open from nine. I won't be here myself, but I'll tell my colleague to expect you.

M: Thank you very much for your help.

W: You're welcome. Thank you for calling.

UNIT 1 Recording 11
W = Woman M = Man

M: Well, I've had some very embarrassing experiences in my life but one of the worst was my very first day at work. I was a trainee solicitor in a law firm and there were fourteen of us trainees there, and everyone was on their best behaviour. Everyone was dressed nicely and the guys had polished their shoes and done their hair you know wanting to make a good first impression and

W: Yeah, I know what you mean. How old were you?

M: Only twenty-three, so I was one of the youngest in the group. Anyway, it started as a typical first day, you know a bit like the first day at school – everyone's not quite being themselves but, you know trying their hardest and you go and get your cup of tea or coffee and you try not to spill it or drop your biscuit on the floor.

W: Yeah.

M: And I remember I was feeling kind of … kind of nervous, maybe a tiny bit shy and then having to pretend to be confident as if to say, you know, 'I'm very professional.' I spent the whole time looking at the others and wondering how experienced they were and …

W: I know the feeling.

M: … and then I had to go to my desk and wait for some work to be given to me and, it was a quiet department so I was waiting and waiting and my shoes were new and were hurting so I kicked them off under the table and then another hour went by, and by this time I was feeling a bit panicky because I didn't have anything to do. I hoped someone would give me some proper work to do. Then the head partner rang me up and told me to come to his office because he'd got some work for me so I grabbed my pen and pad and I went racing round there. And as I walked into his office, he looked me up and down and saw that I wasn't wearing any shoes. I must have seemed ridiculously casual. It was so embarrassing! Thankfully there were no holes in my socks because they were new, too. So I just spent the whole time in his office thinking 'are you gonna say anything, are you gonna tell me off?'

W: Did he say anything?

M: Just before he sent me away he stopped me and he wanted to know why I didn't have any shoes on, and I didn't have a good answer for that. I just said I wanted to feel more comfortable. I thought – I'm never going to fit in at this law firm.

W: And how did he react?

M: He smiled so I think he thought it was pretty funny, but ever since then I've always made sure I keep my shoes on!

UNIT 2 Recording 1
Conversation 1

A: How long have you been working here?

B: I've been here for over ten months now.

Conversation 2

A: How many chocolates have you eaten?

B: I've only had three!

Conversation 3

A: What have you been doing? You're filthy!

B: I've been running.

UNIT 2 Recording 3
S1 = Speaker 1 S2 = Speaker 2 S3 = Speaker 3
S4 = Speaker 4 S5 = Speaker 5

S1: I really can't see the problem. The first thing I did when it all began was I tried to find my house on the website but they hadn't brought the camera van down our road yet, so I was quite disappointed. For me, it's great because it means I can go and look at things like hotels or even cities before I go on holiday … and anyway if someone wanted to look at my house they could just drive past it or walk past it, so I can't see the problem.

S2: It's obvious, isn't it? I mean, they're nothing to do with safety. They're just used by the government to make money. I mean, look at the statistics. In the last year, in my area four cameras have been placed along one stretch of road, and you know what, the number of accidents has doubled. So they obviously don't work as a deterrent. And now your car number plate can be logged so that they can keep track of you wherever you go. I hate it – I hate being watched like that. It's just another example of our surveillance society.

S3: The way I see it, it's an invasion of privacy. It means whenever I go to the supermarket, it's recorded on a chip somewhere and they can find out exactly what I've bought. Why should people have the right to know what kind of food I eat? Or get my details and then send me junk mail? I certainly don't want to be sent adverts from companies I don't know. And this is just the start … I expect next thing you know, the technology will be used to tell us what we can and can't eat.

S4: Me, I'm glad they're there. A few months ago I was robbed by two men at a bus stop not far from where I live but thanks to CCTV, the people who did it were all arrested. It was a bad experience but at least they didn't get away with it. And you see it in the news all the time - that more crimes are being solved because of CCTV cameras. I think we should have more of them. Most people are law-abiding anyway so they've got no need to worry.

S5: I actually think it's an important development. There was a case recently, where there was this big demonstration and lots of people took photos and these were sent to the media. So it means that demonstrators and the police – everyone – has to be more careful because their photos might be sent to the newspapers or posted online. So in general, yeah, I feel it's a good thing.

UNIT 2 Recording 5
Conversation 1

A: Do you think you would ever have cosmetic surgery?

B: Me? No I don't think so I'm really against it actually, I think it's …

A: Really, why?

B: It can be quite dangerous some of the implants you can have, um –

A: Yeah, I know what you mean.

B: Take the case of Mike's girlfriend – she actually had some Botox injections in her forehead.

A: Did she?

B: Yeah, and she couldn't, you know she couldn't –

A: Couldn't move her face?

B: Yeah, she couldn't smile or frown – her face was just frozen solid.

A: Although if someone's really, really overweight and it becomes a health problem, do you think maybe then they should have some kind of surgery, you know, such as liposuction to get rid of fat?

B: Oh I see, for health reasons maybe, yes, I suppose so, I mean you've got a point there, but I still don't like the sound of it. I wouldn't do it myself.

A: I might, if it was to do with my health.

Conversation 2

A: Do you ever download music for free?

B: You mean illegally? No, I think I'm probably one of the few people that don't do it. I've always paid whether it's the track price or the album price.

AUDIOSCRIPT

A: Why? I mean nobody I know pays.

B: Well the way I see it, it's just theft, isn't it? I mean …

A: Oh I totally disagree.

B: I mean, artists have copyright on their songs, so you're stealing from them. It's as simple as that.

A: But it's a well-known fact that musicians get very little money from CD sales anyway. So they don't lose out. I mean, they want people to hear their music.

B: Hmm. I'm not so sure about that. If people share the music without paying, how can musicians make any money?

A: Well, the famous ones, they don't need more money and for newer groups, file-sharing is the way they get known so they don't have to spend a fortune, you know, on things like record companies and managers and …

B: Yeah, but …

A: … anyway, nowadays singers and groups make most of their money from concerts.

B: Hmm. I'm still not convinced. Aren't you worried about being found out? For instance, what about that woman in America? Because of the hundreds of tracks she downloaded illegally, she got fined something like two million dollars.

A: Two million dollars? Ouch!

B: Yeah, so maybe you'd better think again.

A: Hmm.

Conversation 3

A: Have you seen this plan in the local paper for changes to the city centre?

B: Oh, you mean the idea to ban cars from the centre?

A: Yes and only allowing buses. What do you think of the idea?

B: Oh, I'm in favour of it. I think it'd be really good for the environment, you know for cutting down pollution.

A: Well I don't know, apparently it's been shown that buses are more polluting than cars.

B: How can they be? But even if they are at the moment, it seems to me that they're bound to get better, you know, they'll get replaced with electric buses or something like that.

A: Maybe.

B: Does that mean you're against it?

A: Yes, on balance, I think I am. I mean, according to the article, when they did a trial in another town there was a reduction in shop sales – apparently almost ten percent.

B: That doesn't sound right, if more people came in on buses. I suppose the main thing is to put money into making sure you have a good public transport system.

A: Okay, I mean I agree to some extent, but actually, I think the town centre works perfectly fine as it is.

B: But it's clogged up. You know, you can't move, it's polluted.

A: It's a bit clogged up but if you're patient you eventually find somewhere to park.

B: Well I just hope they decide soon.

A: Yeah.

UNIT 2 Recording 7

W = Woman M = Man

W: Excuse me, hello, sorry to bother you, have you got a minute?

M: Ah, yeah sure.

W: Do you mind if I ask you some questions? I'm just doing a survey on happiness.

M: Right.

W: I'll read out the questions to you and you can just tell me what you think if that's okay.

M: Yeah fine.

W: Great. Um, could you look at this list of five things so you've got, ah, number one car, then two is friendship, three good food, four money and five free time. So which two of these would you find it the most difficult to live without?

M: Which two, the most difficult to live without?

W: Yes.

M: Ah, well I couldn't live without friendship I'm, I'm a very social animal I need, um, family and friends around me so it can't be that one. Um – oh no sorry that is, to live without … yes …

W: That's one.

M: That is one, so …

W: Then we just need one more.

M: … friendship is definitely one of them. Ah …

W: Yes, number two, okay.

M: Oh, that's difficult. Free time I don't have any anyway, ah, I could lose the car, I think that wouldn't be a problem. Um, do you know what …

W: How about money?

M: … sad as it is, it's probably money, because money actually …

W: Money, no most people …

M: … you know leads to happiness in, in indirect ways I think.

W: Okay, so I'm gonna put number two and number four for that one. And also how happy would you say you are, on a scale of one to five, five being very happy?

M: Today or just generally?

W: I think generally.

M: Oh generally okay, um, oh, ah, three or four, um – three and a half.

W: Ah

M: Can I have half?

W: No.

M: Oh, okay. Um, well you've made me laugh I'll have four.

W: Oh lovely I'll put you down for four. And what would you say is missing from your life, so what would make you happier?

M: Ah, probably, ah, working nearer to home?

W: Okay.

M: That's, I think you know … just generally the time that would give me …

W: Right.

M: … with family.

W: So maybe it's free time then …

M: Yeah, yeah.

W: …more of that. Okay that's lovely thank you ever so much for taking part, really do appreciate it.

M: You're welcome.

W: Okay, bye bye.

UNIT 3 Recording 1

K = Katie Derham A = Alison Rice
C = Charlie Connolly

K: The buzz word de jour is 'niche travel'. Rather than the usual beach flopout, we're turning instead to a growing band of small tour operators offering Thai cooking weeks, trips to Sri Lanka for tea lovers, the ultimate trekking or trekkie experience or poignant visits to obscure battlefields. Well, I'm joined here in the studio by Alison Rice, who's been a travel writer for many years and Charlie Connolly, author and broadcaster, who among other things has travelled the globe in search of the legacy of Elvis Presley. Welcome to you both. Alison, let's start by turning to you first. This definition of niche travel these days, what does it mean to you?

A: I think some people would say we're just talking about activity holidays where, instead of just lying on a beach you follow a particular interest or hobby with like-minded people. Walking holidays, gardening, cookery, painting, yoga, bird-watching – you remember when bird-watching was just for geeks? There's masses of bird-watching holidays. Battlefields, music, theatre festivals – these are all pegs around which we can build a holiday.

C: I do believe in going to a place for a reason and rather than just 'cos there's a nice view or something. I'm a big believer in people. I think people make a place and the atmosphere of a place.

K: What would your favourite niche holidays be that you've come across recently?

A: For me, it's definitely singing. If you google 'singing holidays' you'll find 416,000 entries. Whole choirs go on holiday now, or if you want to just join a choir, you can join a holiday where you learn a piece, rehearse it through the holiday, sailing down the Nile, there is one in Malta next year where you'll be singing the Messiah … and then the holiday ends where you put on a concert for the locals.

C: There is a tour you can do of Chernobyl. It's a one day tour from Kiev and you get to view reactor number four from a hundred metres away, and you get to visit the dead town of Pripyat, which is … there are schoolbooks still in the school, and posters up on the wall, and calendars. And they do say it's a hundred percent safe – you're tested for radiation levels when you go and when you come back.

K: Well, *The Traveller's Tree* messageboard has been littered with postings on this subject.

We've heard about Fairtrade holidays in Cuba and southern India, Inca treks, one from a contributor called Portly, who thoroughly enjoyed a historical cruise on the Black Sea. But thank you also to Dilly Gaffe who said, 'Never mind niche. Give me a five-star luxury hotel any time!'

UNIT 3 Recording 4
Conversation 1

A: Oh, you must have seen it …

B: No, I've never even heard of it. How does it work?

A: Well it sounds really stupid, but I'll try to describe it. The way it works is that there are two teams, with two celebs on each team.

B: Two what?

A: Celebs. Celebrities.

B: Oh, right.

A: So anyway, there's a studio with a swimming pool and, at the end, about twenty metres from the pool, there's a wall, actually a giant wall covered by another 'wall', or maybe a sort of curtain …

B: I don't get it. A wall covered by a wall?

A: Yeah, but it's really like a single wall.

B: OK

A: And the two people from the first team stand at the edge of the pool facing the wall. Then what happens is that the host says 'Bring on the wall!'

B: He does what?

A: He says 'Bring on the wall!' Like that, very dramatically. Then the wall starts moving quite fast towards the two people.

B: Who are in front of the pool.

A: Yeah and after a few seconds, the curtain lifts off the wall and there's a funny-shaped hole and they have to get through it.

B: They have to get through where?

A: Get through the hole. They have about five seconds to get themselves into the same position as the shape in the hole so that it goes past them and they don't get knocked into the pool.

A: Uh-huh.

B: Yeah, and that's the best part because nobody knows what shape the hole will be until the last moment. It could be anything person-shaped, and …

A: What do you mean, person-shaped?

B: Well, maybe bent over or maybe with one foot in front of the other and one arm up at an angle, like this.

B: So what's the point?

A: Well, basically the point is NOT to get knocked into the pool. If they don't stand exactly in the shape of the hole, the wall will knock them into the pool. The teams take it in turns to have a go and the winning team is the one who gets through the most shapes.

B: It sounds pretty stupid to me.

A: You sort of have to see it to get it. It's incredibly popular.

Conversation 2

A: I like it because it's basically a mix between a general knowledge quiz and kind of psychological game.

B: So how does it work?

A: Well, there are nine people standing in a semi-circle in a very dark studio with spotlights of one colour – maybe blue or red – so it looks very dramatic. Each one is standing behind a kind of metal podium.

B: Standing behind a what?

A: A kind of desk, made of metal. Anyway, the host stands in the centre.

B: Who stands in the centre?

A: The host, the woman in charge. Anyway, the first thing they do is answer general knowledge questions. She fires questions at them one by one, and the object is for the team to win money by answering a chain of questions correctly.

B: Sounds like any old quiz.

A: Yeah but if someone gives a wrong answer they lose all the team's money. The key thing is to bank the money as you go along.

B: Bank the money?

A: Yeah, before a contestant answers their question, they can say 'Bank' and then the total money so far is safely stored and a new chain is started from zero.

B: Whoah! It sounds complicated.

A: It isn't, when you get the hang of it. So then after they've finished each round, they have to vote on who should get eliminated, you know, who should leave the game: the person who is 'the weakest link' in the team.

B: So that's the person who got most answers wrong?

A: Yeah, but what usually happens is that people start voting strategically, sometimes they vote off a strong player so that they can win.

B: So the winner's the last one left?

A: When there are two left, it's the person who gets the most questions right and then that person wins all the money in the bank.

B: I still don't understand why it's so popular.

A: Well, the main reason everyone watches it is because of the host. She's very aggressive – like a sergeant in the army – and she can be really rude to the contestants but instead of being offensive it's actually very funny. I can't really explain. You need to see it.

B: What's it called again?

UNIT 3 Recording 6
Conversation 1

A: You have to sauté the potatoes.

B: You have to do what?

Conversation 2

A: The first player writes an anagram of the word.

B: The first player writes what?

Conversation 3

A: You go to the webinar site.

B: You go where?

Conversation 4

A: Basically, the aim is to beat the rival team.

B: The aim is to beat who?

UNIT 3 Recording 7

I'm not the kind of person who likes extreme activities like bungy jumping or sky diving and, in fact, I'd never do any of those sorts of things. So the activity I'd like to recommend may seem quite boring to some of you, and very simple: it's jumping off of a three metre platform into water.

Anyway, I'll try to explain why it was so special. A few years ago I was at a lake with a friend, and there was a jumping platform about three meters above the surface of the lake, you know the sort of thing, made of wood and, anyway, people were jumping off it into the water and having a good time, so we decided to try it. We waited till there was no one around, because neither of us was feeling particularly courageous. I remember walking to the edge of the platform and looking down and thinking to myself, 'the water is a long way down!' I felt really nervous but eventually I gathered my courage and walked back a few steps, then I ran and jumped into the water.

Actually, I didn't exactly jump into the water, I jumped into the air, or that's what it felt like. Air all around me, for ages. It felt like some of the longest few seconds of my life. I was determined to keep my eyes open, but involuntarily they closed out of fear. I braced myself for impact, which came eventually of course, and it almost hurt, the way I hit the water and travelled quickly to the muddy bottom. I swam to the edge and climbed up to the level of the platform again. My friend had just done her jump, and was also climbing out. I was amazed how scared I'd felt, and at the fact that I hadn't been able to keep my eyes open. I told myself that if I did it again, I could surely keep my eyes open, and relax and enjoy it. I drew in a deep breath, ran, and jumped into the air … and it was exactly the same as the first time.

I'd recommend this experience because it really makes you understand something about fear, in a situation where, in fact, there's no danger. Maybe for some people it's not a big deal, but for me it was because it taught me a lot about myself and how well I can control my feelings, or not.

UNIT 4 Recording 2

I = Interviewer L = Larry Smith

I: In the 1920s, Ernest Hemingway bet ten dollars that he could write a complete story in just six words. He wrote, 'For sale: baby shoes, never worn.' He won the bet. An American online magazine has now used that to inspire its readers to write their life story in six words and they've been overwhelmed by the thousands who took up the challenge. They've published the best in a book which they've given the title of one of the submissions: *Not quite what I was planning*. I asked the editor, Larry Smith, what made him think of the idea.

L: Well, on the site, *Smith Magazine*, we tell stories in all sorts of different ways. Our whole

AUDIOSCRIPT

idea behind the site is that story-telling should be egalitarian, you know, democratic. Everyone has a story, we say that over and over. That's our tag line. But in telling different types of stories since we launched a couple of years ago, we found that you had to give people parameters. So playing off the great literary legend, the Hemingway story, we thought, 'Let's ask our readers their six-word life story, a memoir' and see what happened. We really didn't know what would happen.

I: And what did happen?

L: It was incredible. In a couple of months we got fifteen thousand entries and I was just blown away. Funny, poignant – I really believe that everyone has a story and most of us aren't going to write for the *Guardian* but I was just so inspired by how serious and intense folks took the six-word memoir challenge.

I: OK, but before we look at the examples. It's one thing … because the Hemingway is a story but it's not a story of a life. That seems to be a bit of a challenge to fit that in six words.

L: Well, it's interesting because some folks clearly tried to tell a whole story of a life in six words, and you can tell, and other times they're telling a moment in their life, right at this moment, something that they're feeling right now. Or perhaps something that's been an evergreen, a thread throughout their lives.

I: Give us some examples.

L: 'Wasn't born a redhead. Fixed that.' This woman took life under control. Whether she just always felt that her soul was a redheaded soul or simply at some point in life she was going to make a switch. She could have quit her job. She changed her hair colour.

I: But a lot of them are … they're quite sad or there's a sense of regret or disappointment in a lot of them.

L: I didn't expect that. I thought people would come back with a lot of funny things, some playful things, plays on words … but those are really interesting reality. People really told us, 'It's tough out there.' 'Found true love. Married someone else.' 'Never should have bought that ring.'

UNIT 4 Recording 4

A = Amy B = Barbara C = Carl

C: So, Amy, when's your flight?

A: Tomorrow at one. It's twelve hours so I need a good book. Any ideas? Barbara?

B: Well, I've just finished *The Girl with the Dragon Tattoo* and …

C: Didn't they make a film of that?

B: Yeah, apparently it's really good.

A: I haven't read it. It's a sort of thriller, isn't it?

B: Yeah, it's a kind of mixture between a thriller and a detective story, set in Sweden. I thought it was great. I mean I'm a big fan of detective novels anyway but what I really liked about it was the main character, the girl.

C: … with the dragon tattoo?

B: Yeah. She's really edgy, strange, kind of brilliant but really messed up at the same time.

C: I'm not that keen on detective novels and the modern ones are usually too violent for me, so I don't think I'd like it.

A: Well, it's definitely a possibility. What would you recommend then?

C: What about *Life of Pi*? Have either of you read it?

A: No.

B: I started it but I just couldn't get into it …

C: It's brilliant. It's about this Indian kid who's stuck on a boat in the middle of the ocean with a dangerous tiger, and a zebra and some other animals

A: Sounds very strange.

C: No, it's actually all about courage and survival. It'd be really good for a long plane journey – you won't be able to put it down for the whole twelve hours, it's so exciting, you'll just want to know what's going to happen next.

A: Uh huh.

C: But you didn't finish it?

B: No, actually, to be honest, I couldn't stand it, and I gave up after about a quarter of the way through. I suppose I'm not really into fantasy and

C: It's not really fantasy, it's er, what do they call it, magic realism.

B: Whatever, I just couldn't get into it. Amy, why not try one of the classics? You know, something like *Pride and Prejudice*? Do you like Jane Austen?

A: I dunno, I mean, I've seen the movie and the TV adaptation and I liked them, but I dunno, she's not exactly an easy read.

B: Oh, you should try it. I've read it about, what, ten times and it has to be the most romantic story ever written … The thing I love about it is the writing, the English that she's used is so beautiful.

A: I know what you mean but it just seems a bit, well, a bit serious for a plane journey.

C: Yeah, I agree. I love it too, but maybe not for a plane journey.

A: Actually, you know what? I might try the first one you said, *The Girl with the Dragon Tattoo*. What's the overall story? You know, without giving too much away?

B: Well, it's about …

UNIT 4 Recording 7

Fawlty Towers I absolutely love *Fawlty Towers*, I've seen this hundreds of times and it's my absolute favourite. It always makes me laugh – in fact, it makes me cry with laughter sometimes … can't get enough of it. And the main character, Basil Fawlty, played by John Cleese, is absolutely brilliant. It's like a lesson in comic acting; the more bad things that happen to this man the more we laugh.

My favourite scene is the scene with Mrs Richardson and Basil Fawlty. And, it's very, very cleverly done. Mrs Richardson wears a hearing aid and Basil Fawlty hates Mrs Richardson – she's a terrible grumpy old complaining customer who he really doesn't like. So he comes into the room and he mimes at her – so he moves his mouth but he doesn't make any sound – so that Mrs Richardson turns up her hearing aid so that she can hear him. And then he mimes again and he moves his mouth again not making any sound so she can't understand why she can't hear him, so she turns up her hearing aid again. And then once he's sure that her hearing aid is on full volume he shouts at her, 'Mrs Richardson!' – of course which deafens her and, it's, it's, it's very, very funny and it's amazing because he gets his own back on her 'cos she's been awful to him so, he, you know, he kind of wins in the end but, – Oh it's just brilliant. If you've never seen it you really should see it. There were very few episodes made. I think there were only –only ever one series, maybe eight episodes … something like that … I'm not entirely sure about that, but not very many made and, they're – they're really, really fantastic. Every one is absolutely priceless.

UNIT 5 Recording 2

1 There's been a breakthrough.
2 It's a trade-off between cost and safety.
3 The long-term outlook is very good.
4 The downside is I get paid less.
5 There's only one drawback.
6 There's been a breakdown in communications.
7 What was the outcome of the meeting?

UNIT 5 Recording 3

I = Interviewer E = Expert

I: We often hear that competition is beneficial but how exactly does it work?

E: OK. Let's imagine a Coke machine somewhere, anywhere, selling a hundred cans a day. Now, Pepsi comes along and puts up a machine next to it, how many cans would each machine sell?

I: Fifty?

E: That's what most people think. In fact, each machine would probably sell two hundred cans a day, unless the market was saturated.

I: That's hard to believe … What's the explanation?

E: Well, what happens is that the question in the consumer's mind is no longer 'Should I get a Coke or not?' but 'Which soft drink should I get?' Choice makes people want things.

I: Ah, that's interesting. What about pricing?

E: Well, there are several schools of thought on this. People are expected to think 'If I see two similar products at different prices, I'll buy the cheaper one' but, in fact, that's often not how consumers behave. For example, if I were to introduce a new lipstick and I wanted to compete with a product priced at €4.99, should I price mine above or below the competition?

I: OK – I have a feeling you're going to tell me above, but it seems natural to undercut your competitor.

E: We've found that with certain types of products, if you price your product just above the competition's price – so let's say €5.49 – you'll actually end up with a bigger share of the market.

I: Why's that?

E: We intuitively feel that if something costs more, it's better. People will pay more provided the difference is small. They'll think, 'Well, why not? I deserve the best.'

I: OK. Turning to the appearance of advertisements, what tricks are used to make products more appealing?

E: Take this advertisement for a hamburger chain. Big picture of a juicy hamburger with fresh tomatoes and lettuce …

I: Makes me hungry just looking at it.

E: Yes, it's fine to look at ….as long as you don't eat it. It probably has a hundred percent beef in it, real tomatoes and lettuce … but to make it so shiny, a food stylist has painted the meat with oil or maybe lacquer; and what appears to be steam rising off the meat is probably cigarette smoke blown onto the hamburger just before the picture was taken.

I: I've just lost my appetite.

E: And look at these advertisements for watches. What time is it on this watch?

I: Ten past ten.

E: And on these?

I: Ten past ten – in all of them. Why's that?

E: There are two theories. One is that with the hands in this position, the face of the watch conveys a smile. The other theory is that it's a bit like a tick symbol. In either case the consensus is that the message is positive.

I: And if a watch showed 8.20 it wouldn't sell as well?

E: Presumably not. 8.20 is a very sad-looking time.

I: What about colour in advertising?

E: It's crucial. We have built-in associations for every colour, for instance red is associated with risk and with energy, so you see it in adverts for energy drinks, cars and sports equipment. Green on the other hand denotes safety, so it's often used for medical products. Yellow and orange supposedly stimulate the appetite, so they're used for food ads; blue on the other hand suppresses the appetite … it's linked more to intellect and precision, so you see it in adverts for high-tech products. And purple is an interesting one: surveys show that around seventy-five percent of young children prefer purple to all other colours. So you'll see bright purple in advertising for toys for example.

I: Well, thank you. I'll never shop the same again. And neither will our listeners.

UNIT 5 Recording 4

1 I'll buy it if you bring the price down.
2 I'd buy it if it weren't so expensive.
3 If I were to get a luxury car, it'd be a Ferrari.
4 I'll come as long as you let me pay.
5 You can't come in unless you're a member.

UNIT 5 Recording 5

M1 = Man 1 M2 = Man 2 W = Woman

M1: OK, let's try to do this quickly. We've got just a few minutes. Who's taking notes?

M2: I'll do that.

M1: Good. OK, let's brainstorm.

W: Colour. Purple vegetables.

M2: Purple vegetables. Yeah.

M1: Or a competition. A prize to kids who eat their two veggies a day.

M2: OK …

M1: Or a gardening programme in schools.

M2: What do you mean?

M1: If kids grow vegetables, they'll want to eat them.

M2: Right.

W: Have the opposite? What happens if you don't eat your veggies.

M2: I'm not sure about that.

M1: Hey, we're brainstorming.

W: OK. How about this? Forbid them from eating vegetables, at school at least. No veggies allowed. Then they'll want them.

M2: I'll write it down … Any more?

M1: Something with recipes, like put vegetarian recipes on the back of cereal boxes.

M2: Or on websites.

M1: Viral campaign. Short video with a celebrity. A famous rap star rapping about eating vegetables.

W: OK.

M1: Is that it?

UNIT 5 Recording 6

M1 = Man 1 M2 = Man 2 W = Woman

M1: OK, let's look at the list and cut it down. Here, I'll put these up on the screen.

M2: How do you feel about this idea? The purple vegetables? You know kids, they love purple.

W: Actually, that could be a problem. We're trying to sell something healthy, and we put a chemical in it to make it look attractive.

M1: Good point, yeah. What about having a competition? If the prize is right, children will do anything.

W: Oh, so whoever eats the most vegetables in an hour wins?

M1: No, I was thinking of whoever eats two vegetables a day for a week or something …

W: To be honest, it wouldn't be my first choice.

M2: It's not original enough. And too difficult to organise.

M1: Would you consider the gardening campaign? We set up little vegetable gardens near schools … maybe even have a competition …

M2: Yeah, they could send in photos to a website, and …

W: Well frankly, I think it's too complicated to set up. We need something that's fairly simple in terms of organisation. Something that we can control and monitor easily.

M1: How does the recipe idea strike you?

M2: It doesn't grab me. Sorry.

W: I was going to say the same. To put it bluntly, it's all wrong. It wouldn't mean anything to the kids, maybe only to their parents.

M1: Fair enough.

W: Uh, with respect, I think we're on the wrong track here.

M1: Yeah?

W: I think it'd be great if we could get kids into vegetarianism.

M2: What do you mean?

W: Well, you know how all children love animals … we could use that to make them want to stop eating meat, maybe use cute pictures of animals next to meat.

M1: Oh no, that's gross! Anyway, the point is not to make children vegetarians, just to get them eating a more balanced diet.

M2: I agree. I know this sounds weird but we could go for a 'negative' campaign. It could be done in a funny way. We could use fantasy characters in a cartoon …

M1: As a matter of fact I was thinking of that myself. The ones who don't eat their veggies are the weak ones …

W: Yeah …

M1: So what do we think?

M2: At the moment I'm torn between the cartoon and the viral campaign … a rapper would be perfect …

W: Suppose we try combining the two ideas, and have a viral campaign but not with a celebrity, with cartoon characters?

M2: I like it.

M1: OK, let's go with that.

UNIT 5 Recording 8

W = Woman M = Man

W: We would like to introduce to you an idea that will change the way you eat: Yummy Utensils. As you can guess, we're talking about knives, forks and spoons that you can eat.

M: You'll never have to throw plastic knives, forks and spoons in the rubbish again. At the end of your lunch, after you finish eating, you simply eat your utensils, like this.

W: Yummy Utensils are made of a special vegetable and flour mixture, are strong enough to cut meat and pierce salad, but easy to digest after you chew them.

M: They're tasty too – a bit like pretzels. Here, would you like to try one?

W: What makes our idea special is that it's not just practical, and it's not a simple gimmick.

M: No, Yummy Utensils are not just practical and fun, they're also environmentally friendly. Just think of all of the resources that go into making plastic utensils, which are just thrown into the rubbish and become a permanent part of the waste that we litter the planet with. Yummy Utensils are made from natural ingredients, using the same processes as are used to make bread products, and of course create no rubbish at all.

AUDIOSCRIPT

M: Even if you don't eat your Yummy Utensils and throw them in the rubbish, they dissolve within days. So there's no damage to the environment.

W: We envisage this product being sold in supermarkets, in the same section where you buy picnic supplies. But don't be surprised if they're sold in the snack section – they taste better than some snack foods. And they're certainly better for you.

M: We think that Yummy Utensils will be a hit with families in particular, since they're the biggest consumers of disposable utensils.

W: And kids love having a fork or spoon they can eat. We've done some market testing and it was amazing how much the children enjoyed them.

M: In the future, we are planning to develop a sweetened version which will make Yummy Utensils the perfect dessert.

W: Thank you for your attention and we welcome any questions.

UNIT 6 Recording 1

1 We must go. We mustn't go.
2 I can come. I can't come.
3 You should listen to me. You shouldn't listen to me.
4 We're supposed to go. We're not supposed to go.
5 You ought to ask. You oughtn't to ask.
6 You're allowed to come. You're not allowed to come.

UNIT 6 Recording 3

Part one

OK … so … I've got the date … Thursday the twentieth of May, 2004. Dear the future me, I hope this letter has found its way to you/ me. As I write this I am sixteen in year eleven; and as I read it, I am twenty. Wow! I will have changed so much. I can only guess what I will be like at twenty. I envisage myself at Oxford Uni, sitting… oh, this is embarrassing … sitting under a tree by the river in the college grounds. I think I'll be wearing something floaty and a bit indie, but I bet when I get this, it'll be raining.

As I read this, I'll have already remembered that I fancied Tom Squires … there you go, Tom … I'm looking at him now. I wonder if I'll ever have the guts to tell him. I know, I'm a romantic. I hope that hasn't changed. My plans for myself in the following years are to find a man, someone good-looking, romantic and intelligent who shares my interests – or just Tom. Either way, I hope I'll have someone. I don't remember this … and then I think I'll have three children with long brown hair and green eyes.

Well, I'll stop now even though I want to write everything I can down, but I'm running out of time. I hope I'm happy in 2008, and I hope this letter makes me feel good about who I was, or am, as I write this. Keep smiling, and while I can't really say bye, but good luck for the future and keep dreaming. Don't change too much, and be happy with who you are – I like who I am now more than any other time. Love, Laura.

UNIT 6 Recording 4

Part two

It all sounds very shallow looking back and reading what I thought I'd be doing or hoped I'd be doing. I think my sixteen-year-old self might have been disappointed with where I am, but because I as my twenty-year-old self have sort of grown up and matured. I'm absolutely ecstatic with where I am, and it doesn't have to be this perfect sitting-by-a-lake kind of image.

UNIT 6 Recording 6

P = Presenter V = Vince J = Julia D = Dan Z = Zara

P: And up next, it's time for 'Just tell me I'm wrong.' Today's topic: how young is too young or, perhaps more accurately, how old is old enough? We've received hundreds of emails and text messages about the right age for a child to have a mobile phone, stay home alone, wear make-up, get their ears pierced, babysit for younger kids … and we've got our first caller, Vince. Go ahead, Vince. You're on.

V: Hi. My situation is that my nine-year-old kept asking me to get her a mobile, so I bought her one a few months ago. Then, last week, I got a bill for over two hundred pounds, so I warned her I'd take the phone away from her if it happened again.

P: So I gather your point is whether she's too young to have a mobile?

V: Yeah, yeah, that's right.

P: Er, surely it's the parents' responsibility to set some sort of guidelines ahead of time.

V: So what you're saying is I should have given her some rules?

P: Basically, yes. When she first got the phone. OK, thanks Vince. Next caller is Julia. What's your question, Julia?

J: About the mobile phone thing. I've got an eight-year-old and I worry about him all the time if I can't reach him. You know … anything could happen …

P: So in other words, you want him to have a mobile.

J: And have it on at all times. But he doesn't want one.

P: Fair enough. Let me ask you a question. When you were eight years old and there were no mobile phones, what did your mother do? I bet you were allowed to go out on your own. Isn't that an important part of growing up and developing a sense of independence and responsibility?

J: So what you're getting at is that I'm being overprotective?

P: You could say that.

J: Yeah, but don't you agree that the world used to be a safer place?

P: Surely that's what every generation says. Anyway, thanks for your question, Julia. Let's go to our next caller. Dan, you're on.

D: Hi, my question's also about technology.

P: OK. Go ahead.

D: Well, my son, Seth, he's twelve and, up till recently, he was a normal twelve-year-old,

you know, he used to go out with his friends, play football with me, you know … we had a great relationship

P: So, Dan, from what you're saying, I'm guessing he doesn't want to spend so much time with you now and you feel …

D: Oh no, it's not that. It's just that he spends all his time on the computer now.

P: Isn't that just normal nowadays?

D: It's hard to say. Sometimes at the weekend he spends all day in his bedroom on the computer, on social networking sites or playing games. I don't think it's right. I mean for one thing, he never gets any exercise.

P: Don't you think it's just a stage he's going through? I used to spend hours in my bedroom listening to music when I was that age.

D: You mean I should just relax and let him get on with it?

P: Yeah, he'll grow out of it. And you can't force him to go and play football if he doesn't want to.

D: I guess not. Thanks.

P: OK, our next caller is Zara. You're on.

Z: Um, I was wondering how you would deal with a thirteen-year-old wanting to get pierced ears?

P: Thirteen years old? Doesn't she simply want to be like her friends? I imagine a lot of them have pierced ears.

Z: Well … that's it. I'm not talking about a she.

P: Oh, if I've got it right, you're upset because your thirteen-year-old son wants to get his ears pierced.

Z: That's right.

P: Ah … so it's because he's a boy rather than his age?

Z: I suppose so.

P: Well, what's he like socially? Does he have friends who've got …

UNIT 6 Recording 8

W = Woman M = Man

W: I'm going to speak in favour of the statement: 'Age discrimination should be illegal at work.' The first point I'd like to make is that selecting a person for a job on the basis of their age is unfair. It's as bad as choosing someone because of their gender or race or religion. People should be selected for a job because of their abilities and suitability and not because they are a certain age. For example, if a sixty-year-old person is able, physically and mentally, to do a job they should be judged on the same basis as a thirty-year-old.

M: I want to speak against the statement. I would like to start off by saying that I fully support equal opportunities for people applying for a job. However, I would like to pick up on the point made by Sarah when she said 'if a person is able, physically and mentally, to do a job.' I think we need to be realistic here. As people age, this can affect their energy, their ability to react quickly and their memory. In some jobs it may be vital for people to have high levels of energy, for example in a creative industry such as advertising. Or people need to be able to react quickly, for instance if they are a lorry driver, or be able to concentrate for long periods of time if they are an airline pilot. It is simply a fact of life that, as we age, our mental and physical capabilities deteriorate and that, for certain jobs, younger people are better.

UNIT 7 Recording 1

1 All of us are from Spain.
2 Quite a few of us live nearby.
3 Several of us don't drink coffee.
4 A few of us smoke.

UNIT 7 Recording 2

P = Presenter H = Hoaxer

P: Welcome to Insight, where our topic for the day is hoaxes, specifically photo hoaxes. My producer had to go to great lengths to actually get a hoax photographer to agree to appear on the show, on the condition that we promise to keep his identity secret. So, I'd like to welcome my guest to the show.

H: Thank you.

P: For starters, can you explain why you want to remain anonymous?

H: Two reasons really. People don't like hoax photographers, because people don't like to be fooled in this way. We make them feel stupid. Also, hoaxers often use photographs taken by someone else, and without permission, and the original photographer could sue us … or a newspaper can sue you if they discover you've sold them a hoax.

P: You're playing it safe then.

H: You could put it that way.

P: I see. Now I asked you before the show if you'd ever earned money for your hoax work, and you said that you often work with the police and detectives. What exactly do you do for them?

H: Well when a politician, for example, appears in a published photograph in any … embarrassing situation, say accepting money… sometimes the police ask me to decide if the photograph is a hoax, and then they see if they can find out who did it.

P: Right. OK, well, let's look at some photographs that we found on the Internet – some hoaxes; some not. Talk us through these photographs if you would.

H: OK, this picture of a plane crossing a road looks like a hoax simply because it's such an extraordinary sight. Also, it looks a bit like a composite photo…

P: What's that?

H: When you combine two or more photos, that's a composite. It's easy to put a picture of a plane over a picture of a road, and then put this traffic light here on the right on top, like a sandwich.

P: So it's a hoax photo.

H: No, it's actually real. I wasn't sure myself, but when I found out it was Beijing Airport, I asked a friend who lives in Beijing, and he told me he had seen it with his own eyes a number of years before. There used to be a taxiing runway that actually crossed the road! It's all changed now, of course, and these days Beijing has one of the most modern airports in the world.

P: Sure. Hmm … so … then this one could be real. A suitcase in the top of a tree is such an extraordinary sight, maybe that's why it looks a bit fake.

H: Well, even if you've never seen a suitcase that's fallen from a plane into a tree – and who has? – your common sense tells you that there would be more damage to both the tree and the suitcase.

P: Then it IS a hoax photo.

H: Yes, a classic composite photo.

P: Remarkable. Now this one could be real, the man jumping over the canyon. I remember seeing this on the Internet. They said that there was a 900 metre drop underneath. But you're going to tell me it's a composite photo.

H: Not necessarily. This is an interesting example from a number of standpoints. You have to ask yourself how it is that someone was there to take a very well composed photograph of the man jumping. It's too-well composed.

P: So the whole thing was planned. Still, it's dangerous…

H: Well, in a photograph you never see the whole picture. It looks dangerous, but in fact just below the bottom of the frame here is the ground connecting these two rocks. At most he would have fallen a few metres.

P: How do you know that?

H: This is a quite well-known place for adventure tourists who visit the Grand Canyon.

P: Have you been there?

H: No, but I've seen photographs.

P: Ah, how do you know those weren't hoaxes…

UNIT 7 Recording 3

Conversation 1

A: Can you believe those people who won the lottery?

B: Sorry?

A: Those people who won 43 million euros each.

B: Lucky them! That must be one of the biggest prizes ever.

A: Yeah, but the amazing thing is the two winners are from the same town.

B: So?

A: and they've won separately.

B: What, you mean they didn't do it together?

A: No, they don't know each other.

B: You're kidding. That's absolutely incredible! I mean …

A: Yeah, it's such an amazing coincidence. They're saying that …

Conversation 2

A: Hi.

B: Hi. Have you seen this picture? Look.

A: No.

B: What do you think it is?

A: It's difficult to say, but I gather it's some sort of painting. It's quite pretty. It looks like one of those done by a child or I guess it could be a computer image.

B: Wrong! It's actually a photo of some bacteria they found on the moon.

A: Really? There's no way I would have guessed that. Let me see again. I suppose it does look like bacteria now I come to think about it.

B: Mind you, I don't believe it. I think it's a tabloid …

Conversation 3

A: Did you see that story about the kid in Ethiopia?

B: No.

A: It was on the breakfast news this morning. It was about this girl who was being chased by some men. And three lions came out and chased away the men and then stayed and protected her.

B: That is incredible. Why on earth would they do that?

A: What, the lions?

B: Yeah.

A: Maybe they heard her crying. You know, and thought she was a cub.

B: Perhaps …but it sounds a bit weird. Why didn't they just eat her?

A: Good question. Er, maybe …

B: That reminds me of a story …

Conversation 4

A: He looks in a bad mood.

B: Let's look. What happened?

A: He's got to pay a fine. Apparently he left his car in the wrong place.

B: He's got to pay a fine!

A: Yeah.

B: And he's the one who's always talking about reducing car use and taking public transport.

A: Yeah. That's so hypocritical.

B: I thought you liked him.

A: Yeah, well, sometimes he can be such an idiot but he's …

UNIT 7 Recording 7

M = Man W = Woman

M: Did you hear this story in the news about this guy that swapped a paper clip, for a house?

W: No.

M: It sounds a bit out there but apparently what happened was he started … he was at his desk looking for a job or phoning up about jobs …

W: Yeah.

M: … and, um, he saw a paper clip on his desk, and he thought, I wonder what I can do with this paper clip – whether I can swap it for something.

W: Oh.

M: Anyway, so he got onto the internet and he made this website – I think it's called the-red-paper-clip dot com.

W: Right.

M: And he put this, this on the internet, photographs it, puts it on, and sees if anyone wants to swap something with him.

W: And did, did anything happen?

M: Yeah, so first of all, I don't remember all the details but as I recall two Vancouver women, um, took up the first challenge and they swapped the paper clip with, I think it was a pen shaped like a fish they had found …

W: Random.

M: Yeah – they had found on a camping trip, yeah random. But he meets up with all these people he doesn't just send the things. And so then from that, I believe, this guy in Seattle wanted the pen and, swapped it for a door knob. And the door knob, was swapped for something to do with camping, –

W: Oh so he kept trading up each time.

M: Yeah he kept trading, trading up so, and then that was swapped for a beer keg I think. Apparently what happened was all these people were … the same sort of thought patterns as him and they wanted to sort of meet up and it was about a social event as well.

W: Ah.

M: Anyway, the next thing he got was a snow globe and, according to the report, it said a film director wanted it and said he'd swap it for a part in his film. And then this town decided, they had this house in this town, and that they would swap the house for a part in this film.

W: No! So he went all the way from the red paper clip to getting a house.

M: … a house. And my impression was that he, he was just crazy at the beginning but he, he ended up having this – I'm not sure how good the house was but, well, yeah.

W: Well, better than a paper clip.

M: I know basically that's what happened.

W: Wow!

UNIT 8 Recording 2

I = Interviewer S1 = Speaker 1
S2 = Speaker 2 S3 = Speaker 3
S4 = Speaker 4 S5 = Speaker 5
S6 = Speaker 6 S7 = Speaker 7
S8 = Speaker 8

I: Now I've always thought it has to do with what time of day you're born. I arrived at ten o'clock at night and consequently I'm an owl – coming to life late in the evening and capable of dancing till dawn – which is a pity really because this job requires that I am a lark, getting up every morning at 5.30. Well, which are you and why?

S1: I am up usually between five and half past most mornings. I'm bright and breezy, I sing in the morning. I'm wide awake. I love watching the sunrise. Whenever we go on holiday, my husband thinks I'm mad because quite often I get up with a camera and I'm out there at half past four, five o'clock in the morning watching the sunrise and taking photographs. And I just

love it, it is just so peaceful and so beautiful. It's a lovely part of the day.

S2: Definitely not a morning person. Evening, without a doubt. I despise getting up with a passion. There is a real, real sense of dread, and, oh no, and there's sort of lots of denial about no, it didn't really go off. And I sort of set it again for five minutes later, then set it again for another five minutes later, and I stay there until the absolute last second.

S3: If I'm groggily out at nine or ten in the morning, I do look at other people walking their dogs, or walking along with a bounce in their step and I just think, 'Where does it come from? How can you do that? Should I just eat more vegetables or more fruit or should I get up earlier to be more awake?' None of it works.

S4: My father and my mother are very much sort of early birds, so when I was a teenager I'd sleep in and have comments all the time like, 'You're sleeping your life away, you've wasted the best part of the day', and it's taken me until very very recently actually to be able to stop the guilt at getting up late …

S5: Going to bed earlier seems like you're planning ahead and thinking about the next day, so it seems oriented around whatever work you have to do the next day. It's just quite a nice feeling being awake and nobody else is there. You just feel like you're the one in charge or something, you know what's going on.

S6: Late evening is best for me to be focusing rather than partying. That's when I'm really thinking straight. Everyone's going to sleep at home here when I'm really mentally becoming most awake. That's when I really feel at my sharpest

S7: At the end of the day, nine o'clock, ten o'clock, I'm exhausted, and so I want to go to bed. Anybody mentions 'party' to me and I cringe.

S8: David and I always joked before we had children that it would be great because he would be great in the mornings and I would be great in the evenings, and to a certain extent that's true, but finding time in the middle just to talk to one another is trickier.

I: What are you, lark or owl? And what are the effects? Do let us know on the message board on the website.

UNIT 8 Recording 4

S1 = Speaker 1 S2 = Speaker 2
S3 = Speaker 3 S4 = Speaker 4
S5 = Speaker 5 S6 = Speaker 6

S1: I do prefer to keep to deadlines and if I don't I tend to get a bit stressed out, I don't like to disappoint people and I like to feel as though I'm quite organised. I don't mind working late sometimes if it's to get something finished, and I feel much more satisfied getting something completed at the end of the day and I'm more likely to go home and relax. But, otherwise, I'll end up going home and just thinking about everything that I've got to do the next day, so that stresses me out more.

S2: I think it's really important for transport, public transport to be punctual when you're working, and that, that's – that's just normal but I think when I'm on holiday I'm a bit more relaxed about whether trains or buses are a little bit late, obviously you don't want to waste a whole day waiting for your transport when you want to get from A to B and you want to make the most of your holiday but, yeah, I think I'm definitely more relaxed when I'm abroad than when I'm in my own country …

S3: Yeah I was, taught from an early age that time keeping's really important. Because of that I find it quite annoying when other people don't have that same sort of line of thought. An example I can give is my friends at university, they were always late. It makes me feel incredibly frustrated because, obviously, you're there on time waiting and it can be quite lonely at times.

S4: I generally don't have a problem at all with people turning up late because it gives me time 'cos I'm generally running late anyway so, it gives me plenty more time to get myself ready. If we're preparing for a dinner party, and people turn up late it really doesn't worry me at all. It gives me plenty more time to get ready …

S5: If I'm holding a dinner party and people come late then usually I'm quite annoyed because I'm quite organised and so the food will probably be ready, and so I'll be a little bit cross that perhaps the dinner will be ruined.

S6: Deadlines are important but I try not to let them stress me out too much, I just try to forget about the pressure and get the work done. As for working late, I don't mind working late, we all have to do it from time to time.

UNIT 8 Recording 5

J = Jim L = Liz

J: Here's your coffee.

L: Thanks, Jim. Oh, I needed that.

J: No problem. Hey, Liz, there's something I've been meaning to talk to you about.

L: Oh yeah?

J: It's just that …well … you know you borrowed some money from me last week?

L: Oh, right. It was ten euros, wasn't it? I don't actually have that on me at the moment.

J: It's not that, it's … well … I hope you don't take this the wrong way, but, um …

L: Right.

J: … it's just that this isn't the first time I've lent you money and er, well you haven't paid it back. I mean, I know it's not a lot, just small amounts each time but it kind of adds up quite quickly … I dunno. Do you know what I mean?

L: Yeah. Sorry. I didn't realise. I know I'm terrible with money. I just forget. Look, I promise I'll give it back, but could you wait a week? Until I get paid.

J: Well, actually, you've said that once before. I don't want you to get the wrong idea, but … it, you know, never happened. And it makes things slightly awkward. It makes me feel just a bit annoyed. Do you see where I'm coming from?

L: Oh. Yeah. I suppose so.

J: Look, I've got a suggestion. I'd feel better if we could work out how much is owed and then you could pay me back a little each week, you know, however much you can afford. How does that sound?

L: Yeah, yeah. That sounds reasonable.

J: Okay, great so …

UNIT 8 Recording 8

W = Woman M = Man

W: So what about you, do you have any family rituals or traditions?

M: We have a, we have a family ritual for the children's birthdays, and, that – this involves coming down for breakfast, um, before the children come down, we lay a paper, table cloth, and we write in little coloured sweets we write their name and it says if it was Will for instance it would say 'Will is twelve'.

W: Ah lovely.

M: And then the, all the extra little coloured sweets they get put into a bowl so that they're allowed this treat of having sweets for breakfast which is very unusual. And then all their presents are laid out on the table in front of them, and then, and they come downstairs and you say right it's ready for you to come downstairs now and as they come in we sing Happy Birthday to them, and there are all their presents and it says 'Will is Twelve', and then the other child, there's four years' difference between them, always has to have an un-birthday present, just 'cos otherwise they get upset that one of them's getting more –

W: Ah

M: – more presents than all the other ones. And, we take a photograph of that and I've now got a collection of all these photographs, which go 'Will is One', 'Will is Two', 'Will is Three', 'Will is Four' so there's this sort of continuity that goes all the way through –

W: That's lovely.

M: And he's twenty five now, so we're starting to wonder at what point do we stop doing this.

W: Do they do the same for you and your wife?

M: No not really no it's, – we don't because we're a bit too old for it.

W: For the coloured sweets.

M: Yes, and it was just something that we invented for the children, it's not a family tradition it hasn't come down from either of us we just invented it for the first child when they were one and it's just carried on like that, but we, of course we can't stop it now, you know he's aged twenty six – when he's thirty we'll go 'Will is Thirty'.

UNIT 9 Recording 2

Conversation 1

L = Lise J = Jeff

L: So what happened was, I was sitting in a café and this young couple – they looked like tourists – asked me to take a photo of them. And I took their photo, and they thanked me and left and then I looked at my seat and realised my handbag had gone, with my mobile, wallet, credit card, keys, everything.

J: No! What did you do?

L: Well, there was a guy on the next table and he saw I was really upset and I explained about the bag and he asked me which bank I was with and he said he worked for that bank and gave me a phone number and let me use his mobile to phone them and stop my credit card.

J: And you believed him?

L: Yeah, I mean I was in a real panic. I was really grateful for his help. Anyway, I phoned the number and talked to a woman from 'the bank' and gave her my name and address and my account number.

J: She sounded genuine?

L: Yeah, completely. I could hear the sounds of the call centre behind her. And she asked me to key in my PIN on the phone and she said they'd stop my card.

J: Wow. So it was a double scam. They got your bag and your bank account details?

L: Yeah, unfortunately. Of course, the guy could get my PIN from his phone.

J: So who actually took your bag?

L: Well, it must have been stolen when I wasn't looking.

J: Right.

L: So it can't have been the young couple because I was looking at them all the time I was taking the photo. Their job was just to distract me.

J: Was it the guy at the next table, then?

L: I think so. He must have taken my bag when I wasn't looking. Then he could have hidden it in his case or he might have given it to another member of the gang.

J: And then he gave you a fake number.

L: Yeah, and they must have used a recording of a call centre so that it sounded like the real bank.

Conversation 2

D = Dan I = Ingrid

D: I was badly tricked a few years ago when I was working in a jewellery shop.

I: You never told me about that. What happened?

D: Well, this woman came in and was looking at necklaces. She was young, attractive, well-dressed, and then a guy came in shortly afterwards and he was just looking around. But then the woman went to pay for a very expensive necklace that she'd picked out, and when she was counting out the money onto the counter, the guy grabbed her, flashed his police ID and said he was arresting her for paying with counterfeit money.

I: No! Wow!

D: So he took the cash and the necklace as evidence, wrote down his contact details, and promised me he'd bring the necklace back by the end of the day. I didn't suspect anything. Then he took the woman away, presumably to book her at the police station.

I: And he didn't come back?

D: No, and stupid me, I didn't even begin to suspect anything until it was closing time, so then I phoned the police and they had no idea what I was talking about. That was it, end of story.

I: How much was the necklace worth?

D: £600. And my boss took it out of my salary. That's why I quit.

I: So the police ID must have been a fake.

D: That's right. I just didn't check it.

I: And wait a second, was the woman a real customer?

D: No, the woman must have been working with the guy. She couldn't have been a real customer, or she wouldn't have gone with him …

I: But she might have had fake money.

D: I really don't think so.

I: Talk about an ingenious scam …

UNIT 9 Recording 5

P = Police officer A = Alain

P: Hello, police. Can I help you?

A: Yes, I'd like to report a crime. I've been robbed.

P: I'm very sorry to hear that, sir. OK, I'll need to take a statement.

A: A statement?

P: To write down some details, if that's all right.

A: Yes, sure.

P: Could you give me your name please, sir?

A: Alain Girard.

P: Right. That's Girard with a J?

A: No, G, and it's Alain spelled A-l-a-i-n.

P: Right, Mr Girard. Could you tell me exactly when the incident happened?

A: Just now. About an hour ago.

P: Could you be more precise?

A: Excuse me?

P: Could you give me the exact time?

A: I think at 2.50 or 2.55.

P: That's about 2.50 on the seventh of June. And where did it happen?

A: Park Avenue.

P: Can you pinpoint the exact location?

A: Pinpoint?

P: Tell me exactly where.

A: Oh. It was near the entrance to the park. Just about fifty metres inside.

P: OK. Could you tell me what happened?

A: I was walking out of the park, and a man was running towards me and he hit into me hard –

P: He collided with you?

A: Yes and he said 'sorry' and something else, then before I realised what had happened, he had run on. It was only about thirty seconds later that I realised my wallet had gone and that he must have taken it when he hit me, collided with me.

P: But did it cross your mind that it wasn't just an accident?

A: No, it never occurred to me that he'd done it on purpose.

P: Did you run after him?

A: No, my mind just went blank and I stood there not knowing what to do.

P: But you were OK? Not hurt?

A: No, just very shocked.

P: OK. Could you tell me exactly what your wallet looked like and what was in it?

A: It's brown, leather and it has my credit card and about 250 euros and –

P: Hold on a minute, credit card … about 250 euros, yes?

A: And a photo of my girlfriend.

P: OK. So you saw the man. Can you give me a description?

A: Erm, about twenty, white, quite tall. And he was wearing a sweater, grey colour with a … you know … erm, something you put over your head …

P: A hood? He was wearing a hoodie?

A: Yes, that's the word. So I didn't see his face, not clearly. But he looked as if he was just out jogging, you know, he was wearing some sort of dark trousers, for running or for the gym.

P: Tracksuit bottoms?

A: Yeah. I can't remember anything else, it all happened so quickly.

P: So that's a tall white male, about twenty, wearing a grey hoodie and dark tracksuit bottoms?

A: That's right.

P: And did he have any other distinguishing marks or features?

A: Sorry?

P: Anything special or different from normal? For example, a scar on his face or anything like that?

A: No, he just seemed like a normal guy, out running. Nothing special. Except …

P: Yes?

A: He reminded me a bit of that actor, Vin Diesel. But younger. Do you know who I mean?

P: Vin Diesel, yeah. I'll put it down. And you said he said something to you.

A: Yeah but I didn't catch what he said. It was too quick.

P: Right, one last question and then I'll take your contact details. Were there any other people in the vicinity?

A: Vicinity?

P: In the surrounding area – nearby. Any witnesses who saw what had happened?

A: No, there was no one nearby, in the … vicinity.

P: Right, now I just need to take your contact details, Mr Girard, and I can also give you a phone number to ring if …

UNIT 9 Recording 8

W1 = Woman 1   M = Man   W2 = Woman 2

W1: So we really need to decide then, what it is we get rid of and what is absolutely essential to keep on the life raft, I think that's probably the most important thing isn't it?

M: I'm sure it's easy to get rid of a few things, isn't it?

W2: Like what?

M: Well, I'm not sure about the lighter. I mean, we can't really start a fire on a raft, can we?

W2: No.

W1: I suppose it depends on what the life raft is made out of, doesn't it?

M: Yeah, but it's not exactly top priority to be able to cook a hot meal, you know, when you really just need to survive.

W1: So no lighter?

M and W2: OK.

W1: OK. So what do you think is important?

W2: I'd say that a blanket is essential.

W1: Interesting choice. What for?

W2: Well, you can use it for a lot of different things. To keep you warm obviously, but you can use a blanket as a towel if you get wet –

W1: If you fall in the water.

W2: … for example. And a blanket can protect you from the sun.

M: That hadn't occurred to me. Okay, I'm convinced. So what else?

W1: Well I can't see the point of taking the hand mirror can you?

M: Actually, I can. Because if …

UNIT 10 Recording 1

E = Edith Bowman   J = James King

E: Right, another two couple of films to look at. Now, I heard about this and I really want to see it. Are you starting off with Let the Right One In?

J: I certainly am. Creepy, creepy horror film this one. It's the story of a twelve-year-old boy, real loner boy, real kind of geek at school, bullied at school, who befriends his new neighbour, who's a twelve-year-old girl. She happens to be a vampire. And this is set in very snowy and very bleak Sweden. It's a brilliant, brilliant film, it really is very, very good, because I think it's so bleak, because it's a very – although it is a horror film, it's a very quiet horror film, you know it's very sort of slow, and really carefully paced, really not showy at all. And because of that, I think really, really chilling and actually sometimes you're laughing, and the most horrific things are happening on screen because this boy, you know he's in love with this girl, he wants to help her. You know, and even though really horrible things are happening on screen, you

actually giggle a bit, and I love that … when you really don't know how to feel, you just feel uncomfortable.

E: Almost the film is running your emotions for you.

J: Absolutely. And I think a really unforgettable film. They are going to do an American version of this, which could be quite good. I think it's the guy who made Cloverfield, Matt Reeves has said that he wants to make an American version of this. But go and see this original version because it really, it really does show you that, you know, in horror films, restraint can be a very powerful thing, and it doesn't just have to be really loud and just loads of blood and guts. You can have something that's really poignant and –

E: … and beautiful.

J: … and beautiful at the same time as being really chilling. And the two kids in this are well, just awesome. I haven't stopped thinking about it since I've seen it, it's a really special film, Let the Right One In.

E: How many stars?

J: One, two, three, four, five stars!

E: Yay! Oh, wow …

UNIT 10 Recording 4

Conversation 1

W = Woman   M = Man

W: So here we are in Greenwich Village.

M: It looks very different from the rest of New York.

W: Yeah, the streets are quite narrow and the buildings aren't as high.

M: It does look quite village-like.

W: Yeah, but it's quite big. It extends out west that way to the Hudson River, north above Washington Square. We'll go up there in a bit.

M: And you lived here?

W: When I first came to New York, yeah. In an apartment just around the corner, on West Third Street. Actually, you can see the building over there.

M: Near The Blue Note Jazz Club?

W: Yeah.

M: I've heard of The Blue Note.

W: It's pretty famous. There are some great jazz clubs around the neighbourhood, and that's one of the best. We can see a show there one night if you want.

M: That'd be great.

W: Now up here on the left is the Café Reggio. It's where I used to hang out and read when I wasn't working.

M: Looks good.

W: Their cappuccino is great. The story goes that the original owner brought cappuccino to America. You can see the original cappuccino machine inside.

M: Cool. We could stop and have a coffee.

W: Maybe a bit later? Let's head over to Washington Square Park and then circle back.

M: OK – lead the way!

…

W: A lot of these clubs we're walking by have a real history. As I'm sure you know, Greenwich Village has always been a centre of artistic life – very bohemian. It's always attracted famous writers, dancers and poets. And in the sixties, it was a big part of the folk music scene: Simon and Garfunkel, Joni Mitchell, Bob Dylan, you know.

M: Before my time! Now what's this?

W: This is Washington Square Park. We'll walk into the park on this side. Can you play chess?

M: A bit, yeah.

W: Any of these guys here would be happy to challenge you to a game of chess. They're here all day, every day

M: Maybe next time – I'm not that good! What's the arch over there? It looks like the Arc de Triomphe in Paris.

W: Well it should, that's the Washington Square arch. It was modelled on the Arc de Triomphe and built in 1889 to celebrate the hundredth anniversary of the inauguration of George Washington as president.

M: Could we sit down a second? I need a break.

W: Why don't we retrace our steps and go back to the Café Reggio?

M: Sounds good. I could really do with a coffee.

Conversation 2

W = Woman   M1 = Man 1   M2 = Man 2

M1: So, this is Radcliffe Square.

W: Wow! Is this right in the centre then?

M1: Pretty much.

M2: What's that?

M1: Hold on. Let's just get off our bikes … Right, so that building in front of us is the Bodleian, named after the founder – Thomas Bodley. Believe it or not, despite the fact that it's circular, it's actually a library.

W: Cool!

M1: Yeah, it gets a copy of every book published in the UK.

M2: Who can use it?

M1: Any student at the university. Of course, each college also has its own library – you know the university's divided into colleges, right?

M2: Right. How many colleges are there?

M1: Just under forty. Well, thirty-eight to be exact.

W: So that means thirty-eight libraries?!

M1: Mm but they're not all as big as the Bodleian. Anyway, we'll need to get back on our bikes for the next bit …

…

M1: Can you hear me if I talk as we cycle along?

M2: Yeah.

W: OK, but don't go too fast. I'm not very steady on this thing!

M1: So, here's the famous Bridge of Sighs, connecting two sides of Hertford College.

M2: I've seen the original.

M1: What, of the bridge? In Italy, you mean?

M2: Yeah, it's in Venice. Beautiful.

M1: OK. We'll go past New College and then onto the High Street.

M2: Is that New College there?

M1: Yep.

W: How 'new' is new?

M1: Roughly 1370.

W: You're kidding!

M1: No, really! Interestingly, the oldest college was actually only founded a hundred or so years earlier! Uh-oh, watch out on this corner …

M1: That's the 'Schools'. It's where the students take their exams. Apparently, the biggest room can seat somewhere in the region of 500 students although I haven't seen it myself. Anyway, we're turning right here. The street's cobbled, so be careful.

M2: How many students are there at the university in total?

M1: To be honest, it depends. In term time, you'd probably get upwards of twenty thousand.

M2: Many international students?

M1: Some, but most are from the UK. We'll finish by cycling down this way to Christ Church. We can actually go inside if we're quick. It's well worth a visit.

M2: Christ Church is another college?

M1: Yeah, the biggest and probably the most famous. Have you seen any of the Harry Potter films?

M2: No …

W: I have!

M1: Oh, well you'll recognise the Great Hall. It's where they have the feasts in Hogwarts School. You know that bit when Harry …

UNIT 10   Recording 6

1 It's roughly 1,500 metres in length.
2 There are upwards of 35 corridors.
3 It's just under 1,200 metres above sea level.
4 It's somewhere in the region of 715 km.
5 It's two metres or so at its thickest point and then it narrows.
6 You get approximately 370 to the euro.

UNIT 10   Recording 7

S = Sarah   T = Tim   N = Nigel

S: Right well we have our shortlist for the new feature that we're going to put into the town centre, which one gets your vote Tim?

T: I'm really in favour of the   the state-of-the-art multiplex cinema I think that it would be most useful and beneficial for the community. I think it will be used a great deal, I think it would bring jobs to the area, and I think it would provide entertainment and activities for young people.

N: The only thing that would concern me though is that that's going to be very, very expensive.

T: Um hm.

S: I mean, I personally would prefer the botanical garden.

T: Oh.

S: Because I think that that will satisfy the needs of many different age groups. I think it would be very good for wheelchairs, for … for blind people, for people with disabilities, there would be areas that would be excellent for young people, and lots of learning opportunities in the education centre. And we know from past experience that the older age group certainly enjoy gardens.

T: The only thing that would concern me on that is that you mention youth, but I don't think that you're going to get as many young people involved in a botanical garden. I think if it was interactive then it would be … but just as a thing that was showing I'm, I'm not so sure.

N: Well I don't want to harp on about costs again but we have to consider the maintenance of this botanical garden. There are very high maintenance costs involved.

S: Oh so, Nigel what, what would you prefer?

N: Well, my vote would go to the theatre workshop space for young people. And I know we said we don't want to discriminate against any … we don't want to leave out certain members of our society, but I think we've got a problem in this town about kids getting bored, hanging around on street corners, they need something to do and a theatre workshop space is going to get them … it's going to give them a routine, it's going to give them a motivation, and then when they do their shows, they're bringing along their grandparents, their parents, I feel it's very inclusive.

T: Can you see the older generation, wanting it, liking it?

N: I think the older generation want to be sure that kids aren't hanging about the streets with nothing to do.

S: And could that, theatre workshop space be used for other things as well?

N: Absolutely.

S: Could it be used for meetings, for other sections of society?

N: … Aerobics … there's going to be a sprung wooden floor so there'll be dance classes, yoga, pilates, multi purpose …

Pearson Education Limited
Edinburgh Gate
Harlow
Essex CM20 2JE
England

and Associated Companies throughout the world.
www.pearsonlongman.com

© Pearson Education Limited 2011

The right of Frances Eales and Steve Oakes to be identified as authors of this Work has been asserted by them in accordance with the Copyright, Designs and Patents Act 1988.

First published 2011

ISBN: 978-1-4082-1933-1

Set in Gill Sans Book 9.75/11.5

Printed in Slovakia by Neografia

Acknowledgements

The publishers and authors would like to thank the following people and their institutions for their feedback and comments during the development of the material:

Reporters: Brazil: Stephen Greene, Damian Williams; **Germany:** Rosemary Richey; **Italy:** Elizabeth Gregson, Elizabeth Kalton; **Spain:** Eleanor Keegan; **Turkey:** Grant Kempton; **United Kingdom:** Ben Beaumont, Kirsten Colquhoun, Andrew Doig, Fay Drewry, Eileen Flannigan, Chiara Farina, Sarah Gumbrell, Tad Larner, Fran Linley, Jacquelan McEwan, Zella Phillips, Chris Rogers, Dan Woodard

We are grateful to the following for permission to reproduce copyright material:

Text: Extract 2.1 from Comic Relief, www. comicrelief.com, Reproduced by kind permission of Comic Relief, copyright © Comic Relief 2010. Registered charity 326568 (England/Wales); SC039730 (Scotland); Extract 4.1 adapted from "The Star Thrower" by Loren Eiseley, http:// www.starrbrite.com/starfish.html; Extract 4.2 from Longman Active Study Dictionary, 5th edition, Pearson Longman (2010) pp.812,781, copyright © Pearson Education Ltd; Extract 4.3 from "Many lie over books 'to impress'", 11 December 2008, http:// news.bbc.co.uk/2/hi/ uk_news/education/7776046.stm, copyright (c) The BBC; Extract 5.1 adapted from "The Focus top 10 world's worst inventions", BBC Focus Magazine, 01/03/2007, pp74–75, copyright (c) BBC Focus; Extract 5.1 after "Bicycle chosen as best invention" 5 May 2005, http:// news.bbc. co.uk/1/hi/technology/4513929.stm, copyright (c) The BBC; Extract 7.3 adapted from Ideas from 'Six topics that keep the tabloids in business', http://www.drewrys.com/, reproduced by kind permission of John Drewry; Extract 8.2 from Longman Active Study Dictionary, 5th edition, Pearson Longman (2010) pp.697,79,620,541,21 7,601,939,264, copyright © Pearson Education Ltd; Extract 8.2 from Longman Active Study Dictionary, 5th edition, Pearson Longman (2010) pp.938,492, copyright © Pearson Education Ltd; Extract 9.1 after "Memory on trial", BBC Focus Magazine, 01/01/2009, pp58–61 (Ridgway, A.), copyright (c) BBC Focus; Extract 9.2 from Longman Active Study Dictionary, 5th edition, Pearson Longman (2010) p.792, copyright © Pearson Education Ltd; Extract 10.2 from Longman Active Study Dictionary, 5th edition, Pearson Longman (2010) pp.258,616, copyright © Pearson Education Ltd; Extract 10.2 from

Longman Active Study Dictionary, 5th edition, Pearson Longman (2010) pp.378,827,652,508, 703,935,620,776,608,981, copyright © Pearson Education Ltd

In some instances we have been unable to trace the owners of copyright material, and we would appreciate any information that would enable us to do so.

Illustration acknowledgements: Dan Hilliard: 15, 47; Mariko Yamazaki: 33, 44, 45, 72; Eric Smith: 37, 95, 151, 153, 155, 156; Matt Herring: 62, Lyndon Hayes: 161, 162.

Photo acknowledgements: The publisher would like to thank the following for their kind permission to reproduce their photographs:

(Key: b-bottom; c-centre; l-left; r-right; t-top)

7 **Corbis:** Ken Seet (l). **Photolibrary.com:** Patrick Renice (cl). **Rex Features:** Brian Harris (r); Garo / Phanie (cr). 8 **Rex Features:** John Alex Maguire (t). 9 **Shutterstock.com:** Antonio Jorge Nunes (t); (c); Rui Vale de Sousa. 10 **Getty Images:** Betsie Van der Meer. 11 **Getty Images:** amana images (r). **Photolibrary.com:** Patrick Renice (c). **Rex Features:** F1 Online (l). 13 **BBC Photo Library:** (t). 16-17 **Photolibrary.com:** DesignPics Inc.. 19 **Alamy Images:** D. Hurst (t). **Corbis:** Kevin Dodge (cr). **Photolibrary.com:** simon katzer (cr). **Rex Features:** Tony Kyriacou (l). 20 **Rex Features:** Nils Jorgensen (b). 21 **Press Association Images:** English Lakes Hotel Group (t). 23 **Rex Features:** Kevin Foy (t). 24 **Rex Features:** Richard Crease (b). 26 **Corbis:** DreamPictures (l). **Photolibrary. com:** Maria Breuer (c). **Thinkstock:** Comstock (r). 27 **Getty Images:** AFP. 28-29 **Shutterstock. com.** 29 **iStockphoto.** 31 **Endemol UK:** (cr). **Getty Images:** Robert Gilhooly / Bloomberg (l). **Photolibrary.com:** Imagesource (cl); Radius Images (r). 33 **Photolibrary.com:** Ron Nickel (t). 34 **Thinkstock.** 35 **Alamy Images:** Anders Ryman (tr). **Photolibrary.com:** Egmont Strigl (l); Shaneff Carl (br). 36 **Robert Harding World Imagery:** Bruno Morandi. 38-39 **BBC Photo Library:** (t). 38 **Endemol UK:** (b). **FremantleMedia Image Library:** (l). 40-41 **Getty Images:** Stephen Frink. 40 **Photolibrary.com:** Morales (tc); (tl). 43 **Alamy Images:** David Crausby (cr). **BBC Photo Library:** (r). **Photolibrary.com:** Ghislain & Marie David de Lossy (l); Christian Ohde (cl). 46 **Robert Harding World Imagery:** D H Webster. 47 **Alamy Images:** Stocksearch (br). **Getty Images:** (l). **Shutterstock. com.** 48 **Corbis:** Creasource (b). 49 **Getty Images:** Gareth Cattermole (t). **Nature Picture Library:** John Sparks (b). 50-51 Trevor Clifford. 52 **BBC Photo Library:** (br). 52-53 **Photolibrary. com:** Superstock. 55 **BBC Photo Library:** (r). **Corbis:** Image Source (cr). **Image courtesy of The Advertising Archives:** (cl). **Photolibrary.com:** Mike Kemp (l). 56 **Corbis:** (cl). **iStockphoto:** pagadesign (tl). **Rex Features:** Jean-Philippe Van Damme (tc). **Shutterstock.com:** Galushko Sergey (bl); (cr, tr, br). 57 **Thinkstock.** 58 **Alamy Images:** James Callaghan (r). **Getty Images:** Martha Holmes (tl). **Rex Features:** Sonny Meddle (bl). **Thinkstock:** (c). 59 **Corbis:** Rick Gayle Studio (cr). **Getty Images:** Tim Boyle (t). **iStockphoto:** U ur Koban (bl). **Shutterstock.com:** Mikhail Tchkheidze (cl); (br). 60 **iStockphoto:** Radu Razvan (c); (r). **Shutterstock. com:** (cl). **Thinkstock:** (l, cr). 63 **Photolibrary. com:** Rubberball. 64 **BBC Photo Library:** (b). 64-65 **Rex Features:** Paul Brown. 67 **Alamy Images:** Ben Simmons (r). **Corbis:** Christian Hacker. **Getty Images:** The Image Bank (cr). **Photolibrary.com:** George Shelley (l). 68 **Rex Features:** OJO Images.

(t). 75 **Getty Images:** Suzanne and Nick Geary (t). **Rex Features:** Stewart Cook (b). 77 **Alamy Images:** Ben Simmons. **BBC Photo Library:** (l). **Corbis:** Image Source. **Reuters. Rex Features:** Phil Ball (cl). 80 **BBC Photo Library:** (l). **Rex Features:** Mark Campbell (r). 81 **BBC Photo Library.** 83 **Getty Images:** Robyn Beck / AFP (t). **South West News Services:** (br). 85 **Rex Features:** Image Source. 87 **Alamy Images:** Judith Collins (t). 88-89 **BBC Photo Library.** 91 **Corbis:** Gerolf Kalt (l); Sonntag (cl); **iStockphoto:** (cr). **Photolibrary. com:** Konrad Wothe (r). 92 **Alamy Images:** picturesbyrob (l). **Dreamstime.com:** (b). **Getty Images:** Paul Chesley (r). 94 **Rex Features:** Carson Ganci . 97 **Photolibrary.com:** Odilon Dimier. 98 **Corbis:** dward Bock (r). **iStockphoto:** (l). 99 **Photolibrary.com:** Comstock (r); Jean-Pierre Boutet (l). 100-101 **Getty Images:** Gulfimages. 100 **4Corners Images:** Thiele Klaus (tl). **Photolibrary. com:** Hideki Yoshihara (c); Chad Ehlers (r). 103 **Alamy Images:** Rosemary Calvert (r). **Corbis:** Christian Schmidt (cr). **Photolibrary.com:** Maria Teijeiro. **Rex Features:** Garo / Phanie (l). 104 **Reuters:** Dylan Martinez (t). 105 **iStockphoto:** Rich Legg (t). **Press Association Images:** (b). 106 **Photolibrary.com:** Eric Nathan (b). 107 **Objective Productions:** (t). 109 **Shutterstock. com:** (b); S.Borisov. 110 **Alamy Images:** face to face Bildagentur GmbH (t); Justin Leighton (bl). **Corbis:** Malek Chamoun (br). 112 **Reuters.** 112-113 **Getty Images:** Ros Roberts. 115 **4Corners Images:** Piai Arcangelo (cr). **Getty Images:** Leland Bobbe (bl); Antony Nagelmann (cl). **iStockphoto:** (r). 116 **Kobal Collection Ltd:** Paramount Pictures / Vaughan, Stephen (t); Universal Pictures (b). 117 **Rex Features:** (t). 118 **Kobal Collection Ltd:** Film 4 / Celador Films / Pathe International (l). **Rex Features:** FoxSearch / Everett (r). 119 **Kobal Collection Ltd:** New Line Cinema (b). **Rex Features:** Jason Mitchell (t). 121 **Photolibrary.com:** (t, b). **Press Association Images:** (c). 122 **Alamy Images:** Peter Titmuss (r). **Photolibrary.com:** JTB Photo (c). **Thinkstock:** (l). 123 **Alamy Images:** Ben Nicholson (t). **Lonely Planet Images:** Kim Grant (r). **Rex Features:** Image Source (bl). 124-125 **Rex Features:** Mikko Stig. 124 **Getty Images:** Jim Dyson (t). 148 **Alamy Images:** David J. Green (tr). **Getty Images:** Andrew Bret Wallis (tl). **Thinkstock:** (b). 149 **Getty Images:** (bc/right); AFP (tl); Stone (cl). **Pearson Education Ltd. Photolibrary.com:** Norbert Probst (bc/left). **Shutterstock.com:** (br). 150 **Corbis:** Marie-Reine Mattera (t); Darren Greenwood (cl); Ashley Jouhar (bc/right). **Getty Images:** (tr); Stone (cr); David Leah (bc/left). **Thinkstock:** (Bottom top left, Bottom top right, bl, br). 152 **Alamy Images:** (br). **Rex Features:** Andy Lauwers (bl). **Shutterstock.com:** (tl, tr, cl, cr). 156 **Photolibrary.com:** Evox Images (t). 157 **Pearson Education Ltd:** (tl, tc/left, tc/right, cl, cr, r, bc/ right, br). **Shutterstock.com:** (tr, l, bl). **Thinkstock:** (bc/left)

All other images © Pearson Education

183079